Books by W.S. Merwin

Opening the Hand   1983
Finding the Islands   1982
The Compass Flower   1977
The First Four Books of Poems   1975
(INCLUDING THE COMPLETE TEXTS OF
*A Mask for Janus, The Dancing Bears,
Green with Beasts* AND *The Drunk in the Furnace*)
Writings to an Unfinished Accompaniment   1973
The Carrier of Ladders   1970
The Lice   1967
The Moving Target   1963
The Drunk in the Furnace   1960
Green With Beasts   1956
The Dancing Bears   1954
A Mask for Janus   1952

PROSE

Unframed Originals   1982
Houses and Travellers   1977
The Miner's Pale Children   1970

TRANSLATIONS

From the Spanish Morning   1985
Four French Plays   1985
Selected Translations 1968-1978   1979
Osip Mandelstam, Selected Poems
(WITH CLARENCE BROWN)   1974
Asian Figures   1973
Transparence of the World (Poems by Jean Follain)   1969
Voices (Poems by Antonio Porchia)   1969
Products of the Perfected Civilization
(Selected Writings of Chamfort)   1969; 1984
Twenty Love Poems and a Song of Despair
(Poems by Pablo Neruda)   1969
Selected Translations 1948-1968   1968
The Song of Roland   1963
The Satires of Persius   1960
The Poem of the Cid   1959

Four French Plays

Four French Plays

Translations by
W.S.Merwin

With a Foreword by the Translator

Atheneum   1985   New York

Robert the Devil: originally published in a limited edition by The Windhover Press at The University of Iowa, Iowa City, 1981; copyright ©1981 by W.S. Merwin.

The Rival of His Master: originally published in the Tulane Drama Review; copyright ©1962 by W.S. Merwin.

Turcaret: originally published in The Classic Theatre, Volume 4, *Six French Plays*, edited by Eric Bentley, published by Anchor Books (Doubleday) in 1961; copyright ©1961 by W.S. Merwin.

The False Confessions: originally published in The Classic Theatre, Volume 4, *Six French Plays*, edited by Eric Bentley, published by Anchor Books, (Doubleday) in 1961; copyright ©1961 by W.S. Merwin.

Library of Congress Cataloging in Publication Data

Main entry under title:

Four French plays.

    Contents: Robert the Devil / Anonymous, 14th century —
The rival of his master ; Turcaret / Alain-René Lesage — [etc.]
    1. French drama—Translations into English.
2. French drama—18th century—Translations into
English. 3. English drama—Translations from French.
I. Merwin, W. S. (William Stanley), ———
II. Miracle de Notre Dame de Robert le Diable. English.
1984. III. Le Sage, Alain René, 1668–1747.
IV. Marivaux, Pierre Carlet de Chamblain de, 1688–1763.
Fausses confidences. English. 1984.
PQ1240.E5F57   1984   842'.008   84-70390
ISBN 0-689-11501-6 (pbk.)

Foreword: Four French Plays

The subject of history is always out of reach, or seems to be. Apparently that is a condition of history. It is especially evident in the history of an art like the theater, which depends with a peculiar finality on the moment of performance, an unseizable instant which has been prepared for, rehearsed, and—as the French put it, *répété*—(beforehand) and which may indeed be repeated, afterward, but can never be the same, and flows away, by stages, altogether, leaving at last scripts, costumes, program notes, pictures, recollections, souvenirs, dates, for something that many people once wanted to see and hear because of a particular abundance of life in it, which they could recognize. The attempt to record any such moment, making use of some amalgam of data, description, impressions and opinions, is limited by its nature, as all history is, but with the added handicap of having to pretend to recall, with its circumstances, a deliberate flash of fantasy, an evanescent artifice, a projection of what appeared to be, for that instant, ourselves. The manifest impossibility of any such enterprise, and at the same time the need for it, may be why the history of the theater and of performing arts is particularly prone to nostalgia and fetishism, insisting that the life that was once there and was so ardently acclaimed is still present in the least of its trappings.

The same difficulties would haunt an effort to convey the living quality of a puppet play in an Asian village a thousand years ago and of a production off Broadway, even assuming an equal familiarity with the languages, the audiences, and the expectations. And the scripts, the "plays," partake of such history. On the one hand there they are, they are the words (probably), with the overt fixity of words. On the other hand they are part of the ephemera of performances, and something of what they have presented repeatedly now eludes us once again. Apparently that is a condition not only of the theater but of language. We save the scripts, when we do, as literature, and for the same reasons that we preserve other literary remains. And if they have been the scores for performances, and the performances have been valued, the hope remains that they may be coaxed into producing performances of life again.

These four plays were all written to be performed, and each of them served as a script in the theater and was played to the audiences of its time, who went to see it because they wanted to. All of them are distinctly European, and all date from before the American Revolution. So that, to Americans of the late 20th century, they elicit the American ambiguity toward Europe and toward the past. (Do we still speak a European language? What do our words say of what we and our culture have forgotten?) They are all, in their language of origin, their conception, their forms, French, and they come to us from conventions of the French theater that are unfamiliar to us and are no longer current in France either. We do not have an acting tradition that would, without effort and the luck of talent, be at home in the lines and the periods that typify and are essential to these plays, nor audiences that would know what to expect and listen for. Yet these translations too were all made to be performed. They were commissioned one by one by the BBC Third Programme in the early 1950's and were all broadcast at the time.

Arranged chronologically, the four plays span a period of at least three hundred years. *Robert The Devil* emerged from a world—part history, part chronicle, part legend—which Shakespeare's Henry IV and Henry V thought of as French, and the story, in some unknown mixture, is compounded of all three. Some of it is obviously legendary, but there is, besides, a legend that it refers to historical personages, and that Robert's father, in fact, was William of Normandy, William The Conqueror. The ascription is unlikely, and the origins of the story of Robert are not known to us at all. Before it was a play it circulated, perhaps for some time, as a rhymed tale recited by *jongleurs* in marketplaces. Variants, in verse and in prose, travelled around the Europe of the fourteenth century. The text of more than one Spanish version has survived into our own time.

The French theater in the vernacular—as distinct from the early pieces of liturgical dialogue recited in the churches, in Latin—began somewhere in the 12th century. (The oldest piece known to us is entitled *The Foolish Virgins*.) There were already full-length plays in Latin, by then, which came to incorporate passages in French and then to be superseded by plays in the common tongue, the language of Picardy or Normandy, the *langue d'oc* or *langue d'oïl*. The miracle plays followed, for two centuries and more: a form that gathered up into its stock personages and broad lines both canonical gospel and local lore. Many of the plays were expressions of the wave of devotion to the Virgin that marked that wracked and anxious time.

Historians of French literature tend to make a finer distinction between the miracle plays and the mystery plays which followed them than is customary in accounts of analogous developments in the English theater. The first of the French mystery plays, indeed, were performed without dialogue; they were mimed, or presented as pageants, or as charades without movements. Their subjects might be Christian, like the miracle plays, or allegorical or mythological, though they continued to be, in general, of a religious nature. But by the mid-fifteenth century they too employed dialogue—to such length that some of them grew into rhymed serials running to thousands of verses, which were performed, like the miracle plays, during the great festivities of the church, over the course of several days or even weeks. They were put on like ceremonies. Near the end of the century one was acted at Chalon-sur-Saone in order to put an end to the plague. Societies of artisans, and market towns, had mystery plays composed in honor of their patron saints. The actors were drawn from all classes except the nobility, and they were almost always men. Christ was played, where possible, by a priest. One curate, in 1437, at Metz, almost died hanging up on the cross for hours reciting three or four hundred lines of verse. The stages might be huge, with all the sets visible at once. The action was full of violence, punishment and reward, and feelings loudly expressed, and the whole genre, for a long time, seems to have provided immense popular satisfaction.

I found a copy of Edouard Fournier's edition of *Le Mystère de Robert Le Diable* in a secondhand book store on a back street in Paris, in the early 1950s. Fournier had dedicated the copy to A.M. Romain, who apparently had played Robert the Devil in a production early in 1879. There is a picture of him in the role, in striped hose and leather doublet, sitting in a heavy chair, looking appropriately lowering. An interest in medieval literature and in the origins of the theater prompted me to buy it and to try, a few months later, to see what I could make of it in English.

The story, as it is presented in the play, is close enough

to a myth to be considered as one. It is the tale of the local bad boy who is saved from the consequences of his wicked ways, and turns out happily in the end. It is cast in a fervently devout mode but the blasphemies and the rewards are wholly of this world. And the play manages to be pious without being altogether edifying, unless we can believe in the protagonist's real change of heart. But in order to do that we would have to believe in the protagonist more fully and intimately than is possible in Robert's case. Part of the appeal of the play, in its time, may have been less its spectacle of repentance (which was still self-serving, after all) than the fact that the bad boy gets away with it.

The other three plays represent a world that most of Europe thought of as French three hundred years later, after the age of Louis XIV had presented French culture as the pinnacle of civilization. The comedies of Lesage, their humor and their vein of satire, appear as a link between Molière, in the 17th century, and Beaumarchais, later in the 18th. Lesage was born during the age of Louis XIV and seems to pertain to both centuries. *Crispin, His Master's Rival*, and a novel, *The Limping Devil*, were his first mature works. Both of them, and a comedy entitled *Don César Ursin*, appeared in 1707, when Lesage was almost forty. He had read widely in Spanish literature, and a passion for independence had prompted him, from the beginning, to support himself and his family on what he could earn with his pen, first translating and later making adaptations from Spanish. All three of the works in 1707 were based upon or had been suggested by Spanish predecessors: the novel, as Lesage tells us, owed its conception to Fray Antonio Guevara's *El Diablo Cojuelo*, and the original notion for *Crispin* came from a minor work of Hurtado de Mendoza's. But both are recognizably the writings of Lesage. The style is clean, swift and elegant, unerringly artful yet surprisingly natural. The tone—light, smiling, assured—conveys a constant, hovering irony. It is not hard to see that Lesage's great mentors were Molière and Cervantes. The satire of Lesage, usually, and certainly in *Crispin*, is rather gentle and indulgent, a running, playful mockery from the viewpoint of worldly good sense. So it appears on the surface, at least. But the title itself, and the role of a Crispin, prefigure Beaumarchais and his *Marriage of Figaro*, seventy-seven years later—the play which was the subject of fierce controversy from 1781 when it was accepted by the *Comédie de Française*, until the first performance in the house of the Comte de Vaudreuil two years later; which meanwhile had been kept from public performance by an order from the King, who had leaped to his feet, on first hearing it read, and exclaimed, "It is detestable! It will never be performed! For it to be harmless the Bastille would have to be done away with!" And which was finally played to an excited audience of liberal aristocrats who, in the words of a famous courtesan on the opening night, sat and "applauded their own death sentence."

Lesage's comedy offers no such open and deliberate challenge to authority and the established order. It is a relatively slight, charming piece, its mockery good-humored. When the intrigues are discovered nobody is punished seriously, and the two scheming valets on whom the plot turns are pardoned and set up in business "to make honest folk" of them.

Turcaret is another matter. *Crispin* had been a success, and it is not surprising that Lesage decided to write again for the stage. This time he did not turn to Spain for his subject. Years before, in his late twenties, when he had just married and was feeling the need of a steady income, Lesage had taken a job with a tax "farmer" in the provinces: one of the breed of private tax collectors whose ways and whose careers began, in France, under the auspices of Colbert, in 1781, and who rapidly came to be detested and despised from one end of the country to the other. Lesage had not stayed with that employer for long, but he had come away from the position with bitterness and a disgust for tax collectors and financiers which he displayed for no other form of human endeavor, and which time did nothing to mellow.

Which is not surprising. In the last two decades of the 17th century and the beginning of the 18th the French national debt grew at a terrible pace—largely because of the need to pay for the upkeep and activities of the military—and the private tax farmers squeezed money wherever they could, schemed, maneuvered, and individually became enormously rich at a dazzling rate. Lesage was not only in good company in his loathing of them, he was not the first writer of his time who set out to pillory them and, if literature could accomplish it, to destroy them. The theme was relatively new to the theater. In spite of the brilliance of Molière's satire, Chamfort, late in the 18th century, a philosopher with small regard for the world of money-changers, found it remarkable that "Molière, who spared nothing, never fired a shot at the financiers. It is said that Molière and the comic authors of his time had their orders, on this subject, from Colbert." Molière had come closest in *L'Avare*, but the vice he had mocked there was general cupidity, miserliness, giving oneself up to assigning an excessive and finally exclusive importance to the amassing of money. He had depicted the distorting effects, the blindness, the bloating, the withering, of this malady. And La Bruyère, in *Les Caractères*, published in 1687, had spoken eloquently of the vile consequences of the attachment to wealth. The specific plague of nouveau-riche tax farmers, manipulators and extortionists which had settled upon France late in the 17th century had been assailed by Jacques Robbe in 1682, in a play called *La Rapinière ou L'Intéressé*. And the subject had been returned to from time to time in the next two decades, but without major distinction or bloodletting. It had scarcely been scratched when Lesage set out to write *Turcaret*.

The vein of indulgent irony which—if one is to judge from his other writings—was natural to him, must have seemed inadequate to a theme of such corrosive nastiness. And Lesage's usual temper, and the viewpoint of the decent, informed, skeptical man of the world, would not readily sustain the outrage which he clearly felt toward his protagonist and the world that clung to him. Lesage ordinarily portrayed human weaknesses as ridiculous rather than terrible; he revealed falsehood as foolishness rather than as evil. But even in *Crispin* his references to those whose calling was money had been envenomed, and when he turned to *Turcaret* he produced a character who was laughable but not amusing. Yet his intent clearly was not limited to mockery, however well founded. This time his subject was not mere foolishness, but that "filth of souls" which La Bruyère had spoken of in referring to the round of greed, arrogance, and meanness. Evil, the distorted and consistently self-befouled spirit, is in fact not easy to dramatize. It runs to caricature; and *Turcaret*, while credible enough at one level, is a grotesque, a balloon. He is also a woefully common phenomenon, and a great merit of the play, one of its genuinely dramatic virtues, is the portrayal of the world that this central sinister clown gathers around him, people to whom he is real, who despise him for his vulgarity yet covet his means, lend themselves to his fantasy, hang upon his moods, operate on principles little different from his own, and reflect his warped, shallow nature, his unreality. Some critics have complained about it: Lesage has not given them a single character with whom they can feel sympathy, and "the contemplation of misconduct is not enough to rejoice the eyes or the spirit in the theater . . . etc." (F. Sarcey, *Quarante ans de théâtre*, 1872). But the fact that Lesage shows greed constructing a closed world that reflects itself endlessly provides the play's authenticity and its glimpse of infernal horizons.

From the beginning, some of the concern about the justice of the central portrait, and what Lanson called Lesage's "cruel realism" had arisen from taking the subject personally. A cabal of financiers, after the play's first reading at the *Comédie Française* on May 15, 1708, did everything possible to prevent its being performed, going so far (according to Claude and François Parfait, *Histoire du Théâtre Française, 1734-1749*, as to bribe the company not to put on the play. It required a royal edict (the only one of its kind, and its author, who may have been the Duke of Burgundy or the Dauphin himself, remains unknown) in October of that year, to have the play open, finally, on February 14, 1709, performed by a recalcitrant company. The box office receipts make it clear that the piece was a success even so, but it was immediately pronounced a failure, and was mysteriously withdrawn after seven performances. Twenty-one years later it was revived and its success was established, and it has been successfully produced in France in recent years. Lesage's style, for all its balance and elegance, is not so fancy that it should be a problem for modern actors; the title role is a great acting part, and the theme is close enough to the prevailing motives of our own society to make the play remarkably topical.

The skeptical but generally indulgent temper of Lesage's writing has been said by some French critics to be typically French, yet with his Spanish influences and the ubiquity of his theme in *Turcaret* he is an international figure, especially if one contrasts his work, and in particular his manner, with those of Marivaux. The latter, in attitude, style, and tastes, sometimes seems as embedded in French culture, in the French language, and in his own age, as Racine. And like Racine's, his reputation in France differs markedly from his reputation where French is not the first language. Analogies among the arts must never be trusted very far, but it is probably safe to compare his presentation of the French rococo in comedy with Fragonard's and Watteau's in painting. And yet Marivaux's plays, for the most part, were performed, and found sympathetic audiences, and his reputation was made not at the *Comédie Française* with its somewhat parochial severities, but at the *Comédie Italienne*, heir to images, at least, of the *commedia dell'arte*, and far more open than the *Comédie Française* to fantasy and innovation. His novel, *The Life of Marianne*, provided a model for Richardson. His own journalistic writing was modelled on the English *Spectator*. And his principal theme (though he too, in *The Triumph of Plutus*, twenty years after *Turcaret*, produced a satire on financiers) was, after all, erotic love.

The Life of Marianne has been praised as a forerunner of women's literature; in *The New Colony* Marivaux put on stage a league of women banded together to free themselves from sexual discrimination; and in *The Island of Slaves* he spoke out for human equality, his dialogue, and the shifts and turns of his argument sounding, at moments, like remote, elegant, fanciful precursors of Shaw. But apart from these, the ugliness, brutality, corruption and menace of his time scarcely appear in the decor of Marivaux's comedies. They take place in a world of fantasy and their language is a fantasy language, all delicacy, polish, and artifice. Marivaux does not look directly at the outer, actual world of history. He is concerned with the projection of feeling, in a context that scarcely exists. The reality that interests him is emotional, subjective, inward; his approach to it is analytical and his observation of it inexhaustible. He portrays a psychological reality which in itself is a play of illusions. His characters are involved in a game called love, whose substance or lack of it, and whose consequences in particular situations, they are trying to determine. The attempt leads them on and the assurance they seek or claim remains as evanescent as ever. What is discovered repeatedly is the transparent egoism of their considerations, and—if they are lucky and their roles are the right ones in their world—the truth of their feelings.

The False Confessions is one of Marivaux's principal comedies, a good example of the qualities for which he is remembered. The illusion it begins with, and which it pursues with typical grace and precision, is vanity—the wish to attract attention—upon whose sleights and discoveries much of the action turns. It all ends as happily as it is supposed to, in sincerity and the marriage of true lovers. The interest and the value of the play survive in Marivaux's depictions of the feelings of his utterly unexceptional characters and in the celebrated delicacy and elegance of his idiom. Neither steps easily or spontaneously into another time or language, or onto our stage. Yet Marivaux was a man of the theater, and the plays, the parts, have worked in the theater, in our time.

With all these plays, obviously, but with Marivaux perhaps most of all, what we need is the right actors, to surprise us and make us wonder who these people are who seem so foreign to us, who express themselves so differently from anything we are used to hearing, and whose feelings, at the same time, seem oddly like those with which we are intimately familiar.

April 1984, Maui

Contents

ROBERT THE DEVIL
Anonymous, 14th Century
1

THE RIVAL OF HIS MASTER
Alain-René Lesage
75

TURCARET
Alain-René Lesage
109

THE FALSE CONFESSIONS
Pierre de Marivaux
183

Robert the Devil

Anonymous, 14th Century

Characters

THE DUKE	THE POPE
ROBERT	THE HERMIT
BREAKMUG	GOD
TRICKLE	OUR LADY
GARTERS	GABRIEL
POKE	MICHAEL
THE PEASANT	SAINT JOHN
THE MONK	THE CHEESE-WIFE
THE ABBOT	FIRST CRONY
FIRST BARON	SECOND CRONY
SECOND BARON	THE EMPEROR
HUCHON	FIRST KNIGHT
PIERON	SECOND KNIGHT
THIRD BARON	THE MESSENGER
FIRST HERMIT	FIRST PAGAN
THE VALET	SECOND PAGAN
FIRST SQUIRE	THE GOVERNESS
SECOND SQUIRE	THIRD PAGAN
THE DAMOISELLE	THE SENESCHAL
THE DUCHESS	THE DAUGHTER
FIRST SERGEANT	THE PRIESTS
SECOND SERGEANT	

Act One

THE DUKE:
Where, Robert, will your deeds bring you?
For I believe you grow worse and worse
And are more wicked today than yesterday.
I conferred knighthood upon you
So that you would leave off wicked ways
And turn your mind to good deeds
As a true knight should do
Who should be gentle and courteous also
To the good, and his arm sustain them,
But weigh heavy on wicked felons;
And I know and see daily
That you do just the other way,
Holding God and the Holy Church in despite
Which of all your sins is the worst.
   Be warned.

ROBERT:
Father, you do wrong
To blame me; you waste your breath.
You must not hope that I will strive
To do good: I have no gift for it.
But I will not be idle:
Since I am a knight as you say
I will harass the clergy
And beat the monks and cheat them
And steal from them and rob them,
For they have jewels
And good fair sanctuaries
Whose loot I will bear off with me,
And I will leave nothing for them;
And if one of them should complain,
Be sure my wrath will strike him
And take his life from him.
Such is the life I will lead.
Leave me in peace henceforth;
I will leave you here and go elsewhere
Where I have friends as many as I wish.

3

In two months we shall have done
So much that we shall garner
More riches than ever yours could come to.
   Of that I am certain.(*He goes.*)

THE DUKE:
Oh, God! Grief so possesses me,
I do not know what will become of me!
I see my son cannot be constrained,
Toward no right thing will he warm him,
Is fervent, fiery for ill-doing,
And scornful of well-doing.
A count's estate should be his
If he were diligent and wise.
And no more than a robber of folk he is;
Therefore with him I am displeased.
Oh, sweet Lord God, if You please
Grant him Your grace, that it may bring him
To repent the wrongs he has done.
And to pray with holy piety
For Thy mercy before he comes to die.
   Sweet Lord God.

Scene II

ROBERT:
Ho! Either my eyes trick me
Or there I see Breakmug
And his friend Trickle,
Come from some sport wherever they were.
Tell me, without wasting words,
   Where have you been?

BREAKMUG:
That we will tell you, sweet lord.
We come from labouring a little
And acquiring this coffer
   Which I carry.

ROBERT:
And from whom, say straightway,
   Have you stolen it?

TRICKLE:
What his name was I do not know,
But as a monk he was gowned,
And thoroughly he is beaten now,
Since he tried to prevent us
And to raise a defence
    Against us.

ROBERT:
Worthless work; you should
Have cut off his fists
And then killed him, certainly.
Thus I would deal with such folk.
Where is Garters, tell me,
And Poke, and Bluster?
This immediately
    I wish to know.

BREAKMUG:
At your house you will find them,
Sire, or at least there we left them
When in pursuit of the monk we went
    To rob him.

ROBERT:
Jesus! Then our feet must fly
    Till to the house they bring us.

Scene III

ROBERT:
Ho, there! I would speak to everyone,
And tell how things must be done:
I want everyone to be ready,
To come with me, wherever I go.
I mean never to cease
From going from one abbey to another
To harry the monks there,
Until it is said that I have raided
Every abbey in Normandy
And we will seek out their treasures
And bear them away with us,

And their fine jewels likewise;
And if we should find there
Any priest or lay brother
Who says one word to contradict us
Or would resist us,
Without delay let him
  Be put to death.

GARTERS:

Master, by my faith, I agree,
Since such is your will.
Soon we shall have won
  Great riches.

POKE:

Garters, that is true,
And there is reason for saying so;
For these monks are folk who stay
In their hermitages, and spend little,
Trying always to amass more;
And they have great revenues
From the houses that are theirs,
And from their other labours;
It would profit us to pillage them,
  I believe.

ROBERT:

All that is true. Let us decide,
Where we should go first of all;
For in few words I say
I mean like a hawk to strike them,
And in my words so to fright them
And in such a state to set them
That even the wisest
  Will be astonished.

TRICKLE:

And, master, besides the abbeys
We will find in the towns, surely,
Misers with their thousands
Who dare not divulge their money;
And there too we shall labour profitably,
  I do not doubt.

6

BREAKMUG:
That is true. Follow me,
And I will lead you to a man
Whose wealth, they say,
Attains five thousand and more.
He is a peasant, furthermore,
Without expenses to pay;
I think to this day he never
    Ate one good morsel.

ROBERT:
Breakmug, at once, quickly,
Lead us to him, I pray;
Sirs, let us follow after
    Without delay.

POKE:
We are ready to follow.
    Go; hurry.

Scene IV

BREAKMUG:
Master, to you I tell no lies;
Here is that peasant's house;
Let us go in and not pause,
    So I advise.

ROBERT:
Breakmug, I wish the same.
    Who sleeps here within?

THE PEASANT:
No one at all, within here,
By my faith, is asleep, sire;
If you wish anything, there is no one
    But me in all this house.

BREAKMUG:
This is the person, master.
    Of whom I told you.

ROBERT:

Seize him at once, without more words,
Bind together his feet and fists,
And do all without delay,
  As seems best to me.

THE PEASANT:

By so high a Lord as God is,
I cry mercy of you, sweet sirs.
I do not believe that ever
I wronged anyone who is here,
Or have ever seen one of you,
  It seems to me.

ROBERT:

Enough! Do not try so to trick us;
Rather, show us now your treasure
That you have amassed in gold and silver,
Or wretchedly you will die,
For I will cut off your head
  In this place.

THE PEASANT:

Sire, do not doubt that I will do
What you ask, without dispute;
In God's name, come and look, sire,
With a good will I will show it you,
And this coffer open to you.
  Look, sire.

ROBERT:

What coins are these, tell me?
  Are they florins?

THE PEASANT:

Yes, pure lambs and angels;
And all this, gold money minted in Paris;
And these other coins besides,
  Fair and valuable.

POKE:

Have you no silver plate hidden
  Somewhere else?

THE PEASANT:
No, sire, so may God save me,
Except for these six goblets
Which are not well polished
    As you can see.

ROBERT:
Now, Trickle, come; be lively.
Seize these goblets, these sacks
Keep safe for me, and you,
Poke, take this in your hand.
As for you, base peasant,
Give thanks to our company,
Since we have left you your life.
    Now let us go.

THE PEASANT:
Sirs, I pray to God, devoutly
That he may keep you in safety
And bless you, through His Bounty,
    At last with His love.

TRICKLE:
Let us make no further delay here,
But let us go to that abbey
And enter by force there.
I am sure we will find
Great wealth, as I speak truly.
    Master, let us go.

GARTERS:
Certainly there must be
Great wealth in that place,
Jewels, gold and silver
    In any case.

ROBERT:
Let us go, then. Poke, give
Trickle the sack you carry;
Bear it all to my house, Trickle,
    And return straightway.

TRICKLE:
I shall return so quickly,

That you may well marvel. Do you, meanwhile,
Ponder nothing but robbing craftily
    Much and quickly.

ROBERT:
Proceed, sirs, immediately:
We shall not eat again
Till we have rifled, within,
    Both high and low.

POKE:
Let us go; I have no patience.
I could have easily found friends
With whom I might have caroused at leisure.
    Make this worth my while.

BREAKMUG:
When you talk that way I believe
    That you mock us.

Scene V

GARTERS:
Master, look; that one is the monk.
    I know him well.

ROBERT:
Very well, I will go and speak to him:
Monk, I would have you enter the abbey
And show your treasure to me
    Without grudging any.

THE MONK:
And you, that so haughtily
Demand to look within and see
The treasure, who are you?
    Tell me truly.

ROBERT:
Now, Breakmug, draw your sword
And such a blow strike him
As shall, like corn, fell him,

And here kill him.

THE ABBOT:
No, sire, no; by God's grace!
Do not draw sword or knife,
And you will be shown everything;
I will show you high and low,
Only do us no harm,
    I pray you.

ROBERT:
Lead us, then, I advise you,
At once to where we may
See your treasure, or by Jesu
    We shall run upon you.

THE ABBOT:
I consent utterly and wish it.
Come, lords, since you desire it,
And what you wish shall be done.
There, as you see, is our treasure.
Here, first, our cloths of gold,
Here our chasubles, our tunics,
Here in this other place our relics
In their honour and glory,
And adorned, as you see,
With gold and precious stones.
Indeed many, many days'
Labour must have been spent
In fashioning the settings
Where they are set; as you can see,
And their framing was very costly,
    Beyond any doubt.

ROBERT:
Monk, hear now what I say.
Tell me, what is in that coffer?
You have not brought that one before me.
    Why is that?

THE ABBOT:
Sire, it is there that we keep
Sundry things in safety

Which in trust are given us
For safe-keeping.

ROBERT:

So you say, but if I
Am not shown immediately
What is in that coffer, I shall
Have no patience with you.

THE MONK:

Do not press us to see it, sire,
Since there is nothing of ours there;
For if there is anything of worth there
It is not ours.

BREAKMUG:

You there, be still
And do not dispute our master's will
Or upon your pate you will feel
Such a thing, truly, as will
Let you praise God no more
Nor speak another word.

THE ABBOT:

My dear friend, in God's name,
Forgive him his mistaking
For his wits are not strong.
Dear sir, to you I will open
This coffer and show you
What is within.

ROBERT:

Here is a bag sealed with wax.
What is in it? Are these coins deniers?
I am pleased with this place: here is more money
Than wheat or oats in a granary.
Friends, come forward each one.
You must bend yourselves now to this burden
Without waiting here any longer.
Breakmug, first, gather up
These jewels; and you, Poke,
These deniers; and you, Garters,
Carry away all this money;

And you, Trickle,
Help Breakmug with the jewels.
    Leave nothing.

POKE:

It is done, master; go before us;
We will follow you, step for step.
Monks, I have no pity for you.
    And bear away all.

Scene VI

GARTERS:

Let us store it all in our vault,
And after that I shall lead you to where
I will make you master
Of three times as much as you now have;
Or if you know of better places,
    Tell us of them.

TRICKLE:

We are satisfied with what you say,
We shall be rich soon, in this way,
Let us not fail to visit
A single monastery
From here to Mount Saint-Michel,
But fall upon each one, if you agree,
And bear away the choicest
    Of their treasure.

BREAKMUG:

By Saint Mor, Trickle,
All my heart favours such a venture;
If two will go I will be the third,
    Have no doubt.

ROBERT:

Since we have come thus far,
Sirs, I will go with you.
I am sure that the lords of Normandy
Hate us mortally
Whatever they say;

Yet my heart is so stubborn
That I fear no man born,
And I swear to you by God's mercy
That, if I have done ill I will do worse,
For I will leave no lovely woman,
Married or virgin, without first having
My will of her, whether she likes or no,
Let it grieve who it may.
Here is our castle; let us go in
All together, and store there
   What we carry.

POKE:

That would be well done, it seems to me;
   Let us go in, master.

Scene VII

FIRST BARON:

My lord Duke, something must be done
To repair the wrongs wrought by your son.
We come to you as our lord,
Sire, and make our plaint,
And in complaining, lament
His vile misdeeds.
For he violates the nuns,
And is not aghast at his own crimes;
But in all your country
He lets no honest freeman
Live in peace, but robs him,
And if the good man should protest,
At once, besides his other losses,
   He loses his life.

SECOND BARON:

It is true: I know more than six
Who lived in honoured estate
Whom he ruined and brought to shame.
I think there is not his like under heaven,
For from here to Mount Saint-Michel
And from Genays as far as Mante
There is no monastery, as I well know,

Which he does not pillage daily.
Do not suppose that I deceive you:
He ruins them by robbery,
So that nothing of worth remains.
And then, which is worse,
He lusts after and takes by force
Our nieces, daughters, wives:
Daily he seizes them
And no one can prevent him.
We cannot endure this
   Nor contain our wrath.

THE DUKE:

Oh, Lord God! What does this mean?
I never desired anything
As I did a son. Now I have one
Who proves such that I should rejoice
If he might die before my eyes,
Such anger and torment he brings me.
Tell me, lords, what do you advise?
   What can I do?

THIRD BARON:

If it would not displease you
I would tell you what I would do.
Dear sire, I would send for him
And when he had come
I would forbid him to wreak further harm
Or villainy on anyone:
And if in the least thing he defied me,
Without waiting for further provocation
I would seize him and set him in prison,
   And keep him there.

THE DUKE:

With all my heart. Ho! Come here,
Huchon, and you, Pieron Gobaille;
Go and tell my son Robert
To come here at once; I order him to.
I shall see whether he will obey
   My commands.

HUCHON:

Sire, I think he will,

15

As duty binds him to.
We will go now
   And look for him.

Scene VIII

PIERON:
I think we might best
Go at once to his fortress,
There, better than elsewhere,
We may speak with him, and more privately;
If he is not there we shall learn
   Where we may find him.

HUCHON:
You are right; we should do as you say.
Let us go. Ho! There: I see him;
Pieron, we must run.
Sire, God give you good life!
And if it would not displease you
We wish to speak with you
For a moment only, and tell you
   What we have come for.

ROBERT:
How is this, sirs? Tell me: make haste!
   I will listen.

PIERON:
Dear sire, I will tell you.
My lord the Duke, your father,
And madame also, your mother,
Send you greetings; and the Duke bids you
In this to obey him:
He begs and commands you
Without fail to go to him,
   And at once.

ROBERT:
Tell me, so God reward you:
Do you know why I am sent for?
It is not much to ask you;

Answer me.

HUCHON:
We are not sure why.
But so much we can tell you certainly,
Sire: all the greatest barons
Of the country have gathered there,
And there is not one among them
Who does not groan and complain of you,
And they have begged him
　To remedy this.

ROBERT:
And have you come meddling,
Bringing me this message?
Ho, sir! Without delay
Seize these two: I command you:
And gouge out each of their
　Right eyes.

POKE:
Master, by the worshipful Virgin,
Since you bid it it shall be done
With dispatch: wait only a moment;
Breakmug, come here, come,
Take charge of this one and bind him,
And then we will bind that one;
Good friends, sit down
　Here on the ground.

PIERON:
Oh, dear sire, by your mercy,
As we are now let us be:
In God's name do not
　Gouge our eyes out.

ROBERT:
Be still; you will sleep better
When you lie on your beds;
Do it at once, I say;
　Dispatch them.

BREAKMUG:

Let us dally no longer;
I will deal with him without further
   Hesitation.

POKE:
And I think I will do the same
   As quickly as you.

HUCHON:
Oh, woe! In my deep anguish
   I cannot see!

PIERON:
Oh, God! I can recognise nothing
In my pain,
Which in my head, above all, is.
   Oh, God! What shall I do?

ROBERT:
Sirs, I shall now let you
Depart: Go at once without waiting.
This is defiance of the Duke, my father;
   Tell him so.

HUCHON:
Truly, that message will be given him
As soon as we may speak with him,
Sirs, we go from here
   Grieving.

PIERON:
Huchon, let us depart at once
Since he consents to let us go;
I am certain that he
   Is an enraged devil.

HUCHON:
Indeed, he has so wounded our bodies
That I am sure they will never heal.
We will be avenged one day,
   If luck allows it.

PIERON:

There indeed you tell no lie.
But for the present we must suffer;
We must go and humbly present ourselves
    Before the Duke.

HUCHON:
That we must, and recount to him
What we have learned of his son
And what villainy he has
    Wrought upon us.

PIERON:
He can see it with his own eyes.
    Let us go.

Scene IX

PIERON:
My beloved lord, may God
In His bounty preserve you
And your barons who are here also
And at last guide you
    To taste His glory.

THE DUKE:
By Saint Magloire, what is this, Pieron?
Where has your body been so beaten?
And one of your eyes has been gouged out;
    What does this mean?

PIERON:
Dear sire, your son has done this to me,
And to my companion also,
And he told us as he did so
That it was done to defy you.
See in what contempt he held you
    And holds you still.

FIRST BARON:
Surely since he so scorns you
And has wrought such villainy
He can no longer be called your vassal;

19

Sire, it were best not to delay,
But to take counsel and learn thereby
   What can be done.

THE DUKE:
Give me counsel in this matter,
  I pray you.

SECOND BARON:
Sire, most certainly I will.
He seeks to cast shame upon you;
Let him rather be utterly
Banished from all Normandy,
And send word to every town
Commanding the people therein
That each one should keep watch for him
And strive to lay hands upon him
And all those who go with him.
   Thus I advise.

THIRD BARON:
That advice I will not gainsay,
But would have him banished, sire,
Then he will not dare
   To show himself.

THE DUKE:
Huchon, go at once
Into the town to the market-place
And announce there that Robert is banished
And all who are of his company,
Say that no one must harbour them
But each strive to lay hands upon them
And imprison them straightway;
When you have made this proclamation
You will go forth from town to town
Proclaiming this, leaving no place
Unvisited as far as Ville-Dieu
   De Sanchemel.

HUCHON:
Sire, I hope to fulfil
Your command well and faithfully

And with no waste of time.

Scene X

HUCHON:
Now I have walked all the way
To the town and its market-place
And I must here perform my duty.
Oye! Hear ye! I proclaim
To everyone, as I am bidden
By the Duke of Normandy,
That for his crimes Robert the Devil
And his accomplices are banished this dukedom,
And that everyone must strive
To lay hands on him and his followers
And in close prison confine them
If by any means they may
Be taken, whether in forest or field.
Now I have done. I must go elsewhere
    And cry this proclamation.

Scene XI

GARTERS:
Master, we must renounce our ways,
For things go worse and worse with us;
We must go from this country
And make our nests elsewhere
For we are banished, all of us,
    You first of all.

ROBERT:
Tell me, I beg of you,
    Is this indeed true?

GARTERS:
Alas, it is certainly.
I heard the ban with my own ears
Today, and at that proclamation
    My heart failed me.

21

TRICKLE:
Oh, then our fortune fails us.
Therefore, master, consider where
We may go, for we must take ourselves
    From this place.

ROBERT:
Lords, have no fear of anything.
We are in a deep forest
And a strong fortress is ours;
With food we are well furnished;
Be patient till two months have passed.
Before then, by the faith I owe Saint Peter
I will have spared neither the Duke my father
His dear friends, nor his kin
But have touched their hearts with grief.
I set no store by them.
Wait by yourselves in this wood a while
And keep watch here while I am away.
Let no one enter here
    Except yourselves.

BREAKMUG:
Certainly we will do so,
    Have no fear, master.

Scene XII

ROBERT:
Oh, by God's head, can this be so?
Can my father in a rage
Banish me from my heritage?
It is mine, or will be one day
Should some ill hap befall him.
By my head, does he think to bring me
To heel with shame and injury?
If he hopes to do so, truly,
He knows little of my will,
For my intent is still the same,
I will attempt no good thing
But if I have wrought crimes and done evil
Before now, I will wreak worse still

Hereafter, as long as I live;
I do not covet nor desire
Anything that would delight me more
Than to find any occasion
Or chance of wrong-doing.
Ho! Look! I see a house.
I thought no one lived here
But I will discover who it is.
Ho! You! It seems there are
A great many of you. Who has brought you together
   Here in this place?

FIRST HERMIT:
Sire, we have come here to pray
To God, and to serve Him night and day,
And, may it please you, we are poor hermits,
   As you see.

ROBERT:
I do not heed a word you say.
But you will abide here no longer
For you must all die immediately.
Here, taste you of this edge,
And you, would you not say this sword is keen?
You, do you think flight will save you?
After this blow, go as you please.
And you, stand and receive; I love
To make my sport and game with you.
I hate nothing in this world worse
Than folk of your breed, God confound you.
It is done; I am delivered of all you;
Never will you need book again.
Whether you were clerks or laity,
Now you are dead I leave you here.
And for my play and pleasure
I will go and seek brawls
   Elsewhere.

A VALET:
(*Passing*) Sire, God send you blessings
   And give you good day.

ROBERT:
God save you! Tell me

From what place you have come
And where this road leads
   That you follow.

VALET:

I come straight from the Château of Argues,
Sire, where the Duchess will dine shortly,
And I may say there is a great crowd
   Assembled about her.

ROBERT:

Tell me, dear friend, will the Duke
   Be there also?

VALET:

No, of that I am certain.
He has gone down to the river
But he will be home again
   Early in the evening.

ROBERT:

Good. Farewell, friend. God keep you.
And I will not be withheld until
I have had word with my mother,
   Come what will.

Scene XIII

FIRST SQUIRE:

Richard, ill fortune has found us.
Here Robert comes, dressed in iron.
He is a devil of hell,
   Not a man.

SECOND SQUIRE:

In spite of Saint Peter of Rome,
Since I see he is coming here
I will not wait; I am going now
   To escape him.

FIRST SQUIRE:

And indeed I will do the same.

I prefer to flee from him.
He comes with his sword drawn
   Intending no good.

THE DAMOISELLE:

(*To the Duchess*) Oh, be quick; hurry, dear lady,
And lock yourself in your chamber,
Or this is your last hour, make no doubt.
See, here comes your son
With a naked sword in his hand.
See how everyone flees from him!
I must go and lock myself in
   In some safe place.

ROBERT:

Indeed, now past denying I see
What deadly hate the world bears me;
And if God does so too, He does justly.
Everyone shuns, runs from me;
Shame and self-disgust should consume me
For the great misdeed I have done
And the crimes with which I have befouled me.
Yet my mother does not shun me;
That shames me; lady, speak to me,
And stay: do not go from me.
I beg you, if you know, tell me
From what cause might have come
This in me: that I cannot keep me
From evil-doing however it grieve me.
I think that some vile sin
In my father or in you there was
At the hour when you conceived me,
   And from that sin I am so.

THE DUCHESS:

Son, since it must be spoken,
Know that from me the sin came.
Now at once, in God's name
Strike the head from my body.

ROBERT:

Mother, do not hope it of me.
I am worse than wicked, but I should be

25

Worse still, to do such a thing.
But tell me through what sin
I am with evil so befouled,
   I pray you.

THE DUCHESS:
Sweet son, I will tell you then.
When I had been married to your father
A long time, I was not yet a mother,
And still had conceived no child;
Consider, this often enraged me,
And to such degree that in my bed once
Where for my repose I lay,
Driven by this one thought only,
In anger I said: since God will
Make no child in my body,
Then let the devil make one there.
At that time and at that hour
Your father came home from the wood
And found me weeping bitterly.
And the good man straightway,
To allay the anguish in me,
Began to kiss me tenderly.
And it was then you were conceived.
To speak truly, I did not repent.
Your father, like a wise man, often
With pious heart prayed to God
That if it might so befall that I
Should conceive a child, which would please him
That in its life it might be such
As God might love and delight in;
And that so well it might serve Him
That it might come to reign forever
In glory; such his sweet word was.
But I in mad folly
Said: 'The devil's own may he be;
Since God will not quicken me
If I should have a child of you
To the devil I owe him.' And I believe
That it was from that oath that you
Were born with soul so misshapen
   As now you have.

ROBERT:

Oh, Lord God, Thy grace grant me!
For unless I amend me
I see I am doomed eternally.
For the adversary strives after
Nothing but to have my soul.
But I know what must be done;
I shall not sleep soundly
Until I have come to Rome
And to the Pope made confession
Of all the sins and crimes I have done.
Repentance wrings my heart
For the war I have waged always
Against all good men. Now it torments me,
I will stay no longer. I beg you, lady,
To greet my father for me.
He punished my crimes justly;
It is not his banishing me that grieves me,
For I had rather suffer cold and heat
And misery, to attain
Paradise, than on this earth reign.
    Goodbye, Mother.

THE DUCHESS:

Oh, sweet son! For your sake from
This time in bitter grief will I be
Wretched! What shall I do for sorrow?
I lose my soul, and lose my joy;
I fear that I shall not see him again;
I was puffed with pride and perversity,
Wicked and full of blasphemy
When I gave my son to the adversary.
Oh, my love, and my dear son!
If for this you shunned me
You had good cause and did justly.
    God, take pity upon me!

THE DUKE:

Ho, lady! you see, I am home early.
What is this? I find you in tears?
Will you not at least tell me
    What troubles you?

THE DUCHESS:
Oh, my dear lord, you have not heard:
Our son has gone to Rome,
And swears not to end his pilgrimage
Till the Pope has heard him confess
All the wicked things he has done;
When he had decided this
He begged me to give you
    His greeting, sire.

THE DUKE:
Madame, can it be true as you say?
Does he repent of the misdeeds
He has committed, and the hatreds
    He has heaped on himself?

THE DUCHESS:
My dear lord, of that I am certain;
Do not doubt that remorse wrings him;
For the tears run from his eyes
    When you speak to him.

THE DUKE:
But if he should walk from here to Arles
Out at elbows, on his knees,
Still he would not have atoned for all
His misdeeds, nor half of them.
Even so, may God in His mercy
Watch over him with kind charity
For I doubt that the Pope in any case
Will grant him to see his face;
I fear he may kill himself there,
    Or worse things befall him.

Scene XIV

ROBERT:
Oh, Lord God, who despise never
Nor abandon whatever sinner
So he fix himself upon Thee,
For Thy goodness I thank Thee,
Since Thou has snuffed out within me

The desire for evil-doing.
Indeed, it would be well for me
If I might convert my followers
From their crimes and guide them to goodness.
Come what may, I will speak of it to them
As soon as to my fort I have come.
    God save you all!

POKE:
Welcome, master, and well-timed.
I think a meal would not vex you,
And we were just now about to dine.
    Come and sit down.

ROBERT:
Fair lords, give heed to me:
I have done with wickedness,
And now, my sins to confess,
I am going to the Pope in Rome.
I beg you all: let everyone
From this hour be an honest man
And from wrong-doing abstain.
Repent each one now straightway,
And beg God for His mercy,
    I pray you.

GARTERS:
Do you hear this, lords? Hoy!
Foxes turn into hermits, they say.
Master, as for what you say,
    I will perform nothing.

BREAKMUG:
Garters, I
Will do the same, God strike me;
I seek more robbings and richer quarry
    Than ever.

TRICKLE:
And I also, you may be sure;
Whatever may come, have no fear
That I shall abstain before
    I am dead.

ROBERT:
Since you are agreed all
To persever thus in evil
God will suffer you no longer,
For I in His name straightway
Will take vengeance upon you all.
You first will feel my stroke.
Pass! And you, lie there, Poke;
And each of you thus must pass
Through my hands; try to escape me.
Here, and this moment, you all must die
And render up your lives to me.
Done! Let your sacks sleep where they are,
For from this hour forth you are
Honest men, and no backsliding.
I must set fire to this place
At once, and consume the house.
But now I look, I see the treasure
Which is great, and would be wasted
Unless to some good end I put it.
Ha! I will do better, as a I can.
I will lock this door with a key.
Never again will I live here.
I will go to that abbey
And tell the Abbot my plan
And what I would have done
  With the treasure.

Scene XV

THE MONK:
Lord Abbot, here comes that one
Who has wrought us so much harm.
We must hide wherever we can,
  Lest he find us.

THE ABBOT:
No, I have no wish to move
For the moment from where I am;
I think he will do me no harm
  This time.

30

ROBERT:

Lord Abbot, I come before you
As a sinner seeking grace,
And beseeching your forgiveness
For the great injuries I have wrought you.
Sire, receive me charitably,
For indeed I repent bitterly
The crimes I have done since my childhood;
Besides, in such disgust and horror
I held them, that without showing any
Mercy, as earnest of good faith I
Have killed all the robbers who followed me,
Because all were fixed in their intent
Not to turn aside from stealing.
To the Duke my father carry
This key, and require of him
To go with you to my manor,
There you will find great treasure
Which from you and others I have stolen,
Which I would have returned again
To all those who can say
What and how much from them was taken.
I charge you both with this,
For I depart at once for Rome
To seek, such is my intention,
The Pope's absolution.
   Farewell, Lord Abbot.

THE ABBOT:

Robert, do you not rail at me
And say this in mockery?
Before God, will you not bring us
   To worse ruin than before?

ROBERT:

Sire, I do not deride you.
Go; when you have come to my fortress
You will find all your jewels there;
Take them again, without waiting,
And the rest in God's name return
   As I have said.

THE ABBOT:
Than fret yourself no further,
But consider this done already
For it will be performed exactly
   As you have asked me.

ROBERT:
Until I am absolved and quit
Of my crimes I shall have no ease.
Adieu! And I beseech: may it please you
   Pray for me.

THE ABBOT:
Now, Brother Hugh, I
And yourself must at once go
To the Duke and tell him
   Of this thing.

THE MONK:
Let us go, sire; and I am
Bold to say that God in this man
Has worked a miracle, since from poison
The antidote he has wrought,
   And good from evil.

THE ABBOT:
Indeed, good brother, I think it is so.
For from a lion raging and fierce
A lamb he has made, thus sweet
And thus meek; God's name be praised.
There is the Duke, by our good chance.
   Let us speak to him at once.

Scene XVI

THE ABBOT:
My lord the Duke, God preserve you
From evil, and in joy keep you;
And keep you well, my lady
   The Duchess.

THE DUCHESS:
Sire, may His Holy Will
  Be done in us.

THE DUKE:
Lord Abbot, what news
  Do you bring us?

THE ABBOT:
Good news and fair, my dear lord.
Your son, in whom you should
Take great joy, with many
Salutations sends you this key,
And begs you in kindness to do
One thing, and in this wishes no wrong:
He asks that you and I may go
To his fortress, for we shall find there
As he has told me, great treasure
Which from churches he has sacked
And stolen from the laity; and further
He asks that it may all be
Paid back again, restored to its owners,
So that each may receive what was his.
He has killed the robbers
Who were his followers
Because they would not forswear
Their robbery, nor be
Persuaded to repent.
To the Pope in Rome he has gone
Directly, all unskilled in the way.
Sire, will you now tell me,
If you please, what you intend;
For I believe he will yet be
An honest man, and do much good,
  Or so I hope.

THE DUCHESS:
God aid him and strengthen him!
My soul, such sorrow I have for him.
In God's name, is he going on foot
  Or mounted?

THE ABBOT:

He is going, so God from evil guard me,
On foot, to suffer the journey more sharply.
And so bitterly does he
Repent him, that when he went from me
I feared that his heart would burst
Into two pieces, truly,
With such flow of tears he bewept
   His misdeeds, lady.

THE DUKE:

Now God in His grace preserve him,
Body and soul. Let us go
To the fortress, Lord Abbot, and waste no more
Time, but take up the treasure,
Then send criers proclaiming everywhere
That if any against Robert complain
Of goods stolen, let such a one come
To us, and we will restore them to him
As soon as he makes it known to us.
As for you, has he wrought you
Any loss in all your life?
   Tell me no lie.

THE ABBOT:

Loss, sire? The abbey
He reduced to beggary:
Its treasures he took away,
And the jewels, wrongfully,
Which he says still at his castle are;
He bade me take them again
As soon as I should see them,
   Of that be sure.

THE DUKE:

Lord Abbot, all this will be fulfilled;
You will have what is yours; that is just.
Let us three wait here no longer
   But go to the castle.

THE ABBOT:

Dear lord, let us go; I agree,
   Since it is your wish.

Act Two

ROBERT:
Oh, Virgin, by whom peace was made
Between man and God, then
When God became a man in thee,
Oh, lady full of amity,
Upon the sinner I am take pity,
I who until now did evil only,
Yet, oh, Virgin most sweet, unfailing,
I desire and am filled with longing
To atone for what I have done
And with full penitence pay,
That my soul go not to hell.
To thee I come, lady, to thee my prayer make
Who to all sinners are the redression,
And comfort of the comfortless.
Lady, in well-doing guide me,
That the adversary may not have me.
Oh, God, so far I have come,
I see the Pope seated there on his throne;
Will he not suffer me to fall
At his feet and crave benediction?
I shall beg it of him: Sire, take
   Pity on me.

FIRST SERGEANT:
Oy! What is this ruffian doing here?
Get up, by all bad luck, get up,
Or mark my words, you will never
   Again go upright.

SECOND SERGEANT:
He wants us to beat him still harder,
And I shall admit no weariness
Until I have given him enough.
Are you from the Place Maubert?
Feel this, and this. Get out, villain,
   Or worse will befall you.

35

THE POPE:
Hold there, hold! Let him be.
No more; do not touch him.
Let nothing hinder his saying
   What he wishes to me.

ROBERT:
Holy Father, my lord, I beg you
   To hear my confession.

THE POPE:
Tell me first of what nation
You are, and what station;
Whether you are a knight, or a priest
   Or a layman.

ROBERT:
That I will tell you this moment,
Since I must make it known to you;
I am the Duke of Normandy's son,
But I regard myself and am,
Sire, meaner than a dog's worth,
I am before God so abominable.
Robert my name is, called also The Devil;
For the love of God give me counsel
Or else I am lost, I see clearly;
   (That briefly is my story.)

THE POPE:
Are you that same Robert, truly,
Of whom everywhere they say
That he has so many misdeeds done
That no one can number them?
In God's name I conjure and charge you
To work no more wickedness, neither here
Nor, wherever you meet him, to any creature,
   From this day forth.

ROBERT:
Sire, such is my will; but may it
Please you, without more delay
To hear the confession of my sins;
   That would be kindness.

36

THE POPE:
That indeed I will do. In God's name
  Kneel down here before me.

ROBERT:
Holy father, I beg you, for charity,
Do not turn in horror from my misery.
When my father married my mother
A long time passed, I speak truly,
And no child was born to them;
My mother grew sad at this,
And such wrath worked in her
That when she conceived me, sire,
In spite and rage she said
That if she might conceive a child
She would give it to the adversary.
So that ever since I was born
Such was my evil fortune
That my wishes were all for wickedness;
In short, I was so outrageous
And so bold in my wickedness,
That not one, but everyone fled me
As soon as they saw me.
None ever did so much evil
As I have, like the villain
  That I was.

THE POPE:
Robert, tell me the truth in this:
I think that grief at the wrongs you have done
Weighs heavy on you, and you repent.
  Is that so?

ROBERT:
Hear me, sire, while I tell you;
Truly, such remorse I have
And I repent so bitterly
The crimes I have committed, sire,
That often I cannot say a word
Repentence so grips and wrings
My wretched heart, and so constrains me,
That I take no joy any more
In sport and laughter; and riches repel me;

Everything that was once my pleasure
Now seems rough and bitter to me,
    Such my remorse is.

THE POPE:
Since it is so, I think
I can counsel you simply:
Along the Rhône river make your way
Perhaps three leagues, not further,
To acquit yourself better before God.
There you will find a hermitage
And a wise confessor there;
His name I need not give you;
He is a pious and holy man;
Tell him I have sent you to him
So that he may hear your confession
And lay upon you a penance;
Say in everything I submit you
    To his command.

ROBERT:
Holy Father, I shall go there
Since he is a worthy man
And you so bid me. God preserve you!
I shall set out now, at once,
To have holiness for my soul.
And Lord God, by Thy grace,
Grant me life, time and place
To serve Thee so worthily
    That I may come thus to salvation.

Scene II

ROBERT:
Now I have come nearly
To the end of my journey, for there I see
The hermitage to which the Pope sent me,
And from this place I have walked to
I can see the holy hermit.
I shall go nearer. Sire, for my sins'
Redression the Pope sent me here,
For you to hear my confession

As my need is.

THE HERMIT:
Fair, sweet brother, I am willing,
Since the Pope has sent you to me.
Now tell me at once what I must hear,
    And I shall listen.

ROBERT:
Sire, for my soul's sake
To God and to you I make
Confession of all the sins I have done;
And to tell from the beginning truly,
I am Robert of Normandy
Who have committed every crime
In the world; when I was a child
I struck our neighbours' children
And so cruelly abused them
That for surname people called me
The Devil, and the name stayed with me.
In my childhood so wicked I was,
Holy Father, I murdered my master
Who had come to teach me my letters;
When I had become a knight
I gave myself to robbery
And to pillaging abbeys,
Sacked monasteries, and many
Nuns I have violated,
Brought many men to poverty
And their goods taken away:
Worse I have done, which grieves me;
Seven hermits I have killed, sire,
Whom I found in a hermitage
Serving God in their goodness.
Countless crimes I have done.
In God's name I pray you, and by
His holy passion, for charity
Upon me take compassion,
For I am mindful of my sins.
Lay upon me some penance
    And I will do it.

THE HERMIT:
Sweet son, that I will do,

But for today remain with me,
And when you have waked tomorrow
I will counsel you clearly
And tell you what you must do.
Let us dine now, my dear friend,
And afterwards we will sleep
   Until tomorrow.

ROBERT:

I swear to you by my hand,
Sire, so great is my repentance,
That I neither desire nor could eat
   Anything.

THE HERMIT:

Then to outwit hunger
Lie down on this bed here;
Do not wait any longer;
I will go and sleep elsewhere
Until tomorrow, my dear friend,
   Until daybreak.

ROBERT:

Sire, I will perform straightway
Whatever you ask, right or wrong.
I shall sleep here in this place.
   God be with you.

THE HERMIT:

And I in another place
Will lie down. Good night, friend.
By no means, now that he is
At rest, will I go to bed.
I shall go into my chapel
And pray for him devoutly.
Sire, who for the salvation
Of men offered Thyself upon
A cross to hang, and to die there
To snatch back the souls in pain,
Sire, though monstrous his
Wickedness was, for this sinner
Who longs by Thy grace to be remade
I pray to Thee: pardon him

For his sins, and give me
Guidance and counsel me clearly;
Tell me what penance to lay
Upon him for his ill-deeds.
Alas, sleep weighs so heavy
Upon me, I cannot hold it off,
I cannot. I must sleep in this place
    From sheer weariness.

Scene III

GOD:

Gabriel, I bid you go
Down to the earth, and with him you
Michael, and you, John, my dear friend.
Go into that chapel
Of my good friend, who calls to me.
Mother, come here beside me.
I would give him guidance in this
    As he beseeches me.

OUR LADY:

Son, since he begs you to counsel him
It would not be right to fail him;
Angels, rise up straightway,
And about my Son and me
As we go, bearing us company,
    You must sing.

GABRIEL:

Lady, what desire soever
Is yours, we will refuse never.
Friend Michael, tell me now,
    Which song shall it be?

MICHAEL:

Gabriel, let us, you and I,
Pronounce this rondel, for joy:
Oh, hearts of men praise everlastingly
The Virgin; for her purity
Above the angels she was raised high;
She who for her meekness

Is in heaven's highest place.
Oh, hearts of men praise everlastingly
The Virgin; for her purity.
For so is she full of grace
That who serves her in truth will be
    Blessed everlastingly.

Scene IV

GOD:
Friend, listen to the truth I say;
What in your goodness you ask of Me
I give you. What penance to lay
On this sinner, as piously
You inquire: Say that he
Must act as though he were a madman;
And at all times, wherever he may be
For a year he must not one word say
But be dumb; for his bodily
Hunger, besides, he must eat
Nothing at all except what
From the dogs he may take. It does not
Please Me to ordain lighter
    Penance than this.

OUR LADY:
Now, indeed you should
For your faith's sake rejoice and be glad,
Since God comes here to speak to you
And I also, who am His mother.
Let us return, let us return now
    At once together.

SAINT JOHN:
Lady, that would be best, I think.
You two angels go before
Singing, and I will follow after,
And with you I will sing
In harmony, as best I can,
    And joyfully.

GABRIEL:
Since you will make a third with us,

This place will no longer know us.
But as we rise up, sing we
Together as folk full of joy.
For so is she full of grace
That who serves her in truth will be
    Blessed everlastingly.

THE HERMIT:
Oh, Lord God, for the joy
And grace Thou hast granted me,
Since in my sleep I have seen Thee,
And Thy sweet mother also,
Most humbly I thank Thee,
And for the thing Thou hast told me,
What penance most justly
On this sinner I should lay
So he may come to honesty
    And to please Thee.

ROBERT:
Alas, in my sloth too deeply
I have slept. I must rouse me
And set myself to find
Where the holy hermit may be
From whom I may have absolution
    And be quit of my sins.

THE HERMIT:
Robert, approach; come here
    To me.

ROBERT:
Sire, I would not dare
Approach you unless you had called me,
Lest you might think that I
    Came presumptuously.

THE HERMIT:
The Holy Father has charged me
To absolve you, as you say;
You must be resolute against wickedness
If you wish to enter into grace;
This is what you must do, friend:

Conduct yourself like a madman
With a great club about your neck hung,
And in whatever place you may be
You must eat no meat, save
Such as from the dogs you may take.
And your time you must pass
In silence. To all this I bind you.
These three points obey,
My dear friend, and I am certain
That God will show you mercy
   At the last day.

ROBERT:
With all my heart, sire, and joyfully
I will do these things you have told me,
And if by such means I may be
Quit of the mortal sins I have done
Praised be the sweet King of the heavens
   And of the earth.

THE HERMIT:
Now go, friend, begin
Your penance, to gain grace
And do not delay
   By even one day.

ROBERT:
I will, sire; I will maintain me
Like a madman, and neither
Take note when they mock me,
Nor one word, nor half a word I will say.
Sire, to God I commend you.
I must take thought and devise
In what guise, and how best to play
   The madman.

THE HERMIT:
Friend, the Virgin, of sweet delights,
Willed me to set this penance on you
That before God your soul might be
   Clean of all crimes.

44

Scene V

THE CHEESE-WIFE:
I think this is a good place
To set down my basket full of cheeses,
For wise men and fools both here pass,
And this is the market-place.
Besides, I have walked far enough.
I will set it here.
Ho, what is this? A madman
In this place laughing through his teeth
At my basket where all the cheeses are.
By the faith I owe Saint Germain
Before he puts his hand in there
I will carry my goods away
And take them to sell elsewhere:
Otherwise he might steal from me
A cheese, or perhaps all I have.
   I will not stay here.

FIRST CRONY:
My good fellows, look at that
Madman, his face and his behaviour;
On one foot he dances, and hops on the other,
And comports himself ridiculously,
So may God a good week give you.
Let us two be so brave
As to approach him more closely
To hear the words he will say,
For I think he will make us laugh before
   We come away.

SECOND CRONY:
Indeed, let us go nearer to him;
By Saint Giles, I have not seen
A madman in this town for a long time.
What is your name? Gilbert?
By my soul, he looks like Trubert.
Come over here behind his back.
I will hit him from behind
A good clout with my five fingers
Now look at me, Robelin.

Who hit you?

FIRST CRONY:
He talks no more than a dead
Donkey. What does he say?
Look how he bursts out
Laughing; what does he find funny?
I will decorate him with charcoal;
It will make the oaf more beautiful.
There now; your face is not
So ugly as it was before; if you
Knew the service I have done you
You would thank me handsomely.
Look at him: would you not say his face
    Was blackened prettily?

SECOND CRONY:
Now, by God, what shall I do to him?
There under his hat I will put
This old scrap of rag, and I
Will tear out some of his hair, so:
One handful, two; there, Jack foot-butt.
And there is a crown fit for your head.
Is he not better dressed now
To clown it before you and amuse you?
Instead of yourself bearing a banner
    I will do it for you.

FIRST CRONY:
I will stay here no longer;
I have looked long enough at his folly;
I am going, for his madness begins
    To sicken my brain.

SECOND CRONY:
I feel pity for his fool ways
And that he cannot even one word say.
He is weeping, indeed yes, he is;
Look at him; it is done; there he goes.
He has amused us for a time
    And made us laugh.

FIRST CRONY:
That is true; tell me, will you come now

And drink with me?

SECOND CRONY:
I will that, by the friendship I bear you.
    Let us go.

Scene VI

THE EMPEROR:
My lords, I am hungry.
Bid them make ready
The tables and set them before me,
    For I wish to eat.

THE SQUIRE:
Sire, your will shall be done
At once, without delay.
You, fetch cloths to spread here.
Remon, the Emperor
Is hungry and wishes to eat.
    Tell the kitchen, quickly.

FIRST KNIGHT:
I will do it, my sweet friend.
Here are the cloths; they may
Better be laid if we two
    Spread them together.
Dear sire, here is your Royal table
Prepared for you; sit down when you please
And your dinner will be served you
    Immediately.

THE EMPEROR:
There is no need to persuade me.
Have no fear; I am seated already.
Now, fetch me food to eat
    This moment.

THE SQUIRE:
Sire, with pleasure, and instantly.
Here is bread, and a bottle of wine.
Now, tell me what your pleasure is,

47

Sire, and at once command me
From which plate you would have me
Cut, and without fail I will do it,
    My loved lord.

THE EMPEROR:
Lords, who has sent among us
This man I see coming towards us?
He would shine out in a thousand
He looks so strange; I think he is mad;
By Saint Paul, it is a great pity.
Do not stand dreaming; call him quickly
And let him be given something to eat
    Here before me.

FIRST KNIGHT:
Here, friend, come forward.
By what name do they call you?
Answer at once; conceal nothing
    From the Emperor.

SECOND KNIGHT:
His manner proclaims clearly that he
Is a simpleton, a madman, truly.
The way he makes a face at us all
And then walks away counting his steps;
Look, here he comes back again, trotting,
With his club around his neck slung
And the burden of it making
    His face run with sweat.

THE SQUIRE:
My friend, you are a good, prudent man.
Sit down here for a little while;
I will serve you, with all care.
You will have as much good meat as you desire;
Do so, my friend; you may believe
    You will eat well.

THE EMPEROR:
Here, Louvet; here, Louvet; good dog;
    Gnaw this joint, Louvet.

FIRST KNIGHT:
Look; he is going up to the dog,
And trying to take his meat away
And the dog keeps hold of it firmly
  With his teeth.

SECOND KNIGHT:
But still he tries to take it away,
While the dog grips it still and struggles;
This is a fine fight, truly,
  And fit for laughter.

THE SQUIRE:
However hard the dog holds
With his teeth, the madman pulls harder;
Look; he grappled the dog by the throat
  And took the meat away.

FIRST KNIGHT:
But wait; see whether the dog will let him
  Carry it away.

SECOND KNIGHT:
I think he will not; but the madman
Bites to the bone as fast as he can
To eat all the meat that is there;
I think he will eat so shrewdly
He will leave the dog no meat
  But the gnawed bone only.

THE EMPEROR:
Let him eat it, I charge you;
It is his madness drives him to do so.
Here, you will have this bread, Louvet;
  Here, Louvet; here.

FIRST KNIGHT:
Look: before the dog has so much
As tasted it he will take that also;
It is done; he has taken it from him
  In spite of him.

THE EMPEROR:
The man amazes me,

So utter is his folly;
He has broken the bread in two
To share with the dog, and given him
The larger piece of the two,
   And not a word spoken.

SECOND KNIGHT:
Mad completely, so much is clear,
And is not from this country,
But strangest of all is that he
Speaks no more than a deaf-mute;
Indeed, with his madness I think he
   Must be a mute also.

THE SQUIRE:
But look at this new strange thing:
The madman at the dog's heels follows,
Runs after him everywhere. In his madness
   He loves him.

THE EMPEROR:
Go after him now, by your oath to me;
And see what he does; watch closely;
Find out if he follows the dog
   Where it goes.

THE SQUIRE:
Sire, so God my strength be,
With pleasure I shall do all you bid me.
I return; and I saw this:
The madman is lying, believe this,
Beside your dog, who has lain down
   Under the stairs.

THE EMPEROR:
If you would serve as would please me,
First, from that place fetch him,
And then bring him instantly
A cot, and pillows,
Coverlet, and two sheets of linen
   For him to lie in.

THE SQUIRE:
Beloved sir, without more words

I will do as you bid me
As soon as I have fetched him forth.
It is done; now at once
I will take a bed to the madman,
And then come back here again.
   (*He goes out, and returns.*)
Beloved sire, hear what I say;
I have taken a bed to him
For his greater comfort, to lie in;
But, sire, believe this, truly,
With his foot he kicked it away;
He had no wish to lie therein,
But beside the dog lay down
   As I say.

THE EMPEROR:
Has he some straw under him?
   Tell me that.

THE SQUIRE:
Yes, beloved sire; a great pile.
When I saw that he
Would not in the bed lie
I brought him a heap of straw,
And in that both he
   And the dog burrowed down.

THE EMPEROR:
Then since it is so, leave them;
   They are content thus.

A MESSENGER:
Beloved sire, there is no time to waste:
You must make ready in haste
To defend your lands and yourself;
The pagans are ravaging our country;
We have had battle with them already
But they proved stronger than we;
And further, sire, they are coming
Here in great force, and their intent
Is to conquer you straightway.
They will wreak devastation upon us,
Sire, unless you counsel us

In this matter.

THE EMPEROR:
Lords, I think we had best
Arm ourselves and go
All together to attack them.
You, go proclaim this immediately
To all my vassals who are not here;
Bid each one arm and hasten
To the battle without delay;
    Do it quickly.

THE SQUIRE:
Indeed, sire, I delight to obey;
This moment, for the love I bear you,
I shall set out to tell them
    All together.

THE EMPEROR:
And let us here arm quickly
    As I have said.

FIRST KNIGHT:
Beloved sire, I
For my part shall obey instantly;
And pray God among us justly
    Deal out honour.

SECOND KNIGHT:
I think He will do so, truly,
For we go forth to fight only
For what is ours; to maintain
    What belongs to us.

THE SQUIRE:
Since I am here, I must not be
Detained further, but here in this place
Make my proclamation, without more waiting.
I am impatient for it to be done.—
Harken to me, great and small,
The Emperor hereby
Commands you, everyone,
To arm and make ready for battle;

For we must fight against the pagans
Who have invaded this country
And wish to have it for their own.
For this fight the Emperor summons
All his men who are not with him
And commands both laymen and clergy,
All, to arm without delay,
    And make ready.

Scene VII

GOD:
Gabriel, I wish you to go
At once to Robert the madman,
And tell him to look in the meadow
Where the clear fountain rises,
There white armour is waiting for him,
And arms also he will find there;
And as soon as this armour is on him
He must go and fight against the pagans
And lend aid to the Christians
    At once, and help them.

GABRIEL:
True God, since you wish it, I
    Shall go from here to that place straightway.

Scene VIII

GABRIEL:
Robert, listen to what I say;
God bids you go immediately
And look in the meadow
Over there where there is a fountain;
Go alone; take no one with you.
There you will find splendid
White armour; arm yourself in that;
And once armed, go against
The pagans, and to the aid
Of the Christians, for through you
They will overthrow the pagans, truly;

53

But when you wish to disarm
Come to the same place again,
And leave those arms and armour
Of great price there where you found them.
And after, if you hear ever
That the Saracens, to defy
The Romans, or contend with them,
Have come to despoil this country again,
Go at once and take up those arms,
And guard and give aid to the Romans,
And such grace will go with them
That the victory will be theirs.
    Which said, I have done.

Scene IX

THE EMPEROR:
At once, lords, now we are armed,
Let us go forward against the Saracens
And defend ourselves like brave men;
Let us charge them there where I see them;
Death, let us deal death to all
    This scum.

FIRST PAGAN:
Sabaudo! Bahe fuzaille,
Draquitone, baraquita
Arabium malaquita
    Hermes zalo!

SECOND PAGAN:
Jupiter naquit Apolo
    Perhegathis.

FIRST KNIGHT:
After them; the dogs run;
After them! At least they have lost
This first battle, certainly,
    God be praised.

SECOND KNIGHT:
With all my heart I praise Him.

Sire, let us withdraw now,
And return into your fortress
　To rest ourselves.

FIRST KNIGHT:
Let us do so, for I think
We shall see no more Saracens today,
Since we have beaten them from the field.
　Let us go, sire.

THE EMPEROR:
Let us go, then; I will not refuse you.
Lords, let us give praise to God
Now, since we are in a safe place;
For today has been favourable to us.
Bring us wine, there, and rich food.
Nevertheless, to ward off mischance,
I command you, let no one disarm
Except for the helmets we have on;
For indeed we do not know
　When they may return.

SECOND KNIGHT:
By my faith, I think they will not dare
Return against us this day again,
Nor form ranks for fighting again,
　Nor take up their place.

THE EMPEROR:
Look at the madman: his face
Is blood-stained in more than one place.
This was a villainous deed,
By my body, whoever did it,
To so bruise him about the face.
For this madman troubles no one;
He is a gentle fool; my displeasure
　On whoever harms him.

FIRST KNIGHT:
I will say, sire, what perhaps
Befell him; while we were in battle
Against the pagans, he also
May have fought against them

55

In his way, and they beat him;
   At least it may be so.

THE EMPEROR:
And so it may be, but by
Saint Philbert, if anyone dare harm him
And I learn of it, do not suppose
But it shall go so hard with that man
That he will have no cause for laughter.
But now, who knows to tell me
Who that knight may have been
Who by his strength and prowess
In the battle brought us
To triumph over our enemies?
   Who can name him?

FIRST KNIGHT:
Here, look, comes the Emperor's daughter
   That has been mute from her birth.

SECOND KNIGHT:
See, she would speak to her father;
She makes signs to tell him something.
   What does she mean?

FIRST KNIGHT:
Towards the seneschal she points
And signifies no.
Now look, in the air she shapes
Armour, and smiles pointing
   Out the door towards the meadow.

SECOND KNIGHT:
Fashions with her arms a fighting
And in her face madness. It is not
   Clear what she means.

THE EMPEROR:
What is it, daughter, that you
Show me by signs? I cannot
Understand them, God give me grace.
Governess, cannot you
Interpret clearly what my daughter

56

Wishes, by her dumb-show,
  To tell me?

THE GOVERNESS:
Beloved sire, she is saying
That the ragged madman there
Was the knight who today fought for you
And so bravely that the Saracens
Were discomfited and put to flight
  By his strength.

THE EMPEROR:
God visit misfortune upon you!
Is this the schooling you give her?
You do not teach her but drive her mad.
Unless you guide her differently
You will not keep your post for long,
And you may be punished yet more dearly.
How could a madman so strike
Panic among knights in battle
That he gained the glory
  Over all the rest?

SECOND KNIGHT:
Such things are not accomplished by fools,
But by men who are skilled in fighting
And full of desire to gain glory
  In the battle.

THE EMPEROR:
That is true as you say;
One needs skill and bravery.
Go, Governess, go
And take my daughter with you
And instruct her differently.
My lords, I marvel at these women;
They seem prudent sensible dames,
Yet will be lunatic suddenly
And you will see the wisest of them
  Are the greatest fools.

THE SQUIRE:
Here is the wine and spiced meat

Which you commanded a moment ago;
Taste of this wine, if you please,
    When you wish to drink.

THE EMPEROR:
With pleasure; I shall sup
    Of this wine first.

THE SQUIRE:
It is as light and clear and fine
    As one could wish.

THE EMPEROR:
It is good and unclouded;
It must be of great age.
Drink, lords, fill and drink
    Here before me.

FIRST KNIGHT:
That we will, beloved sire,
    Now you have supped first.

THE MESSENGER:
Dear sire, you must arm
At once, and all your men,
For by my faith, here
Behind me the pagans come, truly,
Drawn up in ordered ranks
    And charging to meet you.

THE EMPEROR:
At once, lords, without delay;
Let us wait where we are no longer,
But this moment with all haste spur on
    Against them.

SECOND KNIGHT:
None of us needs do more
Than put on his helmet; and we are ready.
Let us go at once, without waiting,
    Since they are so near.

58

THE EMPEROR:
One thing I ask of you.
If the knight in white armour
Should come again to the battle
And should give us aid and succour,
Let him not go, without one of you
Discovering, at whatever cost,
Who he may be, before he can
    Escape out of your hands.

FIRST KNIGHT:
Sire, it shall be done as you say.
Let us go; in God's name let us go
And attack the pagans, and say no more,
But wield stroke and slash
In the battle as well as we may
    To gain glory.

SECOND KNIGHT:
I think we shall gain it, truly,
And that God will give us aid;
For it would be a great horror
Otherwise, if that pagan rabble
Should conquer Christian people
    And make them their slaves.

THE EMPEROR:
Now at once, let each one lay
Hands on his sword, for the attack
Upon those who covet wrongfully
    That which is ours.

FIRST KNIGHT:
Forward! Upon them! Death! Death!
    Death to them all.

THIRD PAGAN:
Hara Mare, fara marez
    Astripodis.

SECOND KNIGHT:
You will have no quarter from me.
    This stroke is yours.

59

THE EMPEROR:

In the name of Saint Mary!
There he is, lords; a noble knight!
How can one man fight as he does?
If he had not come, by my faith
We should all have been overcome
    And destroyed.

FIRST KNIGHT:

But who is he? Where is he from?
I shall find out now if I can.
I shall hide and wait for him
    There by the road.

THE EMPEROR:

He has brought this war to an end.
    Let us go, friend.

FIRST KNIGHT:

My lord knight, speak to me,
And rein in, for love's sake.
He does not deign to wait
But I will make him pause for a while;
With my lance I will strike him
Where best I may wound him.
But there; he rides off in spite of me.
He is either from heaven or from hell;
In his thigh he carries the head
Of my lance, for I wounded him.
And in this place the lance is broken.
Now, I must go to the Emperor
And tell him that I could not stop him
    For all that I did.

THE EMPEROR:

Now, tell me, since God sends you
To us again, what do you know
Of that knight who fought so well?
Who is he? What is his name?
Is he not some famous man?
    Tell me the truth.

FIRST KNIGHT:
Sire, I must admit to you,
I neither took him nor overthrew him,
Though in his thigh he carries
The iron of my lance buried;
There is where it broke off, you see.
Here is where the wood sundered,
But I am grieved now at what
I have done, and remorse wrings me
That ever I should have touched him
   And done him harm.

THE EMPEROR:
Could it be that, in His grace
God so far favoured us
That He sent an angel to us,
   A spirit?

SECOND KNIGHT:
Sire, he is a mortal man.
And of that you can make certain.
Send a crier to proclaim
That whatever man may come
Before you in white armour, bringing
With him the head of this lance here
And can show you also
The wound that the lance-head made,
Will have, without question
Your sweet and pure daughter
And the half of your empire.
   Would you wish it so?

THE EMPEROR:
It would delight me; you have counselled well.
Squire, at once without delay
Go cry abroad this proclamation
   Everywhere, friend.

THE SQUIRE:
I shall do it, sire, straightway
   Without more words, since you wish it.

Scene X

THE SQUIRE:
Here I see a great number
Of worthy people; I shall delay no longer.
Here in the Emperor's name
As he wishes, I shall make proclamation.
Give ear to me, great and small;
The Emperor sends to say
That that man will have his daughter
Who comes before him dressed in white armour,
Bringing with him the broken head
Of a lance, and can show him also
In his thigh the wound it made.
Whatever man may do so,
The Emperor will give him
His daughter, and with that create him
Lord absolute of half
 Of his empire.

Scene XI

THE SQUIRE:
Sire, you believe me, I
Have made a barbarous proclamation;
The Emperor promises to give
His daughter in marriage, sire,
And the half of his empire
To whoever may bring him
The lance-head by which he was
Wounded, in one of his thighs;
But he must be in white armour
And show the wound also
That the lance made; this surely
 Is a mad proclamation.

THE SENESCHAL:
Perhaps it was done to avenge
Someone who roused his displeasure,
Or for some other secret reason.
But truly I love the maiden

And with this love I am so driven
That in no place may I have peace,
For her father cannot abide me,
Nor will suffer me to have her
For wife, at which my heart fails me.
Nevertheless, if I may,
By this one stroke I will win her.
Go to the house of Jehan de Savoy
The armourer, and tell him to send me
A complete suit of fine armour
All of white, whatever it may cost;
And meanwhile I will see
To the lance-head, and wound myself
To fit the Emperor's proclamation;
And then go at once and show myself
  Before him.

THE SQUIRE:
Sir, I shall go and return
  Immediately.

THE SENESCHAL:
Oh, God! How the pain torments me
Here where I have pierced my thigh;
Surely I must have the maiden
Since for her I have suffered such pain;
And to have her I would bear any pain;
This smart is not worth a feather
If by its means I may win the girl
  Whom I desire.

THE SQUIRE:
Sir, to accomplish
Your pleasure I have come
With all haste I could, truly,
And have brought you this
Armour, sir, for your approval.
Put it on first to see
If it fits you well; you can pay
  Afterwards.

THE SENESCHAL:
Give it to me; let me

Try it. I think it fits me well.
Now, carry my helmet, and
  Come with me.

THE SQUIRE:
By my faith, with pleasure, dear sire,
  I will go before you.

Scene XII

GOD:
Mother, and you, John, come
To me; we must descend from here;
And you, Angels, you must come also;
We must go again, now,
To the worthy hermit who hears
  Confessions for Rome.

OUR LADY:
We will descend without delay,
God, dear Son, since it is your pleasure.
Sing, and with no secret voice,
Angels, but so that all may hear you,
As we go, to make all rejoice
  And delight us.

FIRST ANGEL:
Lady, with pleasure, without more words
With a clear voice we shall sing:
Royal Virgin, daughter and mother
Of the Creator Almighty
Of the world and its true Redeemer,
Sweet to all, to none bitter,
Flower of sweetness surpassing all other,
Royal Virgin, daughter and mother
Of the Creator Almighty,
By the most excellent mystery
God became both gift and giver
  Of himself to thee, to do thee honour.

Scene XIII

GOD:
Let My speech not fill you with dread
But delight and sweetness, worthy man;
Go now to the city of Rome
And find Robert, who for his
Actions is thought to be a madman;
Tell him he has made his peace
With Me, and now may end his penance;
Say that he will rise in station
And that now he must embrace
Marriage. With whom? The Emperor's
Daughter, for such is My desire.
   Now go at once.

THE HERMIT:
Sire, who created heaven and earth
And for small things return great blessings
All that You have commanded me
   I shall perform.

OUR LADY:
Arise, Angels, and with lifted
Voices sing as we return;
For what we came to do is done.
   Rise up singing.

MICHAEL:
Now let us all together
Sing with joy to God's mother:
By the most excellent mystery
God became both gift and giver
Of Himself to thee, to do thee honour.
Royal Virgin, daughter and mother
Of the Creator Almighty
   Of the world and its true Redeemer.

Scene XIV

THE SENESCHAL:
Emperor, God increase your glory!
I am he who in the battle

65

Appeared twice, truly,
And twice to your aid came;
Here is the lance-head that pierced me
And wounded me, in my thigh;
And if you desire to see,
I will show you the wound it gave me;
Here it is. Now, if it please you
I would have your daughter to marry.
For the rest of your heritage,
    I leave it to you.

THE EMPEROR:
Seneschal, God amend you!
Is this the truth? Were you
He who came to aid us?
I took you for my enemy,
I tell you that, which is no lie,
    Openly.

THE SENESCHAL:
Sire, in his need a man learns
Who his friends are. What I did
For you, you know already;
    I will say no more.

THE EMPEROR:
You will have my daughter
Without question, as I promised.
You, post without delay
To the Pope, and pray him
To come to us here
And in the Holy Church just there
Marry my daughter and the Seneschal
Who has been my friend, and loyal
    In my need.

FIRST KNIGHT:
Beloved sire, I will go
    And pray him to come.

THE EMPEROR:
And you, Squire, go and say
To the governess to bring

My daughter here without delay;
   I command it.

THE SQUIRE:
Sire, as best I may,
   With pleasure I will do as you say.

Scene XV

THE SQUIRE:
Mistress, you are to conduct
His daughter before my lord;
At once do it; come with me
   And obey.

THE GOVERNESS:
Willingly, my sweet friend.
   Let us go.

Scene XVI

FIRST KNIGHT:
Lords, let none hinder me,
For love's sake. I must speak
To the Pope without delay;
   The matter is urgent.

FIRST SERGEANT:
Do so; I remember you well.
You wait upon the Emperor.
Do not lag back there in the rear
   But come forward.

SECOND SERGEANT:
There is nothing that will obstruct
Or harm you. Enter boldly, sir
And present yourself to the Holy Father
   There where he sits.

FIRST KNIGHT:
Holy Father, if it
Might please you, I will not
Hide the cause from you, but tell
  What brings me here.

THE POPE:
My son, whatever human thing
It be, unless your conscience forbids you,
Pronounce it at once to me
  And I will listen.

FIRST KNIGHT:
I will; and, not to waste
Your time, as briefly as I may;
The Emperor beseeches you,
Sire, to marry his daughter;
May it please you to come
And perform this wedding,
That it may be more grand
  And solemn.

THE POPE:
Fair son, I consent to you.
Rise, lords, and come with me.
And fall back to make a broad lane
  As I pass.

FIRST SERGEANT:
So we shall, God give us grace.
Rise, all, and make way there!
Back, back, or I shall rap you
  With my mace.

SECOND SERGEANT:
Make way there before us;
You people are too curious;
Make way, or I will pay you
  With my fist.

Scene XVII

THE POPE:

Emperor, at your wish I am here.
I have been told that you intend
To marry your daughter. To whom
  Will you give her? Tell me.

THE EMPEROR:
By my faith, sire, to the Seneschal
Who has proved so well
His loyalty, that twice he saved us
In battle, from our enemies;
We had been given over
To death, but for him. Truly
He has well deserved her, sire.
Here now, is my daughter;
It is these two that I
  Would have you marry.

THE POPE:
Seneschal, tell me, is this
  What you wish?

THE SENESCHAL:
Holy Father, there is nothing I desire more
  Than I do this maiden.

THE POPE:
And you know that she is mute?
  She cannot speak.

THE SENESCHAL:
I do, sire, and in no way
  Does that deter me.

THE DAUGHTER:
Father, I see you are a fool
If you believe this traitor.
God who created us everyone
Would not suffer his lie,
His falsehood, his treachery,

69

And for this gave back to me
Speech, which has been lost to me
Since my birth. Do you think that he
Won the battle? By no means, truly.
It was won by another than he
One to God far more friendly;
And when I made signs that day
You could not credit me,
   But I spoke truly.

THE EMPEROR:
Daughter, to hear you
Speak gives me such joy,
That I cannot keep from weeping,
For my joy is full of pity.
Daughter, let me tenderly
   Kiss you.

THE POPE:
My daughter, if you please,
Tell us who the man is
Whom God so loves, as
   You believe.

THE DAUGHTER:
Holy Father, do not doubt.
It is true. There is a meadow
Close by, and a fair dear fountain there;
There, in truth, I saw him
Who saved us, twice arm himself
All in white armour that was there.
And when, after the battle,
He returned, I speak the truth,
I saw him draw from his thigh
A lance-head, which in the ground he buried,
And I can show you that same
Lance-head; the place is not far.
Governess, come with me; and you
   Also, my lords of the guard.

Scene XVIII

THE DAUGHTER:
Fair lords, here is the lance-head;
With great difficulty I took it
From the ground where he buried it.
But I do not know
How the armour came there,
Nor what became of it when
He laid it down, for instantly
    It vanished from my sight.

FIRST KNIGHT:
Sire, she speaks the truth, certainly;
That is the head of my lance,
And to remove the last doubt,
Look: here is the place where it fitted,
And where it broke; Oh, God, look
How it has knitted and joined again
As though it had never been broken.
    Here are wonders.

THE POPE:
Do not marvel; these are blessings
By which God brings us to the truth.
My daughter, tell us
    Where this man is.

THE DAUGHTER:
Sire, by Saint Peter of Rome,
I think that if you look for him
You will find him lying
    By the dog Louvet.

THE EMPEROR:
Holy Father, let us go there,
    And our men can follow after.

Scene XIX

THE EMPEROR:
Look: beside the dog he is lying;
He values himself at nothing.
Rise up, there, and come out
　From that place.

THE POPE:
God send you His grace, good creature!
I am the Holy Father of Rome.
I pray you, if you love me,
　Speak to me.

THE EMPEROR:
He will not answer at all.
I think perhaps he cannot speak.
Friend, show me your thigh
On which you limp, and I
Shall see that you are cured
　Within a month.

THE HERMIT:
Robert, Robert, I recognize you.
My dear lords, do not be vexed;
You will soon understand all this.
You were surnamed The Devil,
But God, your spiritual Father,
When He saw your devotion
And your great contrition,
Bade me command you
To pretend that you were mute,
To conduct yourself like a fool,
And not to eat anything
But what from the dogs you might take.
And because, without fail, you
Have performed this grievous penance,
God, who favours the good always,
In His infinite goodness
Declares that penance at an end
And lifted from you forever;
From this moment you may speak,

For all your sins are forgiven.
And at the same time your
Honours are restored to you;
Your knighthood once more is yours
    As once it was.

ROBERT:
Oh, Lord God, on my knees
I wish to give thanks to Thee,
And praise and magnify Thee,
Since I have received, of Thy mercy,
Peace and concord with Thee
    After my misdeeds.

THE EMPEROR:
Good man, you who know these things,
    Who is this man?

THE HERMIT:
He is a great and noble baron,
Beloved sire, you may be certain;
The Duke of Normandy's son
    And direct heir.

THE EMPEROR:
Robert! I wish without delay,
Fair sire, to give you my daughter
To be your wife; do not
Refuse, for with the gift
Of my daughter I will join upon you
    Half of my empire.

ROBERT:
Beloved sire, I thank you.
Nevertheless, God willing,
From this day forth I desire
    To live as a hermit.

THE HERMIT:
Robert, God has ordained
And willed otherwise for you;
Listen: He commands you through me,
And He has made this clear to me,

73

To take without hesitation
This girl, and never leave her after,
For from you two such a line
Will spring, heed now what I say,
As will make all Paradise rejoice.
   That is to come.

ROBERT:

Since it is as you say,
I will not wish it otherwise,
Beloved sire, I consent
   To your wish.

THE POPE:

My son, you speak well and wisely.
This is what we will do.
Into my palace we will go;
There you will be plighted and joined
In marriage; now come with me.
These priests here will go before us
And escort us, singing
   Some lovely song.

THE PRIESTS:

In that we will not disobey,
Holy Father, since you wish it.
In praise of the Holy Virgin we
Will sing, in whom is no bitterness.
Virgin, we should glorify thee
Since, from Hell to save us,
God became a man in thee,
To draw us out from the foul place
And the mire where Adam thrust us,
   When he tasted of that tree.

The Rival of His Master

Alain-René Lesage

Characters

M. ORONTE, *a bourgeois of Paris*

MADAME ORONTE

M. ORGON, *Damis' father*

VALÈRE, *in love with Angélique*

ANGÉLIQUE, *M. Oronte's daughter, promised to Damis*

CRISPIN, *Valère's valet*

LA BRANCHE, *Damis' valet*

LISETTE, *Angélique's maidservant*

THE SCENE IS LAID AT PARIS

Scene I

VALÈRE, CRISPIN.

VALÈRE: Ah, there you are, scoundrel!

CRISPIN: Let us contain our tempers.

VALÈRE: Villain!

CRISPIN: And let us dispense, if you please, with personal reflections. What is your complaint?

VALÈRE: My complaint, you deceitful wretch? You asked my leave to be gone for a week, and it's over a month since I laid eyes on you. Is that the manner of service which you think a valet owes to his master?

CRISPIN: In faith, sir, my service is more than equal to your payment. To my mind neither of us has more cause to complain than the other.

VALÈRE: I should like to know where you could have been.

CRISPIN: I've been looking to my own fortune. I've been to Touraine on a little expedition with a lord whom I number among my friends.

VALÈRE: Expedition? What sort of expedition?

CRISPIN: Collecting a tax to which the folk of the provinces are rendered liable by the manner in which they play cards.

VALÈRE: You could scarcely have come at a better moment, for I'm quite without money, and you no doubt are in a position to lend me some.

CRISPIN: Not at all, sir: ours was not a generous catch this time. The fish saw the hook and never so much as nibbled.

VALÈRE: There's a gifted lad! Crispin, listen to me, I am willing to forgive the past. I have need of your talents.

CRISPIN: What clemency!

VALÈRE: I am in the most awkward circumstances.

CRISPIN: Your creditors are impatient! That rich merchant, perhaps, to whom you gave a note for nine hundred francs for

77

the thirty pistoles worth of cloth he furnished you, has he obtained sentence against you?

VALÈRE: No.

CRISPIN: Ah! I see. Has Madame the generous marquise, who undertook to pay your tailor herself when he had summoned you, discovered that we were in league with the tailor?

VALÈRE: Wrong again, Crispin: I have fallen in love.

CRISPIN: Oh! Oh! And with whom, perchance?

VALÈRE: With Angélique, M. Oronte's only daughter.

CRISPIN: I know her by sight. Plague take me! A pretty face! Her father, unless I'm mistaken, is a bourgeois who lives in this house here, and is very rich.

VALÈRE: Yes, he has three large houses in the most elegant parts of Paris.

CRISPIN: Ah, an adorable creature, that Angélique!

VALÈRE: He's said to have cash, besides.

CRISPIN: I appreciate the full ardor of your love. But how far have you got with the girl? Is she aware of your sentiments?

VALÈRE: In the week since I gained access to the house I confess I have won her favorable regard; but Lisette, her chambermaid, told me something yesterday which has plunged me into despair.

CRISPIN: Oh, what did she tell you, that discouraging Lisette?

VALÈRE: That I have a rival. That M. Oronte has given his word to a young man from the provinces who is about to arrive in Paris and make Angélique his wife.

CRISPIN: And who is this rival?

VALÈRE: That I have yet to learn. Lisette was summoned just as she was telling me this disagreeable bit of news, and I was obliged to retire without learning his name.

CRISPIN: It appears that we may not be possessed of M. Oronte's three beautiful houses quite so promptly.

VALÈRE: Go find Lisette and have a talk with her on my account; after that we shall see what we can devise.

CRISPIN: Leave it to me.

VALÈRE: I shall wait for you at the house.

He goes.

Scene II

CRISPIN, *alone*: Oh how tired I am of being a valet! Ah! Crispin, it's your own fault, you were always one for trifling. You should be launched upon a dazzling career in the world of finance. The devil, with my wit by this time I could have been bankrupt several times over.

Scene III

CRISPIN, LA BRANCHE.

LA BRANCHE, *to himself*: Crispin, is it not?
CRISPIN, *to himself*: Do I behold La Branche?
LA BRANCHE, *to himself*: It is Crispin, to the life.
CRISPIN *to himself*: It's La Branche, my life upon it!
To LA BRANCHE
Ah, what a lucky meeting! The most affectionate kisses, my dear fellow!
They kiss.
To be honest, having missed you about Paris for some little time, I was afraid some decision or other of the courts might perhaps have withdrawn you from us.
LA BRANCHE: Upon my word, my dear man, I have had a narrow escape since last I saw you. They were determined to give me employment at sea; I looked forward to being included in the latest shipment from la Tournelle.
CRISPIN: In the name of heaven! What had you done?
LA BRANCHE: One night, in an unfrequented street, I was seized with a fancy to detain a foreign merchant in order to ask him, out of curiosity, for news of his country. But he, not understanding French, supposed that it was his purse that I was asking for. He shouted, "Thief!" The watch came. They took me for a felon. They fetched me to the Châtelet, and there I remained for seven weeks.
CRISPIN: Seven weeks!
LA BRANCHE: I'd have been there longer if it had not been for the niece of an old-clothes woman.
CRISPIN: Is it possible?
LA BRANCHE: They were furiously prejudiced against me, but she applied herself so effectively, out of friendship for me, that they came to realize my innocence.
CRISPIN: It's well to have influential friends.
LA BRANCHE: That adventure has made me thoughtful.
CRISPIN: I believe you; you're no longer curious to have the latest news from foreign countries.

LA BRANCHE: No, a pox take them! I've gone back into service. And you, Crispin, are you still at it?

CRISPIN: No, I'm an honorary malefactor, like you. I've gone back into service too, but I've a master who has no money, and from that you can deduce a valet who has no wages. I am less than content with my situation.

LA BRANCHE: As for me, I'm quite content with mine. I've retired to Chartres; I am in the service of a young man called Damis, a likeable youth; he's devoted to cards, wine, women; a universal man. We embark together upon all manner of escapades. And that diverts me, it keeps me out of mischief.

CRISPIN: Ah, the innocent life!

LA BRANCHE: Is it not?

CRISPIN: Indeed. But tell me, La Branche, what brings you to Paris? Where are you going?

LA BRANCHE: To that house there.

CRISPIN: To M. Oronte's house?

LA BRANCHE: His daughter has been promised to Damis.

CRISPIN: Angélique, promised to your master?

LA BRANCHE: M. Orgon, Damis' father, was in Paris a fortnight ago; I was with him; we paid a call on M. Oronte, who is one of his oldest friends, and they settled the marriage between them.

CRISPIN: It is resolved then?

LA BRANCHE: Yes, both fathers and Madame Oronte have signed the contract already; the dowry, of twenty thousand crowns in cash, is ready for delivery. They are waiting only for Damis' arrival to conclude the affair.

CRISPIN: Ah, upon my soul, in that case there is nothing for Valère my master to do but to seek his fortune elsewhere.

LA BRANCHE: What! Your master?

CRISPIN: He is in love with this same Angélique, but since Damis . . .

LA BRANCHE: Oh! Damis will not marry Angélique: there is a slight difficulty.

CRISPIN: Ah! What?

LA BRANCHE: While his father was contracting a marriage for him here he was contracting one for himself in Chartres.

CRISPIN: Ah, that alters the case!

LA BRANCHE: I found my master's wedding clothes all made; I have been ordered to take them to Chartres as soon as I have seen Monsieur and Madame Oronte and withdrawn M. Orgon's promise.

CRISPIN: Withdrawn M. Orgon's promise!

LA BRANCHE: That's what fetched me to Paris.

Starting off to M. ORONTE'*s house.*

Let us not say farewell, Crispin: we shall be seeing each other presently.

CRISPIN, *detaining him*: One moment, La Branche; wait, my boy; I've had an idea . . . Tell me now, does Monsieur Oronte know your master?

LA BRANCHE: They have never set eyes on each other.

CRISPIN: Be damned now, there's a fat trick there for the taking, if you choose. But after your interlude in the Châtelet, I fear you may not have the courage.

LA BRANCHE: No, no! Say the word, say the word. No storm that he's endured discourages a good sailor from putting to sea again. What had you in mind? Were you thinking of passing off your master for Damis, and getting him married to . . .

CRISPIN: My master! Fie upon it! A fine beggar for a girl like Angélique! I had a far better match marked out for her.

LA BRANCHE: Who, may I ask?

CRISPIN: Me.

LA BRANCHE: Damnation, you're right! That's well thought on, to say the least.

CRISPIN: Besides, I'm in love with her.

LA BRANCHE: I approve of your passion.

CRISPIN: I shall assume the name of Damis.

LA BRANCHE: Well said.

CRISPIN: I shall marry Angélique.

LA BRANCHE: With my full consent.

CRISPIN: I shall lay hands on her dowry.

LA BRANCHE: Excellent.

CRISPIN: I shall disappear before the explanations begin.

LA BRANCHE: Let us expatiate somewhat on that point.

CRISPIN: Why?

LA BRANCHE: When you spoke of disappearing with the dowry you failed to mention me. Something there needs correcting.

CRISPIN: Oh! We shall disappear together.

LA BRANCHE: On that condition, I shall be your partner. The affair, I confess, is a trifle hazardous, but my boldness is reawakened and I feel that I was born for great things. Where shall we hide the dowry?

CRISPIN: Deep in some remote province.

LA BRANCHE: Better out of the kingdom entirely I should think; what do you say?

81

CRISPIN: We'll see, we'll see. Tell me, what sort of character has M. Oronte?

LA BRANCHE: An extremely simple bourgeois; his genius is not remarkable.

CRISPIN: And madame?

LA BRANCHE: A woman between twenty-five and sixty; a woman infatuated with herself, and of so vacillating a mind that in the same moment she can believe both sides of anything.

CRISPIN: That will do. Now we must borrow the clothes to . . .

LA BRANCHE: You can use my master's.

Examining CRISPIN's *figure.*

Yes, just so; you are nearly the same size.

CRISPIN: The devil! He has not a bad figure.

LA BRANCHE: I see someone coming out of M. Oronte's; let us go to my lodgings and plan the details of our enterprise.

CRISPIN: Before we do that I must run to the house for a word with Valère, and engage him not to call at M. Oronte's for the next few days. I shall be with you shortly.

He goes out one direction and LA BRANCHE *out another.*

Scene IV

ANGÉLIQUE, LISETTE.

ANGÉLIQUE: Indeed, Lisette, since Valère revealed to me his passion I have been consumed by a secret despair, and I know that if I were to marry Damis I should lose my peace of mind for ever after.

LISETTE: He's a dangerous man, that Valère.

ANGÉLIQUE: How miserable I am! Put yourself in my place, Lisette. What should I do? You must advise me.

LISETTE: What advice could you expect from me?

ANGÉLIQUE: Whatever you're prompted to by your interest in my concerns.

LISETTE: There are only two things which anyone could advise you to do: one, to forget Valère; the other, to defy the authority of your parents. You are too much in love to do the first; my conscience is too delicate to encourage you in the second; it's difficult, as you can see.

ANGÉLIQUE: Ah, Lisette, you rob me of my last hopes.

LISETTE: But wait; it appears to me nevertheless that it may be possible to reconcile your love and my conscience; yes, let us go and find your mother.

ANGÉLIQUE: What shall I say to her?

LISETTE: Confess everything. She loves to be flattered, to be caressed; let us flatter her, and caress her; at bottom, after all, she does have a certain affection for us, and she may perhaps oblige M. Oronte to withdraw his promise.

ANGÉLIQUE: You're right, Lisette. But I'm afraid that . . .

She hesitates.

LISETTE: What?

ANGÉLIQUE: You know my mother. Her mind is so changeable.

LISETTE: It's true that she always agrees with whoever spoke to her last; still, we must try to enlist her on our side.

Noticing MME ORONTE *approaching*.

But here she is; leave us for a moment: I'll signal you when to rejoin us.

ANGÉLIQUE *withdraws to the back of the stage.*

Scene V

MADAME ORONTE, LISETTE, ANGÉLIQUE.

LISETTE, *pretending not to notice* MADAME ORONTE: One cannot but agree that Mme Oronte is one of the most delightful women in Paris.

MME ORONTE: Lisette, you are a flatterer.

LISETTE, *feigning surprise*: Ah, Madame, I didn't see you! The words which you have just overheard were prompted by a conversation which I have just been having with Mlle Angélique on the subject of her marriage. "You have the most judicious," I told her, "the most reasonable of mothers."

MME ORONTE: It's quite true, Lisette; I am not like other women. It is always reason that governs my actions.

LISETTE: Of course.

MME ORONTE: I am neither obstinate nor capricious.

LISETTE: And withal you are the best mother in the world. I would stake my word on it that if your daughter were repelled at the idea of marrying Damis you would never force her to it against her inclination.

MME ORONTE: I, force her! I, render my daughter unhappy! God forfend that I should violate her sentiments in the very

83

slightest! Tell me, Lisette, does she feel an aversion for
Damis?

LISETTE: Well, but . . .

She hesitates.

MME ORONTE: You can conceal nothing.

LISETTE: Since you are determined to know, Madame, I must tell
you that the prospect of this marriage repels her.

MME ORONTE: Perhaps she is in love.

LISETTE: Oh, Madame, that is always the case. When a girl has
an aversion for a man who is chosen to be her husband, you
may be certain that she has a weakness for another. You have
told me, for example, that you detested M. Oronte when he
was first proposed to you, because you loved an officer who
perished at the siege of Candia.

MME ORONTE: It's true; and if the poor boy had not died I should
never have married M. Oronte.

LISETTE: Very well, Madame, Mademoiselle your daughter is of
the same disposition as you were before the siege of Candia.

MME ORONTE: Ah, who then is the gentleman who has found the
secret of pleasing her?

LISETTE: He's that young man who has been here at cards for the
past few days.

MME ORONTE: Who, Valère?

LISETTE: Valère.

MME ORONTE: By the way—that reminds me—he gazed at us
yesterday, at Angélique and me, with such passion in his
eyes! Are you certain, Lisette, that it's my daughter he's in
love with?

LISETTE, *signaling to* ANGÉLIQUE *to approach*: Yes, Madame, he told
me so himself, and he charged me to beg you, on his account,
to grant him an audience so that he may ask you for her
hand.

Scene VI

ANGÉLIQUE, LISETTE, MADAME ORONTE.

ANGÉLIQUE, *approaching, to her mother*: Forgive me, Madame, if
my sentiments are not in agreement with your own; but you
know . . .

MME ORONTE, *to* ANGÉLIQUE: I know well enough that a girl cannot
always regulate her affections to fit her parents' preferences,

but I am tender by nature, I have a good heart, I share your
sufferings. In a word, I accept Valère's suit.

ANGÉLIQUE: I cannot express, Madame, the gratitude I feel for
your kindness.

LISETTE, *to* MME ORONTE: That will not be enough, Madame. M.
Oronte can be somewhat obstinate: if you do not maintain
your case with great vigor . . .

MME ORONTE, *interrupting*: Oh, you need have no fears of that
kind. I shall take Valère into my protection; my daughter
will be married to no one else, you may take my word for
it.

Noticing M. ORONTE.

Here comes my husband; you'll see what tone I take with
him.

Scene VII

ANGÉLIQUE, M. ORONTE, MME ORONTE, LISETTE.

MME ORONTE, *to her husband*: Well timed indeed, Monsieur: I wished
to tell you that I no longer concur with the plan to marry
my daughter to Damis.

M. ORONTE, *to his wife*: Ha! Might one know, Madame, why you
have altered your decision?

MME ORONTE: We have been offered a better match for Angélique.
Valère has asked for her hand. True, he is not so rich as
Damis, but he is gently born, and our consideration of his
nobility should more than outweigh our disappointment at
his fortune.

LISETTE, *in an undertone to* MME ORONTE: That's good.

M. ORONTE, *to his wife*: I have considerable esteem for Valère, and
I would give him my daughter's hand without so much as a
glance at his scanty fortune, if I might do so with honor,
but that is impossible, Madame.

MME ORONTE: Why impossible, Monsieur?

M. ORONTE: Why impossible? Would you have us break our promise to our old friend, M. Orgon? Has he given you any cause
to complain?

MME ORONTE: No.

LISETTE, *in an undertone to* MME ORONTE: Stand fast! Do not weaken!

M. ORONTE, *to his wife*: Then why would you have us insult him
in this way? Only consider: the contract is signed, all the
preparations are made, we await only Damis' arrival. The

thing is too far advanced, do you not agree, for us to withdraw now.

MME ORONTE: Indeed, I had not considered it in that light.

LISETTE, *in an aside*: Farewell, the weathercock is turning.

M. ORONTE, *to his wife*: You are too reasonable, Madame, to think
of opposing this marriage.

MME ORONTE: Oh, I do not oppose it!

LISETTE, *in an aside*: Death and burial! Is this a woman? Not
contradict him once!

MME ORONTE: You see, Lisette, I have done what I could for
Valère.

LISETTE, *ironically, in an undertone to* MME ORONTE: Oh yes, how
fortunate he is that you took his part!

Scene VIII

ANGÉLIQUE, M. ORONTE, LA BRANCHE, MME ORONTE, LISETTE.

M. ORONTE, *noticing* LA BRANCHE: Here is Damis' valet.

LA BRANCHE: Monsieur and Madame Oronte's most humble servant; Mademoiselle Angélique's most humble servant. Good
day, Lisette.

MME ORONTE: Well, La Branche, what news?

LA BRANCHE, *to* M. ORONTE: M. Damis, your son-in-law and my
master, has just arrived from Chartres; he is following hard
on my heels; I came ahead to announce him.

ANGÉLIQUE, *to herself, aside*: Oh heaven!

M. ORONTE, *to* LA BRANCHE: I am eager to see him. But why did
he not come here directly? Considering our present relation-
ship, why should he stand thus on ceremony?

LA BRANCHE: Oh, Monsieur, he appreciates the niceties of conduct too well to permit himself to behave towards you
with familiarity; he is the best-mannered youth in France.
His valet though I am, I have nothing but good to say of
him.

MME ORONTE: Is he polite? Is he a man of discernment?

LA BRANCHE, *to* MME ORONTE: Discernment, Madame! He grew
up among the most brilliant youth in Paris. Oh before heaven,
he's lively in intelligence.

M. ORONTE: And is M. Orgon not with him?

LA BRANCHE, *to* M. ORONTE: No, Monsieur; a violent attack of gout
prevented him from coming.

M. ORONTE: The poor gentleman!

LA BRANCHE: He was suddenly seized with it the very evening before our departure. Here's a letter which he wrote to you. *He hands* M. ORONTE *a letter.*

M. ORONTE, *reading the address*: "To Monsieur, Monsieur Craquet, physician, in Sepulchre Road."

LA BRANCHE, *taking back the letter*: That's the wrong letter, Monsieur.

M. ORONTE, *laughing*: There's a doctor who lives on the same street as his patients.

LA BRANCHE, *taking out several letters and reading the addresses*: I've a number of letters here which I must deliver. Let's see; this one.
He reads.
"To Monsieur Stammer, parliamentary lawyer, Cursing Lane," It's not that one either, let us see the next one.
He reads.
"To M. Glutton, canon of . . ." Bless me, I'll never find the one I'm looking for.
He reads.
"To Monsieur Oronte." Ah! Here is Monsieur Orgon's letter . . .
He gives it to M. ORONTE.
His hand was trembling so when he wrote it that you wouldn't recognize the writing.

M. ORONTE: Indeed, it's quite unrecognizable.

LA BRANCHE: The gout is a terrible affliction. Heaven spare you its visitations, and Mme Oronte likewise, and Mlle Angélique, and Lisette, and all others present.

M. ORONTE, *reading*: "In the midst of my preparations to depart with Damis, I have been taken with the gout and thus prevented. Nevertheless, since my presence is not absolutely necessary in Paris, I would rather not delay with my indisposition a marriage which I desire most dearly and which is the sole consolation of my old age. I commend my son to you; be a father to him as well as to your daughter. I shall approve your decisions. From Chartres. Your affectionate servant, Orgon." The poor man!

M. ORONTE, *seeing* CRISPIN *dressed in* DAMIS' *clothes, to* LA BRANCHE: But who is this young man approaching us? Would not that be Damis?

LA BRANCHE, *to* M. ORONTE: None other.

87

To MME ORONTE.

What do you say, Madame? Is there not something about him which predisposes you in his favor?

Scene IX

CRISPIN, ANGÉLIQUE, M. ORONTE, MME ORONTE, LISETTE.

MME ORONTE, *to* LA BRANCHE: He's not ill-favored, as you say.

CRISPIN, *calling*: La Branche?

LA BRANCHE, *to* CRISPIN: Monsieur.

CRISPIN: Do I behold M. Oronte, my illustrious father-in-law?

LA BRANCHE: You do; his very person.

M. ORONTE, *to* CRISPIN, *kissing him*: Welcome, son-in-law, welcome; come and kiss me.

CRISPIN, *kissing* M. ORONTE: My delight is extreme at being able thus to express the extreme delight I feel at greeting you with a kiss.

Indicating MME ORONTE.

And this, no doubt, is the delightful child who is destined for me?

M. ORONTE: No, my boy, that is my wife. This is my daughter Angélique.

CRISPIN: Confounded pretty family!

Looking at ANGÉLIQUE.

How delightful to have one of these ladies for my wife—

Looking at MME ORONTE.

—and the other for my sister.

MME ORONTE, *to* CRISPIN: How excessively charming.

To LISETTE.

He seems intelligent.

LISETTE, *in an undertone*: And what taste!

CRISPIN, *to* MME ORONTE: What an air! What grace! What noble pride! 'Slife, Madame, you are utterly adorable. Indeed my father said to me, "Wait till you see Mme Oronte, she's the most piquant of beauties."

MME ORONTE: Oh fie!

CRISPIN, *aside*: The most disagree . . .

Aloud.

"If only," he said "if only she were a widow I would marry her at once."

M. ORONTE, *laughing*: I'm much obliged to him, upon my soul.

MME ORONTE, *to* CRISPIN: I have the most overwhelming regard for your father; how vexed I am that he was unable to come with you!

CRISPIN: He is mortified not to be able to attend the wedding. He was looking forward to dancing the jig with Mme Oronte.

LA BRANCHE, *to* M. ORONTE: He begs you to execute the marriage at once, for he is furiously impatient to have his daughter-in-law at his side.

M. ORONTE, *to* LA BRANCHE: Well, well, all the conditions have been agreed upon and signed; we have only to conclude the affair and settle the dowry.

CRISPIN, *to* M. ORONTE: Settle the dowry. Yes, very well said. La Branche! Allow me to give my valet an errand.
Aside, to LA BRANCHE.
Go to the marquis.
In an undertone.
Arrange to have horses waiting this evening, do you understand?
Aloud.
And tell him that I kiss his hands.

LA BRANCHE, *going*: At once, Monsieur.

Scene X

ANGÉLIQUE, M. ORONTE, CRISPIN, MADAME ORONTE, LISETTE.

M. ORONTE, *to* CRISPIN: But to return to your father. I am distressed to the utmost to learn of his indisposition; but I pray you, satisfy my curiosity. What news, tell me, of his lawsuit?

CRISPIN, *anxious, calling*: La Branche!

M. ORONTE: You're quite pale; what's the matter?

CRISPIN, *in an undertone, to himself*: The devil take the question . . . !
Aloud.
I forgot to tell La Branche . . .
In an undertone, to himself.
He might have told me about that lawsuit.

M. ORONTE: He'll be back presently. Well, has the case been decided?

CRISPIN, *to* M. ORONTE: Yes, thank God, that matter's over.

M. ORONTE: And did you win it?

CRISPIN: At great expense.

M. ORONTE: I'm delighted, I assure you.

MME ORONTE: Heaven be praised!

CRISPIN: My father took the case very much to heart; he would have presented his entire fortune to the judges rather than be given the lie.

M. ORONTE: Upon my soul, that business must have cost him something, did it not?

CRISPIN: You may take my word for it! But justice is so fair a thing it's worth paying the price for it.

M. ORONTE: Agreed, agreed; but apart from that the suit must have been a disagreeable business for him.

CRISPIN: Ah, you cannot imagine. He was dealing with the most devious pettifogger, the least reasonable of men.

M. ORONTE: Of men, you say? He told me that his opponent was a woman.

CRISPIN: Yes, his oppponent was a woman, it's true, but this woman had in league with her a certain old man from Normandy, who gave her his advice, and it was he who rendered the business so painful to my father . . . But let us talk of something else; let us say no more of lawsuits; I wish to concern myself with nothing but my marriage and the pleasure of beholding Mme Oronte.

M. ORONTE: Very well, let us go in then, my boy, let us go in; I shall bid them make ready for the wedding.

CRISPIN, *giving his hand to* MME ORONTE: Madame!

MME ORONTE: Daughter, I hardly think that you are to be pitied; Damis has much to be said for him.

CRISPIN, M. ORONTE, *and* MME ORONTE *go*.

Scene XI

ANGÉLIQUE, LISETTE.

ANGÉLIQUE: Alas! What is to become of me?

LISETTE: You are to become M. Damis' wife; that's easy to guess.

ANGÉLIQUE, *weeping*: Ah, Lisette, you know my sentiments, will you not condole with my sufferings?

LISETTE, *weeping*: The poor child!

ANGÉLIQUE: Can you be so hard as to abandon me to my fate?

LISETTE: You break my heart.

ANGÉLIQUE: Lisette, my dear Lisette!

LISETTE: Say no more to me, for I am so moved that I might well give you bad advice; and, as afflicted as I see you are, you would not hesitate to follow it.

Scene XII

ANGÉLIQUE, LISETTE, VALÈRE

VALÈRE, *to himself, at the back of the stage, without first seeing* AN-GÉLIQUE: Crispin told me not to show myself here for several days, as he was planning a stratagem, but he never explained to me what it was. I cannot live in this uncertainty.

LISETTE, *to* ANGÉLIQUE, *on noticing* VALÈRE: Valère is here.

VALÈRE, *upon noticing* ANGÉLIQUE: I am not mistaken; it's she. *Approaching.*
Be gracious, fair Angélique, and let me learn my destiny from your own lips. What decision . . . ? But what is this? In tears, both of you?

LISETTE: Ah, yes, Monsieur, in tears, in despair. Your rival is here.

VALÈRE: What do I hear?

LISETTE: And is to marry my mistress this very evening.

VALÈRE: Just heaven!

LISETTE: If she were at least to live in Paris after her marriage, that would be something; you could weep together, from time to time, over your misfortunes; but to complete the calamity, you will have to shed your tears separately.

VALÈRE: I shall die. But Lisette, tell me, who is this fortunate rival who is to leave me bereft of that which I hold dearest in the world?

LISETTE: He is called Damis.

VALÈRE: Damis!

LISETTE: He is from Chartres.

VALÈRE: I know the region well, and as far as I know there is no other Damis there but M. Orgon's son.

LISETTE: Just so, your rival is M. Orgon's son.

VALÈRE: Ah, if we have no one but Damis to fear, we may reassure ourselves.

ANGÉLIQUE: What do you mean, Valère?

VALÈRE: Let us be sad no longer, delightful Angélique. Damis was married a week ago, at Chartres.

LISETTE: Well!

ANGÉLIQUE: You're jesting, Valère. Damis is here, and is on the point of making me his wife.

LISETTE: He is in the house with M. and Mme Oronte at this very moment.

VALÈRE: Damis is a friend of mine; it is not a week since he wrote to me. I have his letter at my house.

ANGÉLIQUE: What does it say?

VALÈRE: That he had been married secretly, at Chartres, to a young lady of quality.

LISETTE: Married secretly! Ah! Ah! We must look into this matter; I'm sure it's well worth the trouble. Go, Monsieur, and fetch that letter, and lose no time doing it.

VALÈRE, *going*: I shall be back in a moment.

LISETTE: As for us, let us not allow this bit of news to remain idle; I am sorely deceived if we cannot derive from it some advantage. It will serve at least to delay your marriage for a little.

On noticing M. ORONTE, *who sees* VALÈRE *leave*:

Here is M. Oronte. While I proceed to enlighten him, go yourself and inform Madame your mother.

ANGÉLIQUE *exits*.

Scene XIII

LISETTE, M. ORONTE.

M. ORONTE: That was Valère who just left?

LISETTE: Yes, Monsieur, he has just told us something which will astonish you, upon my word.

M. ORONTE: Namely?

LISETTE: My faith but Damis is a fine gentleman to want two wives when so many honest men fret at having one.

M. ORONTE: Explain yourself, Lisette.

LISETTE: Damis is married; he has been wedded secretly to a young lady of Chartres, a person of quality.

M. ORONTE: Good heavens! Is it possible, Lisette?

LISETQE: Nothing could be more positive, Monsieur; Damis sent word of it himself to Valère, who is a friend of his.

M. ORONTE: It's a fable, I tell you.

LISETTE: No, Monsieur, I promise you. Valère has gone to fetch the letter; you have only to examine it.

M. ORONTE: Once again, I cannot believe what you say.

LISETTE: Ah, Monsieur, why do you refuse to credit my words? Is not the youth of today capable of anything?

M. ORONTE: It is true, they are worse corrupted than in my day.

LISETTE: How do we know that Damis is not one of these contemptible rascals who do not scruple to amass several dowries? Besides, since the person whom he has married is of gentle birth, this clandestine marriage will have consequences which will not be particularly pleasant for you.

M. ORONTE: What you say, I must confess, deserves some consideration.

LISETTE: Some consideration! If I were in your place, before I gave up my daughter I should wish to know the truth of the matter.

M. ORONTE: You're quite right.

On noticing LA BRANCHE:

There is Damis' valet; I must sound him out thoroughly. Withdraw, Lisette, and leave me alone with him.

LISETTE, *to herself, going*: If only this news might be confirmed.

Scene XIV

M. ORONTE, LA BRANCHE.

M. ORONTE: Approach, La Branche, come closer . . . I would say you had an honest face.

LA BRANCHE: Oh, Monsieur, without vanity I assure you that I am more honest than my face.

M. ORONTE: I am happy to hear it. Now: your master, it seems, is very successful with the ladies.

LA BRANCHE: In faith, he has a fine appearance. Ladies will be foolish; and he has a certain air about him which charms them. In marrying him off M. Orgon assures the repose of at least thirty families.

M. ORONTE: That being so, I am not surprised that he has married a young lady of gentle birth.

LA BRANCHE: What do you mean?

M. ORONTE: My friend, you must confess the whole truth; I know all; I know that Damis is married, that his bride is a young lady of Chartres.

LA BRANCHE, *aside*: Ooh!

M. ORONTE: You are shaken; I see that what I have been told is the truth; you are a knave.

LA BRANCHE: I, Monsieur?

M. ORONTE: Yes, you, you skulking rascal! I have found out your

93

plan, and I intend to punish you as an accomplice in this criminal project.

LA BRANCHE: What project, Monsieur? Upon my life, if I so much as understand . . .

M. ORONTE, *interrupting*: Feign ignorance of what I am saying, do, you deceitful fellow! But if you do not instantly make a sincere confession of the entire affair I shall deliver you into the hands of justice.

LA BRANCHE: Do as you please, Monsieur, I have nothing to confess to you. It is useless for me to torment my mind; I cannot imagine what cause you can have to complain of me as you do.

M. ORONTE: You refuse to speak?

He calls in the direction of the house.

Ho, there, within the house! Fetch me a constable!

LA BRANCHE, *restraining him*: One moment, Monsieur. Innocent though I am, you proceed upon a note which puts my innocence at a disadvantage. Come now, let us remain calm and get to the truth of the matter. Now, who told you that my master was married?

M. ORONTE: Who? He sent the news himself to a friend of his, named Valère.

LA BRANCHE: Valère, you say?

M. ORONTE: Yes, Valère. What do you say to that?

LA BRANCHE, *laughing*: Nothing; in faith, an excellent shot! Ha! Ha! Monsieur Valère, that wasn't a bad one, upon my soul!

M. ORONTE: What? What do you mean?

LA BRANCHE, *laughing*: We were told, right enough, that sooner or later he'd serve us a dish of his own concoction, and so he did, so he did, as you see.

M. ORONTE: I don't see at all.

LA BRANCHE: You will, you will. In the first place, this Valère is in love with your daughter, I may as well warn you of that.

M. ORONTE: I'm well aware of it.

LA BRANCHE: Lisette is in league with him; she is a party to all his schemes for the success of his suit. I would swear that it was she who told you that lie.

M. ORONTE: It was she.

LA BRANCHE: My master's arrival has thrown them into desperate straits, and as a result what have they done? They have spread a rumor that Damis is married. Valère even goes so far as to make free with a supposititious letter which he pretends to have received from my master, and all this, you realize, in order to delay Angélique's marriage.

M. ORONTE, *aside*: What he says does have the ring of possibility.

LA BRANCHE: And while you are looking into this false report, Lisette will win over her mistress and persuade her to commit some indiscretion, after which you will no longer be able to refuse her to Valère.

M. ORONTE, *aside*: Ho! Ho! His reasoning is quite reasonable.

LA BRANCHE: But upon my word, the deceivers will be deceived. M. Oronte is a man of wit, a man of sense; he's not a person to be meddled with.

M. ORONTE: No, upon my soul.

LA BRANCHE: You can recognize all the tricks that are practiced, all the ruses that a lover may stoop to in order to supplant his rival.

M. ORONTE, *aloud*: Take my word for it. It's obvious to me that your master is not married. Still, you must admire the temerity of Valère's imposture. He claims that he and Damis are the closest of friends, and I would stake my word that they have never set eyes on each other.

LA BRANCHE: I'm sure you're right. Confound it, Monsieur, but you're penetrating! I'll be bound, nothing escapes you.

M. ORONTE: I'm seldom mistaken in my conjectures.

Sees CRISPIN *coming*.

I see your master; I shall have a good laugh with him over his pretended marriage. Ha! Ha! Ha! Ha!

Scene XV

CRISPIN, M. ORONTE, LA BRANCHE.

LA BRANCHE, *pretending to laugh*: He! He! He! He! He! He!

M. ORONTE, *laughing, to* CRISPIN: Son-in-law, do you know what is being said about you? Oh, how delicious! I have been informed by someone—and informed, I may say, with the most absolute certainty—that you are married. It was said that you had contracted a secret marriage with a young lady of Chartres. Ha! Ha! Ha! Ha! Now is that not delicious?

LA BRANCHE, *laughing and making signs to* CRISPIN: He! He! He! He! What could be more delicious.

CRISPIN, *pretending to laugh, to* M. ORONTE: Ho! Ho! Ho! Ho! It's absolutely delicious.

M. ORONTE: Another, I am positive, would have been fool enough to believe them; but as for me, not so fast.

LA BRANCHE: Oh, the devil! M. Oronte is as big a wit as you are likely to find.

CRISPIN: I should like to know who could have been the author of so ridiculous a rumor.

LA BRANCHE, *to* CRISPIN: Monsieur tells me that its originator is a gentleman names Valère.

CRISPIN, *feigning surprise*: Valère! Who is this person?

LA BRANCHE, *to* M. ORONTE: You see, Monsieur, he does not even know . . .

To CRISPIN:

Oh, he's that young man, you know the one, the one whom they say is your rival.

CRISPIN: Oh, yes, yes, I remember; in particular because they said that his fortune was of the slightest and that at the same time he was laden with debts, but that he's set his sights on M. Oronte's daughter, and that his creditors were praying fervently that the marriage would take place.

M. ORONTE: Let them wait, indeed; they'll see her married.

LA BRANCHE, *to* M. ORONTE: He's not a fool, though, Valère; upon my word, he's no fool.

M. ORONTE, *to* LA BRANCHE: I'm not stupid either; upon my soul, not so stupid. And to prove it to him, I'm off to my solicitor this very moment.

He starts off, then returns.

Or still better, Damis, I have a proposition to make to you. I confess, I contracted with M. Orgon to give you twenty thousand crowns in cash; but would you accept, instead of this sum, my house in the faubourg St. Germain? It cost me more than eighty thousand francs to build.

CRISPIN, *to* M. ORONTE: I'm happy to accept anything; but to be candid, I should much prefer cash.

LA BRANCHE: Cash, as you're well aware, is much more portable.

M. ORONTE, *to* LA BRANCHE: Quite true.

CRISPIN: Yes, it fits better into a travelling bag. There is a property for sale near Chartres, you see, and I have a mind to buy it.

LA BRANCHE: Ah, Monsieur, what a handsome estate! If you had seen the property you'd be enchanted.

CRISPIN: I could have it for twenty-five thousand crowns, and I've been assured that it's worth sixty.

LA BRANCHE: Oh, at least, Monsieur, at the very least. Oh, I should say so. Quite apart from everything else, there are two fish ponds where the gudgeon fishing is worth two thousand francs a year.

M. ORONTE: You mustn't let an opportunity like that slip through your fingers.

To CRISPIN.

Very well then, I've fifty thousand francs at my solicitor's, which I had set aside to buy the chateau of a certain financier who's about to vanish; I shall give you half of that sum.

CRISPIN, *kissing* M. ORONTE: Ah, how good you are, M. Oronte! I shall never forget it; eternal gratitude . . . my heart . . . indeed, I am quite overcome.

LA BRANCHE: M. Oronte is the phoenix of fathers-in-law.

M. ORONTE: I shall go and fetch the money now, but I shall go in and tell my wife first.

He starts off.

CRISPIN, *stopping him*: Valère's creditors will hang themselves.

M. ORONTE: Let them! I will have you and my daughter married within the hour.

CRISPIN, *laughing*: Ha! Ha! Ha! How delicious that will be!

LA BRANCHE: Oh yes, yes, how utterly amusing.

M. ORONTE *goes.*

Scene XVI

CRISPIN, LA BRANCHE.

CRISPIN: It seems that my master and Angélique have had an explanation, and that he is acquainted with Damis.

LA BRANCHE: They are so well acquainted that they correspond with each other, as you see; but thanks to my efforts, M. Oronte is thoroughly prejudiced against Valère, and I hope the dowry will be stowed in our saddlebags before his opinion is changed.

CRISPIN, *glancing towards the back of the stage*: Oh heavens!

LA BRANCHE: What is it, Crispin?

CRISPIN: Here comes my master.

LA BRANCHE: What dreadful luck!

Scene XVII

CRISPIN, VALÈRE, LA BRANCHE.

VALÈRE, *at the back of the stage, holding a letter in his hand*. With this letter I can demand to speak with M. Oronte.

97

Seeing CRISPIN, *whom he does not at first recognize.*

But I see a young man; can it be Damis? I must go closer and be sure.

He approaches.

Just heaven! It's Crispin.

CRISPIN, *to* VALÈRE: Precisely. What the devil are you doing here? Did I not forbid you to approach M. Oronte's house? You will destroy everything that my talents have contrived for you.

VALÈRE: There will be no need to employ any stratagems on my account, my dear Crispin.

CRISPIN: Why not?

VALÈRE: I have learned who my rival is; he is a young man called Damis, and I have nothing to fear from him, he is married.

CRISPIN: Damis married! Here is his valet, Monsieur, whom I have enlisted in your interest; he will tell you his news.

VALÈRE, *to* LA BRANCHE: Can it be that what Damis has written to me is not true? Why should he have written to me this . . . ?

He reads Damis' letter.

"From Chartres. You must know, my dear friend, that I was married in this town several days ago. My nuptials were secret; my bride is a young lady of quality. I shall presently be in Paris, where I hope to acquaint you *viva voce* with all the details of this marriage. Damis."

LA BRANCHE, *to* VALÈRE: Ah, Monsieur, now I understand. When my master wrote you that letter he had, it's true, contracted but not performed a marriage. But M. Orgon, instead of approving the contract, gave a large sum to the girl's father, and so hushed up the affair.

VALÈRE: Damis is not married, then?

LA BRANCHE: Just so.

CRISPIN: No, he's not.

VALÈRE: Ah, my lads, I implore your help. What stratagem have you devised, Crispin? You preferred not to tell me a while ago. Do not leave me any longer in this uncertainty. Why this mystery? What are you planning to do on my account?

CRISPIN: Your rival is not yet in Paris. He will not be here for two days yet; before then I hope to render M. and Mme Oronte disgusted with the thought of having him for a son-in-law.

VALÈRE: How do you propose to do that?

CRISPIN: By pretending to be Damis. I have committed not a few extravagances already; I deliver myself of absurd speeches, I perform in a ridiculous manner which is rapidly exasperating Angélique's father and mother. You know what sort of person Mme Oronte is: she loves to be flattered. I address her with the most unheard of brutality.

VALÈRE: And?

CRISPIN: And I shall say and do so many foolish things that I'll wager they'll pack me off before the day is out, and resolve to give Angélique to you instead.

VALÈRE: And is Lisette a party to this stratagem?

CRISPIN: Yes, Monsieur, she's helping us.

VALÈRE: Ah, Crispin, how can I ever repay you?

CRISPIN: Simply for amusement, ask this fellow here whether I play my part well.

LA BRANCHE: Ah, Monsieur, you've a clever servant in that one! He's the slyest rogue in Paris; I can't help but admire him extravagantly. Though to be honest I'm not far behind him, and if our enterprise succeeds you'll be no less indebted to me than to him.

VALÈRE: You may both be certain of my gratitude; I promise you . . .

CRISPIN, *interrupting*: Ah, Monsieur, let us do without the promises; remember that if you were to be seen with us, all would be lost. Go now, and do not allow yourself to be seen here again today.

VALÈRE: I shall leave you, then. Farewell, my friends; I put my trust in your labors.

LA BRANCHE: You may put your mind at ease, Monsieur; only withdraw at once, and leave your fortune to us.

VALÈRE: Remember that my fate . . .

CRISPIN, *interrupting*: No more speeches, I beg you.

VALÈRE: Depends upon you.

CRISPIN, *pushing him*: Go, go I say.

VALÈRE *leaves*.

Scene XVIII

CRISPIN, LA BRANCHE.

LA BRANCHE: He's gone at last.

CRISPIN: I can draw breath.

LA BRANCHE: That was close. I was perishing with fright lest M. Oronte should surprise us with your master.

CRISPIN: I was afraid of that too; but since we need fear that no longer, we are assured of the success of our project. We can now choose the route which we shall take. Have you bespoken horses for tonight?

LA BRANCHE, *looking off*: Yes.

CRISPIN: Good. I say we should take the road to Flanders.

LA BRANCHE, *still looking*: The road to Flanders; yes, that's an excellent choice. I'm for the road to Flanders too.

CRISPIN: What are you gazing at so attentively?

LA BRANCHE: I'm looking . . . yes . . . no . . . God's blood and body, can it be who I think it is?

CRISPIN: Who do you think it is?

LA BRANCHE: Alas, it's his face.

CRISPIN: Whose face?

LA BRANCHE: Crispin, my poor Crispin, it's Monsieur Orgon.

CRISPIN: Damis' father?

LA BRANCHE: None other.

CRISPIN: The revolting old man!

LA BRANCHE: I believe all the devils have been loosed against that dowry.

CRISPIN: He's coming here; he'll see M. Oronte and reveal everything.

LA BRANCHE: We must prevent that if possible. Go and wait for me at the inn.

Alone.

My greatest fear is that M. Oronte may discover me talking to M. Orgon.

CRISPIN *withdraws*.

Scene XIX

M. ORGON, LA BRANCHE.

M. ORGON, *to himself, without at first seeing* LA BRANCHE: I wonder what welcome I shall have from M. and Mme Oronte.

LA BRANCHE, *in an undertone to himself*: You have not seen them yet.

Aloud.

M. Orgon's servant.

M. ORGON, *aloud*: Ah, La Branche! I did not see you.

LA BRANCHE: Indeed, Monsieur! Is it your habit to take people by surprise in this way? Who expected you in Paris?

M. ORGON: I left Chartres shortly after you did, for I decided that it would be better if I were to speak to M. Oronte myself, and that it was neither seemly nor courteous to withdraw my word at the hands of a valet.

LA BRANCHE: You are most fastidious, I see, in observing the proprieties. And so you intend to call upon M. and Mme Oronte?

M. ORGON: That was my plan.

LA BRANCHE: You may thank heaven that you met me here, in time for me to prevent you.

M. ORGON: What! Have you already spoken with them, La Branche?

LA BRANCHE: Ah, indeed I have, upon my life! I have just come from there. Madame Oronte is most horribly enraged with you.

M. ORGON: With me!

LA BRANCHE: With you. "Ho, indeed," she said, "M. Orgon has gone back on his word; who would have believed it? My daughter can never hope for a settlement after this."

M. ORGON: How will it harm her daughter?

LA BRANCHE: That's what I said to her. But when would an angry woman ever listen to reason? She could not be calmed. And she added a number of bourgeois reflections. "No one will think," she said, "that Damis was obliged to marry a girl in Chartres; instead, everyone will suppose that M. Orgon has examined the foundations of our fortune, and having found them untrustworthy, has withdrawn his promise."

M. ORGON: Fi! Can she really believe that they will say that?

LA BRANCHE: You cannot imagine how completely her fury has divorced her from her senses. She has eyes; she recognizes no one. She seized me by the throat and it was all I could do to struggle out of her clutches.

M. ORGON: And M. Oronte?

LA BRANCHE: Oh, M. Oronte I found somewhat more temperate. He merely boxed my ears twice.

M. ORGON: La Branche, you astonish me. Can they indeed view the matter with such passion? How can they disapprove of my consenting to my son's marriage? Have you explained all the circumstances to them?

LA BRANCHE: Excuse me, I told them that since Monsieur your

son had given his word, your daughter-in-law's family was preparing to take the matter to law, a step which you had wisely prevented by joining the two parties in marriage.

M. ORGON: And they did not yield when they heard this?

LA BRANCHE: Yield indeed! They are in no condition to yield! If you listen to me, Monsieur, you will turn around and go back to Chartres at once.

M. ORGON: No, La Branche, I will see them; I will present things so that they . . .

He starts toward M. Orante's house.

LA BRANCHE, *restraining him*: No, Monsieur, I insist; you shall not enter. I cannot allow you to go in and have your face scratched to pieces. If you are fixed absolutely on speaking with them, wait at least until the first transports of rage have subsided.

M. ORGON: That is a sensible suggestion.

LA BRANCHE: Put off your visit until tomorrow. They will be more willing to receive you.

M. ORGON: You are right, their mood should be less violent by then. Very well, I shall follow your advice.

LA BRANCHE: Nevertheless, Monsieur, you must do as you please; you are the master.

M. ORGON: No, no; come, La Branche; I shall see them tomorrow. *He goes.*

Scene XX

LA BRANCHE, *alone*: I am close behind you. But I'm on my way to find Crispin. This time, at any rate, we're out of danger. I've only one small remaining doubt as regards the dowry: I'm vexed that it must be shared with an associate. For after all, since it will be impossible for my master to marry Angélique, it seems to me that I've a clear right to the whole of the dowry. How can I deceive Crispin? I must advise him to flee with Angélique this evening. He loves her, no doubt he will take my advice, and as for me, I'll decamp with the cash. But no. That won't do. I mustn't quarrel with a man who's so well versed in this whole affair as I am myself. He might easily have his revenge one day. Besides, I should be transgressing against our own laws. For we sharks and swindlers are more scrupulously faithful to each other than are your honest folk. There is M. Oronte, coming out of his house on his way to his solicitor's. How lucky to have got

M. Orgon away in time!
He goes.

Scene XXI

M. ORGON, LISETTE.

LISETTE: I repeat, Monsieur, Valère is an honest man, and you
should inquire into the mattter . . .
M. ORONTE, *interrupting*: I have inquired into the matter, Lisette.
I know that you are in Valère's interest, and I am vexed that
you could not contrive between you a better expedient to
oblige me to put off my daughter's marriage to Damis.
LISETTE: What, Monsieur! Do you imagine . . . ?
M. ORONTE, *interrupting*: No, Lisette, I imagine nothing. I am
easily deceived. I have the poorest wit in the world. Go,
Lisette, and tell Valère that he will never be my son-in-law,
he can inform his creditors of the fact.
He goes.

Scene XXII

LISETTE, *alone*: Well! What's the meaning of all that? There's
something there that's quite beyond my grasp.
She muses.

Scene XXIII

LISETTE, VALÈRE.

VALÈRE, *to himself, without at first seeing* LISETTE: In spite of what
Crispin said, I cannot sit quiet and await the success of his
stratagem. After all, I do not know why he forbade me to
come here, for indeed, far from ruining his scheme I should
be able to help it.
LISETTE, *seeing* VALÈRE: Ah! Monsieur!
VALÈRE: Well, Lisette?
LISETTE: You have been a long time fetching Damis' letter; where
is it?
VALÈRE, *taking the letter from his pocket*: Here; but it will be of no

use to us. Far better, tell me, Lisette, how is the stratagem progressing?

LISETTE: What stratagem?

VALÈRE: The one which Crispin has contrived, to favor my suit.

LISETTE: Crispin? And who is Crispin?

VALÈRE: Ha! My soul! He's my valet.

LISETTE: I don't know him.

VALÈRE: That's carrying dissimulation too far, Lisette; Crispin told me that you were helping him with his stratagem.

LISETTE: I do not understand you, Monsieur.

VALÈRE: Ah, it is too much; I am past patience; I am in despair!

Scene XXIV

MADAME ORONTE, VALÈRE, LISETTE, ANGÉLIQUE.

MME ORONTE: I am delighted to find you, Valère, so that I may reprimand you for your behavior. Is it proper, I ask you, for a young gallant to forge letters?

VALÈRE, *to* MME ORONTE: Forge! I, Madame! Who can have employed such slander to lose me your esteem?

LISETTE, *to* MME ORONTE: Ah, Madame, M. Valère has not forged anything. There is trickery somewhere in all this.
Noticing M. ORONTE *and* M. ORGON.
But here is M. Oronte returning, and M. Orgon is with him. Now we shall learn the truth.

Scene XXV

MME ORONTE, VALÈRE, M. ORONTE, M. ORGON, ANGÉLIQUE, LISETTE.

M. ORONTE, *at the back of the stage*: There is knavery in this affair, M. Orgon.

M. ORGON, *at the back of the stage*: We must bring it to light, M. Oronte.

M. ORONTE, *approaching, to his wife*: Madame, on my way to my solicitor's just now I met M. Orgon. He tells me that he came to Paris to withdraw his promise. Damis is, in truth, married.

M. ORGON, *to* MME ORONTE: He is, Madame. And when you are acquainted with all the circumstances of this marriage, you will excuse . . .

M. ORONTE: M. Orgon had no choice but to consent. But what puzzles me is his insistence that his son is in Chartres.

M. ORGON: Beyond any doubt.

MME ORONTE, *to* M. ORGON: And yet there is a young man here who claims to be your son.

M. ORGON: He is an imposter.

M. ORONTE, *to* M. ORGON: And that same valet who was here with you a fortnight ago, that La Branche, calls him his master.

M. ORGON, *to* M. ORONTE: La Branche, you say? Ah, the scoundrel! Now I understand why he dissuaded me, a moment ago, from coming to see you. He told me that you were both in the most fearful rage with me, and that you had used him roughly.

MME ORONTE: The liar!

LISETTE, *in an undertone, aside*: I'm beginning to see where the kettle leaks.

VALÈRE, *in an undertone, aside*: Has my trickster been playing tricks on me?

M. ORONTE, *seeing* LA BRANCHE *and* CRISPIN *approaching*: We shall soon unravel the matter, for here they are, both of them.

Scene XXVI

M. ORONTE, M. ORGON, VALÈRE, MADAME ORONTE, ANGÉLIQUE, LI-
SETTE, CRISPIN, LA BRANCHE.

CRISPIN, *to* M. ORONTE *without at first seeing* VALÈRE *and* M. OR-
GON: Well, M. Oronte, is everything ready? Our mar-
riage . . . Ooh! What do I see?

LA BRANCHE, *to* CRISPIN: Ho! We're discovered. Run!

LA BRANCHE *and* CRISPIN *turn to flee.*

VALÈRE, *stopping them*: Oh! You will not escape us, my fine felons, and you will be dealt with as you deserve.

VALÈRE *seizes* CRISPIN *by the shoulder;* M. ORGON *and* M. ORONTE *seize* LA BRANCHE.

M. ORONTE: Ah! Aha! We have you, you rascals.

M. ORGON, *to* LA BRANCHE: Tell me, La Branche, you villain, who is this other rogue whom you have been pretending was Damis?

VALÈRE, *to* M. ORGON. My own valet.

MME ORONTE: A valet! Just heaven! A valet!

VALÈRE: A perfidious wretch who led me to believe that he was acting in my interests, while he was using the blackest artifice imaginable to deceive me.

CRISPIN, *to* VALÈRE: Gently, Monsieur, gently. Let us not judge on appearances.

M. ORGON, *to* LA BRANCHE: And you, La Branche, you scoundrel, is that how you execute the errands I send you on?

LA BRANCHE, *to* M. ORGON: Come, Monsieur, not so fast if you please; do not condemn folk before you have heard them speak.

M. ORGON: What! You are not so bold as to contend that you are not an accomplished scoundrel?

LA BRANCHE, *tearfully*: I, a scoundrel! Oh indeed! After all one's affectionate service, that's the kindness one earns!

VALÈRE, *to* CRISPIN: Crispin, do you also mean to deny that you're a rogue and a rascal?

CRISPIN, *indignant*: Rogue? Rascal? The devil! You shower me with epithets which do not apply to me in the least.

M. ORONTE, *to* LA BRANCHE *and* CRISPIN: How, then, wretches, do you intend to justify yourselves?

LA BRANCHE, *to* M. ORONTE: Crispin, here, will put the matter in its proper light.

CRISPIN: La Branche will explain it all to you in two words.

LA BRANCHE: Tell them, Crispin. Expound your innocence.

CRISPIN: Tell them yourself, La Branche; you can put them right at once.

LA BRANCHE: No, no, you'll manage the affair much better.

CRISPIN: Very well, then, Messieurs, I'll explain the thing to you quite naturally. I passed myself off as Damis in order to repel M. and Mme Oronte with my ridiculous deportment, and thus to render them favorable to my master's suit, but instead of disgusting them with my impertinent conduct, I was so unfortunate as to win their favor; hardly my fault, that.

M. ORONTE, *to* CRISPIN: Nevertheless, if you had not been prevented, you would have carried the masquerade so far as to have married my daughter.

CRISPIN, *to* M. ORONTE: No, Monsieur, ask La Branche: we came here just now in order to reveal all.

VALÈRE, *to* CRISPIN *and* LA BRANCHE: No colors in which you may paint your trickery will quite blind us; since Damis is married, there was no need for Crispin to play the part which he did.

CRISPIN: Well then, Messieurs, since you will not absolve the innocents, have mercy and pardon the guilty.

He kneels before M. ORONTE.

LA BRANCHE, *kneeling too*: Yes, we throw ourselves upon your clemency.

CRISPIN: To be honest, the dowry tempted us. We are used to trickery; forgive us on the grounds of habit.

M. ORONTE: No, no, your temerity will not go unpunished.

LA BRANCHE, *to* M. ORONTE: Ah, Monsieur, do not be impervious to pity, we beg you by Mme Oronte's beautiful eyes.

CRISPIN: By the tenderness which you cannot but feel for so charming a wife.

MME ORONTE: I pity these poor lads; I beg you to have mercy on them.

LISETTE, *in an undertone, aside*: There's a clever pair of rogues!

M. ORGON *to* CRISPIN *and* LA BRANCHE: You are fortunate, rascals, in having Mme Oronte to intercede for you.

M. ORONTE: I was anxious to have you punished, but since my wife would have it so, let us forget the past. Besides, today I give Valère my daughter; we must concern ourselves only with rejoicing.

To the valets:

And so, you are forgiven; and furthermore, if you will promise me to mend your ways, I will so far extend my generosity as to undertake to answer for your fortunes.

CRISPIN, *rising*: Ah, Monsieur, we promise.

LA BRANCHE, *also rising*: Yes, Monsieur, we are so mortified at not having succeeded in our enterprise, that we renounce all our trickeries.

M. ORONTE: You have wit, but you must employ it better; and in order to turn you into honest folk, I mean to send both of you into business. La Branche, I shall find a good situation for you.

LA BRANCHE: And I assure you, Monsieur, of my good will.

M. ORONTE: And as for my son-in-law's valet, I shall marry him to the goddaughter of one of my friend's agents.

CRISPIN: Monsieur, I shall endeavor to be so obliging as to deserve all of the godfather's kindnesses.

M. ORONTE: Let us delay no longer, but go in.

To M. ORGON:

I hope that M. Orgon will consent to honor my daughter's wedding with his presence.

M. ORGON: I hope to dance with Mme Oronte.

M. ORGON *gives his hand to* MME ORONTE, *and* VALÈRE *his to* ANGÉLIQUE, *preparatory to entering the house of* M. ORONTE.

Turcaret

Alain-René Lesage

Characters

M. TURCARET, *a financier, in love with The Baronne*

MME. TURCARET, *his wife*

THE KNIGHT
THE MARQUIS } *coxcombs*

THE BARONNE, *young widow, coquette*

M. RAFLE, *a usurer*

M. FURET, *a rogue*

MME. JACOB, *a dealer in toilet necessaries, and sister to M. Turcaret*

FRONTIN, *the Knight's valet*

FLAMAND, *Turcaret's valet*

JASMIN, *page to The Baronne*

MARINE
LISETTE } *maidservants to The Baronne*

THE PLACE: THE BARONNE'S HOUSE IN PARIS.

Act One

Scene I

THE BARONNE, MARINE

MARINE: Two hundred pistoles again yesterday!

THE BARONNE: Stop scolding me . . .

MARINE: No, Madame, I cannot remain silent; your conduct is unendurable.

THE BARONNE: Marine!

MARINE: You try my patience to the limit.

THE BARONNE: But what would you have me do? I wasn't born to be niggard and thrifty.

MARINE: That would be asking too much of you. Nevertheless, it's plain to me that you will have to learn.

THE BARONNE: Why?

MARINE: You are the widow of a foreign colonel who was killed last year in Flanders. You have already consumed the small pension which he settled upon you at his departure, and you had nothing left but your furniture, and would have had to sell that, if auspicious fortune had not arranged for Monsieur Turcaret, the revenue-collector, to fall in love with you. Is that not true, Madame?

THE BARONNE: I don't deny it.

MARINE: Now, this Monsieur Turcaret, who is not a particularly charming man, and whom, besides, you do not love, although you intend to marry him, since he has promised to make you his wife: this Monsieur Turcaret, I say, seems to be in no hurry to keep his word and marry you. And you are not impatient for him to carry out his promise and become your husband, for he never lets a day pass without giving you a handsome present. I have no objection to that. But what I cannot endure is to see you being fleeced by a certain rake-about-town, with nothing to his credit but that he calls himself a knight, and who wants only to squander the revenue-collector's pickings on his own amusements. Really, what do you mean to do with this knight?

THE BARONNE: Keep him for a friend. Is one not allowed to have friends?

MARINE: Of course. And certain friends in particular whom one may fall back on as a last resort. This knight, for example: you could always marry him if Monsieur Turcaret should fail you. For he's not a knight of any order that's sworn to celibacy and the defense of Malta. He's a knight of Paris. His only campaigns are at cards.

THE BARONNE: Indeed! I think he's an extremely honest man.

MARINE: My opinion is exactly the opposite. With those passionate airs he gives himself, and that soothing voice of his, and that winning expression, I think he's a complete actor. And my judgement is confirmed by the fact that Frontin, his good valet Frontin, has never said a word against him.

THE BARONNE: What an astonishing prejudice! And you conclude from that . . .

MARINE: That master and valet are a pair of scoundrels who have joined forces to swindle you. And you let yourself be deceived by their artifices, though you've been acquainted with them long enough to know better. It's true that he was the first, after you became a widow, to declare himself your slave. Rather unceremoniously he did it, too; and that pose of sincerity established him so firmly in your favor that he disposes of your purse as though it were his own.

THE BARONNE: It's true that I appreciated the knight's first attentions. I admit that I should have made trial of him before I disclosed my own feelings. And I agree, really, that perhaps you're right to reproach me for all that I've done for him.

MARINE: There's no doubt of it. And I won't cease to torment you until you have flung him out of your house. For, do you realize what will happen, if you continue?

THE BARONNE: Alas! What?

MARINE: Monsieur Turcaret will discover that you want to retain the knight as a friend. And Monsieur Turcaret is not of the opinion that you should be allowed to have friends. He will stop giving you presents. He will not marry you. And if you are reduced to taking this knight for your husband, it will be a miserable match for both of you.

THE BARONNE: You're right, Marine. I hope I may be able to profit by your advice.

MARINE: You'll do well to try. One must look to the future. From now on keep your eyes fixed on a vision of solid security, and profit by Monsieur Turcaret's prodigalities while you wait for him to marry you. If he fails you at last, the world may talk a little, but you will have property to console you, and cash, and jewels, and good notes-of-hand, and rents accruing. And so you cannot fail to find some capricious or restless gentleman who will restore your reputation with a good marriage.

THE BARONNE: I yield to your persuasions, Marine. I will try to disengage myself from the knight, for I am well aware that our attachment will end in my ruin.

MARINE: Ah, at last you have come to your senses. That is the only course to follow. You must fasten yourself upon Monsieur Turcaret and either marry him or ruin him. At the very least you will be able to set yourself up out of the debris of his fortune, and maintain a brilliant position in the world. And let people say what they please; for they will get tired of cackling, their malice will become jaded, and imperceptibly they will grow accustomed to mistaking you for someone as virtuous as themselves.

THE BARONNE: I have made my decision. I will banish the knight from my heart. It is done. I will buoy up his fortune no longer. Nor will I pay his debts any more. He will have nothing further from me.

MARINE: Here is his valet. Give him a glacial welcome. That will be a good way to begin to carry out this grand design.

THE BARONNE: Trust me to do it.

Scene II

THE BARONNE, MARINE, FRONTIN

FRONTIN, *to* THE BARONNE: I have come at my master's wish, and at my own, Madame, to bid you good day.

THE BARONNE, *coldly*: I am obliged to you, Frontin.

FRONTIN: And would Mademoiselle Marine allow one to take the liberty of greeting her, as well?

MARINE, *brusque*: Good day and good morrow.

FRONTIN, *handing* THE BARONNE *a note*: This note, which Monsieur the Knight has written to you, will advise you, Madame, of a certain adventure . . .

MARINE, *in an undertone, to* THE BARONNE: Refuse to accept it.

THE BARONNE, *taking the note*: Merely accepting it does not obligate me to anything. Let us see, let us see what he has sent me.

MARINE, *in an undertone, to* THE BARONNE: Ridiculous curiosity!

THE BARONNE, *reading*: "A countess has just given me her portrait. I am sending it, as a sacrifice, to you. Though you need not compensate me, for this sacrifice, my dear Baronne. For I am so enthralled, so possessed by your charms, that I am not at liberty to be unfaithful to you. Forgive me, my adored one, for writing no more, but I am beside myself with despair. I have lost all my money, and Frontin will tell you the rest. . . . The Knight"

MARINE: If he's lost all his money, I don't see that there's anything more to be said.

FRONTIN: By your leave. Apart from the two hundred pistoles which Madame was so good as to lend him yesterday, and the trifling amount which was all he had of his own, he has pledged his word for a thousand crowns, and lost it: that is the rest of the story. Oh, believe me, there is not an idle word in my master's notes.

THE BARONNE, *to* FRONTIN: Where is the portrait?

FRONTIN, *giving it to* THE BARONNE: Here.

THE BARONNE: He has never spoken to me of this countess, Frontin!

FRONTIN: Madame, she's a conquest which we made inadvertently. We met her the other day at cards.

MARINE: Shuffled in among the jacks.

FRONTIN: She besieged my master; he, merely for amusement, returned her sallies. She, who has a weakness for the serious, took the whole thing in deadly earnest; and this morning she sent us her portrait, when we do not even know her name.

MARINE: I'll wager that this countess is some Norman lady whose entire bourgeois family is milked so that she can maintain a small apartment in Paris, where the furniture comes and goes according to the whims of her luck at cards.

FRONTIN, *to* MARINE: That we do not know either.

MARINE: Oh do you not! You know well enough. Plague it, you are not a pair to make sacrifices foolishly. You know within a ducat what every one of them is worth.

FRONTIN, *to* THE BARONNE: Do you know, Madame, that this past night has seemed an eternity to my master? When he returned home he flung himself into a chair and began to rehearse all the most unfortunate turns of the game, seasoning his reflections with energetic epithets and apostrophes.

THE BARONNE, *looking at the portrait*: You have seen this countess, Frontin. Is she not more beautiful than her portrait?

FRONTIN: No, Madame. And as you can see, hers is not the kind of beauty that is remarkable for its regularity. But she is rather striking; bless me, she's rather striking. Well, at first I tried to convince my master that all his oaths were a waste of breath. But then, realizing that imprecations were all he had to console him for his loss, I let him find what ease he could in his own epithets.

THE BARONNE, *still looking at the portrait*: How old is she, Frontin?

FRONTIN: That I can't say for certain. For her color is so beautifully applied, that I could be wrong by some twenty years or so.

MARINE: In others words she's at least fifty.

FRONTIN: I should think so, for she looks thirty. My master, as I was saying, having considered everything, gave way to his passion and demanded his pistols.

THE BARONNE: His pistols, Marine! His pistols!

MARINE: He will not kill himself, Madame. Not he.

FRONTIN: I refused to fetch them. On the instant, and violently, he drew his sword.

THE BARONNE: Oh, Marine! He's wounded. I'm sure of it.

MARINE: No, no. Frontin restrained him.

FRONTIN: I did. Heedless of the danger, I flung myself upon him. "Monsieur," I said, "consider what you are about to do. One must not despair entirely, simply because of a game of cards. If your grief has made you loathe the sight of day, spare at least your own person. Live for the sake of your beloved Baronne. She has always rescued you from difficulties before now, and you may be sure"—I added, merely to calm his anguish—"that she will not desert you in this."

MARINE, *in an undertone*: Cunning, cunning! The brigand!

FRONTIN: "It's only a matter of a thousand crowns," I went on, "this once. Monsieur Turcaret has a broad back. He can easily support that much more."

THE BARONNE: And then, Frontin?

FRONTIN: Madame, at those words (I ask you to bear witness to the power of hope) he allowed himself to be disarmed like a child; and went to bed and slept.

MARINE: The poor gentleman!

FRONTIN: But this morning, when he awoke, all his distress returned as irresistibly as ever; even the countess' portrait could not dispel it. He sent me out immediately, to come here;

115

and he is waiting for my return, in order to decide his fate. What shall I tell him, Madame?

THE BARONNE: Tell him, Frontin, that he can always depend on me; and that, since at the moment I have no money in hand . . . *She starts to remove her diamond.*

MARINE, *restraining her*: Oh, Madame! Are you dreaming?

THE BARONNE, *putting back her diamond*: You will tell him that I am distressed to hear of his plight.

MARINE, *to* FRONTIN: And that I, for my part, am extremely vexed at his misfortune.

FRONTIN: Oh, he will be desolate, poor Monsieur . . . *Aside.* God shrivel the wench!

THE BARONNE: Tell him, Frontin, that I share his sufferings.

MARINE: And that I feel his affliction very keenly, Frontin.

FRONTIN: In that case, Madame, it is finished; you will never see Monsieur the Knight again. The shame of being unable to pay his debts will keep him out of your sight, for nothing is more painful for the son of a good family. We shall depart at once, by carriage.

THE BARONNE: Depart, Marine! By carriage!

MARINE: They can't afford it.

FRONTIN: Farewell, Madame.

THE BARONNE, *taking off her diamond*: Wait, Frontin.

MARINE, *to* FRONTIN: No, no; hurry and give him your answer.

THE BARONNE, *to* MARINE: Oh, I cannot bring myself to abandon him. *Giving* FRONTIN *her diamond.* Here: here is a diamond worth five hundred pistoles, which Monsieur Turcaret gave me. Go and pawn it, and save your master from the dreadful situation into which he has fallen.

FRONTIN: I will restore him to life. And I will give him an account, Marine, of the enormity of your distress. *He goes.*

MARINE: Oh, indeed you belong together, you and he, you pair of scoundrels!

Scene III

THE BARONNE, MARINE

THE BARONNE: I suppose you're angry with me, Marine. You must be furious . . .

MARINE: No, Madame, I cannot be bothered, I assure you. What does it matter to me, after all, if everything you have goes as it comes? That's your affair, Madame; your affair.

THE BARONNE: Alas, I deserve your pity rather than your reproaches. What you have seen me do was not the action of a free will; for I am enslaved by a sentiment so tender that I cannot resist it.

MARINE: A tender sentiment! Can you afford to indulge in fancies of that sort? Tut and faddle! You love like an old housewife.

THE BARONNE: How unjust you are, Marine! How can I fail to be kindly disposed to the Knight, after the sacrifice which he has made for my sake?

MARINE: Oh, that noble sacrifice! You're as gullible as a child. My death and prayers! It's some old family portrait, for all you know. His grandmother, more than likely.

THE BARONNE, *looking at the portrait*: No, it seems to me I've seen that face, and recently, too.

MARINE, *taking the portrait*: Let me see . . . Oh, of course. It's that female colossus from the provinces whom we saw at the ball three days ago; who had to be begged and teased to take off her mask, and whom nobody knew, when she did remove it.

THE BARONNE: You're right, Marine. She's not ill-favored, this countess.

MARINE, *returning the portrait to* THE BARONNE: After the fashion of Monsieur Turcaret. But if the countess were a revenue-collector, they wouldn't have sacrificed her for your sake, upon my word.

Scene IV

THE BARONNE, FLAMAND, MARINE

THE BARONNE: Hush, Marine. Here comes Monsieur Turcaret's lackey.

MARINE, *in an undertone, to* THE BARONNE: Oh, anything you like, for him. He never brings us any but good news. He's carrying something. Undoubtedly a new present for you from his master.

FLAMAND, *presenting* THE BARONNE *with a small coffer*: Monsieur Turcaret, Madame, begs you to accept this little gift. Your servant, Marine.

117

MARINE: You're very welcome, Flamand! I'd much rather see you than that villain Frontin.

THE BARONNE, *showing* MARINE *the coffer*: Marine, look at this. Observe the workmanship of this little coffer. Have you ever seen anything of such delicacy?

MARINE: Open it, open it. I will reserve my admiration for the inside. My heart tells me we will find it even more ravishing than the outside.

THE BARONNE, *opening it*: What do I see? A note of credit! The matter is serious!

MARINE: For how much, Madame?

THE BARONNE: Ten thousand crowns.

MARINE, *in an undertone*: Good! That makes up for the loss of the diamond.

THE BARONNE: I see another note.

MARINE: Also payable to the bearer?

THE BARONNE: No. This one contains some verses which Monsieur Turcaret has addressed to me.

MARINE: Verses, from Monsieur Turcaret?

THE BARONNE: "To Phyllis . . . Quatrain . . ." Phyllis is me, and he begs me in verse to accept his other note in prose.

MARINE: I am extremely curious to hear the verses of an author who sends such excellent prose.

THE BARONNE: Then listen. The verses read:
"Accept the note enclosed, charming Phyllis,
  And be assured in this fashion
  That always an eternal passion,
  While three and three make six, in my heart still is."

MARINE: Ah, what an exquisite thought!

THE BARONNE: And nobly expressed! The works reveal the author, always. Go, take this coffer into my chamber, Marine.
MARINE *goes.*

Scene V

THE BARONNE, FLAMAND

THE BARONNE: I must give you something for yourself, Flamand. So you may drink my health.

FLAMAND: Oh, I'll not fail to do that, Madame. And in the best, too.

THE BARONNE: Do. There.

118

FLAMAND: When I was with that solicitor, whom I served before, I could bring myself to drink almost anything; but since I have been with Monsieur Turcaret I have grown refined in my preferences, indeed I have.

THE BARONNE: There is nothing like the household of a man of business, for perfecting one's taste.

Scene VI

THE BARONNE, FLAMAND, MARINE

FLAMAND, *catching sight of* MONSIEUR TURCARET: Here he is, Madame. Here he is.

Scene VII

M. TURCARET, THE BARONNE, MARINE

THE BARONNE: I am delighted to see you, Monsieur Turcaret, so that I may compliment you on the verses which you sent me.

M. TURCARET, *laughing*: Ho, ho!

THE BARONNE: May I say that they are the last syllable, for gallantry! Neither Voiture nor Pavillon ever executed anything like them.

M. TURCARET: You are jesting, surely.

THE BARONNE: Not at all.

M. TURCARET: Seriously, Madame, do you find them well turned?

THE BARONNE: No wit could have bettered them.

M. TURCARET: I may tell you that they are the first verses I ever wrote in my life.

THE BARONNE: One would never have said so.

M. TURCARET: I preferred not to enlist the aid of some author, as is the usual practice.

THE BARONNE: One can see that at once. No professional author thinks and expresses himself in that way. No one would ever suspect that one of them had written your verses.

M. TURCARET: I was merely curious to see whether I might be capable of such composition, and love awakened my talent.

THE BARONNE: You are capable of anything, Monsieur, and nothing is impossible for you.

MARINE: You are to be complimented on your prose as well, Monsieur. It's of quite as much value as your verse, to say the least.

M. TURCARET: It's true that my prose has a certain worth. It is signed and approved by four of the treasurers of the commune.

MARINE, *to* M. TURCARET: Give me their approval, and let the Academy say what it pleases.

THE BARONNE: For my part, I cannot approve of your prose, Monsieur. It impels me to quarrel with you.

M. TURCARET: On what grounds?

THE BARONNE: Have you lost your reason, to send me a note of credit? You commit some folly or other of that sort every day.

M. TURCARET: You are jesting.

THE BARONNE: How much is it for, that note? I was so vexed with you that I did not even notice the amount.

M. TURCARET: Good! It's a mere ten thousand crowns.

THE BARONNE: What? Ten thousand crowns? Indeed, if I had known that I should have sent it back to you at once.

M. TURCARET: Tut, tut.

THE BARONNE: But I shall return it to you.

M. TURCARET: Oh, now that you have received it, you would not send it back.

MARINE, *in an undertone, aside*: Oh! I should think not.

THE BARONNE: I am more offended by your motive than by the thing itself.

M. TURCARET: Oh? Why?

THE BARONNE: It seems, from the way you encumber me daily with presents, as though you suppose you need that sort of tie to attach me to you.

M. TURCARET: What a notion! No, Madame, nothing was further from my thought . . .

THE BARONNE: But you are mistaken, Monsieur. I do not love you any more dearly because of them.

M. TURCARET: How candid she is! How sincere!

THE BARONNE: Nothing but the ardor and devotion of your attentions affect me.

M. TURCARET: And how good, at heart!

THE BARONNE: And the pleasure of seeing you.

M. TURCARET: I am charmed by her . . . Adieu, charming Phyllis.

THE BARONNE: What? Are you leaving so soon?

M. TURCARET: Yes, my queen. I was merely passing by, and

stopped in to greet you. I am going to one of our meetings
to oppose the admission of a knave, a ne'er-do-well wastrel
whom someone wishes to introduce into our company. I shall
come back as soon as I can escape.

He kisses her hand.

THE BARONNE: Ah! I wish you had returned already!

MARINE, *curtseying to* M. TURCARET: Adieu, Monsieur. I am your
most humble servant.

M. TURCARET: By the way, Marine, it strikes me that it has been
a long time since I have given you anything.

He gives her a fistful of money.

There. When I give, I give without counting; that's my way.

MARINE: And I accept in the same fashion, Monsieur; that's mine.
Oh, we are the soul of good faith, both of us.

M. TURCARET *goes.*

Scene VIII

THE BARONNE, MARINE

THE BARONNE: He has gone away delighted with you, Marine.

MARINE: And we remain delighted with him, Madame. He has
money, he is openhanded, and he is gullible. He might have
been made especially for coquettes.

THE BARONNE: I can do more or less what I please with him, as
you see.

MARINE: Yes. But here, unfortunately, are a couple who thoroughly offset Monsieur Turcaret.

Scene IX

THE KNIGHT, THE BARONNE, FRONTIN, MARINE

THE KNIGHT, *to* THE BARONNE: Madame, I have come to express
my gratitude. Had it not been for you, I should have broken
my gambler's pledge; my word would have lost its credit,
and I should have been despised by all honest people.

THE BARONNE: I am happy, Sir Knight, to have afforded you this
pleasure.

THE KNIGHT: Ah, how sweet it is to behold one's honor rescued
by the very object of one's love!

MARINE, *in an undertone, to herself*: How tender and passionate he is! How could anyone refuse him anything!

THE KNIGHT: Good day, Marine. Madame, I owe her certain acknowledgments too. Frontin tells me she interested herself in my distress.

MARINE, *to* THE KNIGHT: Oh, yes indeed, bless my soul! I certainly did interest myself in it: it cost us enough.

THE BARONNE, *to* MARINE: Hush, Marine! You indulge in pleasantries sometimes which I do not find at all pleasant.

THE KNIGHT: Oh no, Madame! Let her speak. I love people who are frank and sincere.

MARINE: And I hate those who are not.

THE KNIGHT: She is so witty when she is ill-humored. I am enraptured with the brilliance of her replies. Marine, I, at least, do cherish a genuine feeling of amity towards you, and I should like to give you a few tokens . . .
He pretends to go through his pockets.
Frontin, the next time I win, remind me.

FRONTIN, *to* MARINE: He has no change at the moment.

MARINE, *to* FRONTIN: I've had quite enough of his money. All I ask is that he doesn't come here pilfering ours.

THE BARONNE: Have a care what you say, Marine.

MARINE: It's highway robbery.

THE BARONNE: You are being disrespectful.

THE KNIGHT, *to* THE BARONNE: Do not take her seriously.

MARINE: I cannot remain silent, Madame. I cannot stand peacefully by and watch you being duped by him as thoroughly as Monsieur Turcaret is by you.

THE BARONNE: Marine . . . !

MARINE: Oh, for shame, Madame! It's ridiculous of you to gather in with one hand so that you can throw away with the other. What kind of behavior is that? We shall have all the shame, and Monsieur the Knight, here, will have all the profit.

THE BARONNE: Really, your insolence goes too far. I cannot endure any more.

MARINE: Neither can I.

THE BARONNE: I will discharge you.

MARINE: I will spare you the trouble, Madame. I will dismiss myself. I will not have everyone say of me that I connived at the ruin of a financier and have nothing to show for it.

THE BARONNE: Out of my sight, you impudent creature! And do not return except to render me your accounts.

MARINE: I will render them to Monsieur Turcaret, Madame. And if he is sensible enough to believe me, you will be able to settle them together.

Scene X

THE KNIGHT, THE BARONNE, FRONTIN

THE KNIGHT, *to* THE BARONNE: I must confess, she was impertinent. You were quite right to discharge her.

FRONTIN: Yes, Madame, you were quite right. Imagine! And she a servant! She was as bad as a mother.

THE BARONNE, *to* FRONTIN: She's an everlasting pedant who gives me no peace.

FRONTIN: She meddled. She gave you advice. She would have been the ruin of you in the end.

THE BARONNE: I have wanted, for a long time, to get rid of her. But I am a woman of habit, and I do not like strange faces.

THE KNIGHT: It would be disagreeable, nevertheless, if in the first flush of her anger, she were to go to Monsieur Turcaret and give him impressions which would be as inconvenient to you as to me.

FRONTIN, *to* THE KNIGHT: Damn me if she doesn't. Your serving-wenches are like your bigots: they perform charities out of spite.

THE BARONNE, *to* THE KNIGHT: Why should it disturb you? I have no fear, whatever she says. I am provided with wit, and Monsieur Turcaret is not. I do not love him, and he is in love. I shall convince him that her dismissal is an indication of my virtue.

THE KNIGHT: Excellent, Madame; one must profit by everything.

THE BARONNE: But I fancy it is not enough for us to be rid of Marine. We must contrive to execute, besides, a plan that I have formed.

THE KNIGHT: What is your plan, Madame?

THE BARONNE: Monsieur Turcaret's lackey is a dunce, a fool; he will never be of the least service to us. And I should like to replace him with some clever person, some superior genius made to govern mediocre minds and keep them perpetually in those situations where they can be of most use.

FRONTIN: Some superior genius! I've caught your drift, Madame: you refer to me.

THE KNIGHT: Indeed, Frontin would not be wasted, from our point of view, in the employ of a public treasurer.

THE BARONNE: I should like to place him there.

THE KNIGHT: He would render us a good account, would he not?

FRONTIN: I am jealous of the notion. One could not imagine anything better. In faith, Monsieur Turcaret, I will show you the country, upon my word.

THE BARONNE: He has made me a present of a note of credit for ten thousand crowns. I must change the form of that valuable, and have the money for it. I know of no one to whom I can entrust the transaction. I must ask you, sir, to undertake it for me. I will give you the note. Redeem my diamond; I shall be most happy to have it again; and you can give me an account of the remainder.

FRONTIN: That is only too just, Madame; and you need have no fear as to our probity.

THE KNIGHT: I will lose no time, Madame. You will have the money at once.

THE BARONNE: Wait here for a moment; I will fetch you the note.

Scene XI

THE KNIGHT, FRONTIN

FRONTIN: A note for ten thousand crowns! What a windfall! And what a woman! One must be as lucky as you are, to fall in with one like her. Do you know, I find her a shade too credulous for a coquette.

THE KNIGHT: You're right.

FRONTIN: It's not a bad return for the sacrifice of our old ninny of a countess, who hasn't a sou.

THE KNIGHT: That's true.

FRONTIN: Madame the Baronne believes that you have lost a thousand crowns, pledged against your word, and that her diamond is in pawn. Will you return it to her, Monsieur, with the remainder of the note?

THE KNIGHT: Of course I will return it to her!

FRONTIN: What! All of it, without any new article of expense?

THE KNIGHT: Certainly. I shall take great pains to see that it is all there.

FRONTIN: You have moments of integrity. I would never have expected it.

THE KNIGHT: I would be a miserable bungler, to risk breaking with her so cheaply.

FRONTIN: Ah, I beg your pardon. I judged you rashly. I was afraid you had decided to do things by halves.

THE KNIGHT: Oh no! If ever I show her my heels, it will not be until after the total ruin of Monsieur Turcaret.

FRONTIN: After his destruction, you mean? His disintegration!

THE KNIGHT: And I court the coquette only so that I may ruin the financier.

FRONTIN: Excellent: in those generous sentiments I recognize my master.

Scene XII

THE KNIGHT, THE BARONNE, FRONTIN

THE KNIGHT, *in an undertone to* FRONTIN: Hush, Frontin; here is the Baronne.

THE BARONNE: Go, Sir Knight; go at once and change this note, and return me my jewel as soon as possible.

THE KNIGHT: Madame, Frontin will bring it to you immediately. But, before I leave you, suffer me, enchanted as I am by your generous conduct, to express to you . . .

THE BARONNE: No, I forbid you; not a word of that.

THE KNIGHT: What constraint, for a heart as full of gratitude as mine is!

THE BARONNE, *going*: I will not say farewell, then, since I trust I shall see you again, presently.

THE KNIGHT: Ah, could I leave your side without so sweet a hope! *He escorts* THE BARONNE, *who enters her chamber, then he goes.*

Scene XIII

FRONTIN

FRONTIN, *alone*: I am intrigued by the pageant of human existence! We pluck a coquette; the coquette devours a man of means; the man of means has others whom he plunders. And the sum of it all is as entertaining a light-footed progression of knaveries as a man could wish for.

Act Two

Scene I

THE BARONNE, FRONTIN

FRONTIN, *giving her the diamond*: As you see, Madame, I have
wasted no time. Here is your diamond. The man who had
it in pawn returned it to my hands the moment he saw the
sparkle of your note of credit, which he plans to invest at a
nice honest rate of interest. My master, whom I left with
him, will be here presently with the remainder.

THE BARONNE: I am at last rid of Marine. She meant, in fact,
what she said. I had supposed she was only feigning; she has
gone. And so, Frontin, I am without a chambermaid. I charge
you to find me another.

FRONTIN: I have one in mind already. She is a sweet, agreeable
girl, exactly what would suit you. She could see everything
in your house turned upside down, without saying a word.

THE BARONNE: I love that sort of person. Do you know her particularly well?

FRONTIN: Most particularly well. We are even related slightly.

THE BARONNE: In other words, she is to be trusted.

FRONTIN: As myself. I am her guardian. I have charge of her
wages and profits, and it is my duty to supply all her little
wants.

THE BARONNE: She is in service at the moment, I suppose?

FRONTIN: No, she left her last situation several days ago.

THE BARONNE: What was the reason?

FRONTIN: She was in service with people who lead a life of re-
tirement, and receive none but seemly and serious visitors.
A husband and wife who love each other; extraordinary people. In short, it is a dreary house, and my young charge was
bored there.

THE BARONNE: Where is she at this moment?

FRONTIN: She is lodged with an old prude of my acquaintance,
who harbors out of work chambermaids out of charity, so
that she may keep track of what goes on in families.

THE BARONNE: I should like her to begin here today. I cannot do without a girl.

FRONTIN: I will send her to you, Madame; or fetch her here myself. You will be delighted with her. I have not told you all of her little talents: she sings and plays most deliciously on all sorts of instruments.

THE BARONNE: Frontin, she sounds an exquisite creature.

FRONTIN: I will answer for her. I may tell you that I intend her for the Opéra; but I wish her to be formed and polished in the world, first; they are no use at the Opéra until they are fully developed.

He goes.

THE BARONNE: I cannot wait to see her.

Scene II

THE BARONNE

THE BARONNE, *alone*: This girl should be a great pleasure to me. She will amuse me with her songs, where that other only annoyed me with her sermons.

Scene III

THE BARONNE, M. TURCARET

THE BARONNE, *noticing* M. TURCARET; *to herself*: But here is Monsieur Turcaret. Dear, how agitated he seems! Marine must have been to see him.

M. TURCARET, *out of breath*: Uff! I don't know where to begin, perfidious thing!

THE BARONNE, *aside*: She has spoken to him.

M. TURCARET: I have heard all about you, deceitful person! I have heard everything about you. I have just been rendered an account of your double-dealings, of your felonies.

THE BARONNE: The beginning is charming; and you employ very pretty words, Monsieur.

M. TURCARET: Let me speak. I want to inform you of what you are. Marine has told me. This splendid knight, who came here a little while ago, I had good reason to be suspicious of him. He is not your cousin, as you pretended to me. You

127

proposed all along to marry him, and to show me the door—
me!—when I had made your fortune.

THE BARONNE: I, Monsieur? You suggest that I love this knight?

M. TURCARET: Marine assured me that you do, and that whatever
figure he cuts in the world is paid for out of your purse and
mine. And that you sacrifice to him all the presents that I
give you.

THE BARONNE: Marine has a pretty tongue! Was that all she told
you, Monsieur?

M. TURCARET: Do not answer me, felon! I have proof that will
cover you with confusion. Do not answer me. Speak: what,
for example, has become of that large jewel which I gave
you the other day? Show it to me this minute. Show it to me.

THE BARONNE: Since you take that tone, I will certainly not show
it to you.

M. TURCARET: Hum! And what tone, death and damnation, what
tone do you presume to suggest that I take? Oh, do not think
that you will be let off with a few reproaches. Do not think
that I am such a fool as to break with you without tumult,
and depart without a thunderclap. I will leave the marks of
my wrath behind me. I am a decent man, an honest man.
Good faith, that's my passion. I have none but legitimate
attitudes. I have no fear of scandal. Ah, you are not dealing
with an abbot, as you will learn to your cost.
He goes into THE BARONNE'S *bedchamber.*

Scene IV

THE BARONNE

THE BARONNE, *alone*: No, I am dealing with a lunatic, a man possessed! . . . Oh very well; do, Monsieur: do just as you please.
I shall not attempt to hinder you, I assure you . . . But . . .
what do I hear? . . . Heaven! What a shambles! . . . He has
quite literally gone mad . . . Monsieur Turcaret, Monsieur
Turcaret, I shall make you pay dearly for your passion.

Scene V

M. TURCARET, THE BARONNE

M. TURCARET: Well, I am halfway to consolation. I have already
smashed the large mirror and all the best pieces of china.

THE BARONNE: By all means break the rest, Monsieur. Why do you not continue?

M. TURCARET: I will continue when I please, Madame . . . I will teach you to juggle with a man like me . . . Now then, that note of credit which I gave you a little while ago: I'll have it back. Give it to me.

THE BARONNE: You'll have it back! And what if I've given that to the Knight, as well?

M. TURCARET: Oh, if I thought you had!

THE BARONNE: What a fool you are! I pity you, truly I do.

M. TURCARET: Indeed, indeed! Instead of throwing herself at my feet and begging me for mercy, she still says that it's I who am wrong; she still says that it's I who am wrong!

THE BARONNE: Of course.

M. TURCARET: Oh! To tell you the truth, I'd be delighted if, as a treat to me, you would undertake to convince me of that.

THE BARONNE: And so I should, if you were in a state to listen to reason.

M. TURCARET: What could you say to me, traitress!

THE BARONNE: I shall say nothing to you. Oh, what an uproar!

M. TURCARET, *out of breath*: Very well! Speak, Madame, speak. I am controlled; I am calm.

THE BARONNE: Then listen . . . All the extravagances that you have just perpetrated stem from a false report of Marine's.

M. TURCARET: A false report! Death and damnation! It's nothing of the . . .

THE BARONNE: Do not swear, Monsieur. And do not interrupt me. Remember that you are controlled; you are calm.

M. TURCARET: I will not say a word. I will restrain myself.

THE BARONNE: Do you know the real reason why I dismissed Marine?

M. TURCARET: Yes. Because she defended my interests too warmly.

THE BARONNE: On the contrary. It was because she never ceased to reproach me for my fondness for you. "Could anything be so ridiculous," she would say to me twenty times a day, "as to see the widow of a colonel sighing for Monsieur Turcaret, a man of no birth, no wit, of the grossest and most common appearance . . ."

M. TURCARET: You need not quote the details, if you please. That Marine is an impudent wench.

THE BARONNE: "When there are at least twenty gentlemen, all of the first quality, any of whom you could have for a husband if you chose to. Whereas you refuse your consent even to

129

the persistent suit of the family of a marquis who adores you, and whom you are so feeble as to sacrifice for the sake of this Monsieur Turcaret."

M. TURCARET: It is not possible.

THE BARONNE: I take no credit for it, Monsieur. This marquis, with regard to his person, is an extremely presentable young lord; but his conduct and his way of life are not at all suited to me. He comes here from time to time with my cousin, the Knight, who is a friend of his. I discovered that he had won over Marine, and that is why I discharged her. She has gone straight to you and peddled you a pack of falsehoods in order to avenge herself, and you have been so credulous as to take her at her word. Should you not have considered, at the time, that it was an irate servant who was addressing you; and that, if I had had any cause to reproach myself, I would not have been so imprudent as to dismiss a maidservant whose indiscretion I had cause to fear? Tell me: should you not naturally have considered such a thing?

M. TURCARET: I agree, I should, but . . .

THE BARONNE: But, but you are wrong. She told you, among other things, did she not, that I no longer had that large diamond which, merely in jest, you placed on my finger the other day, and then forced me to accept?

M. TURCARET: Oh yes. She swore to me that this very morning you gave it to the Knight, who, she says, is no more your cousin than Jean de Vert.

THE BARONNE: And what would you say if I were to show you that same diamond, here and now?

M. TURCARET: Oh, in that case I'd say that . . . But you can't.

THE BARONNE: Here it is, Monsieur. Do you recognize it? You see how far one should credit the testimony of certain menials.

M. TURCARET: Oh, that Marine! What a scoundrel! Now I recognize her trickery, and my injustice. Forgive me, Madame, for having doubted your good faith.

THE BARONNE: No, your behavior was inexcusable. Go: you are not worthy to be forgiven.

M. TURCARET: I admit it.

THE BARONNE: Should you have let yourself be persuaded so easily to turn against a woman who loves you so tenderly?

M. TURCARET: Alas! No . . . Oh, how miserable I am!

THE BARONNE: You must confess that you are an extremely silly man.

M. TURCARET: Yes, Madame.

THE BARONNE: An absolute gull.

M. TURCARET: I agree. Oh, Marine, Marine, you villainous baggage! You cannot imagine all the lies that that unscrupulous jade regaled me with . . . She told me that you and Monsieur the Knight regarded me as nothing better than a cow to be milked. And that if I gave you everything today, you would have your door shut in my face tomorrow.

THE BARONNE: The wretch!

M. TURCARET: That's what she said. It's an absolute fact. I'm not a man who makes things up.

THE BARONNE: And you were silly enough to believe her even for a moment!

M. TURCARET: Yes, Madame. In that respect I behaved like an utter fool . . . Where the devil were my wits?

THE BARONNE: Are you sorry for your credulity?

M. TURCARET, *throwing himself on his knees*: Oh, bitterly, bitterly! I entreat you a thousand times over to forgive me for my anger.

THE BARONNE, *raising him*: You are forgiven. Rise, Monsieur. Your jealousy would be less quick if your love were less ardent, and the excess of the one permits me to forget the violence of the other.

M. TURCARET: What magnanimity! . . . I must confess that I am a great brute!

THE BARONNE: But seriously, Monsieur, do you believe that a woman's heart could hesitate for a moment between you and the Knight?

M. TURCARET: No, Madame, I do not believe it, but I fear it.

THE BARONNE: What can be done to disperse your fears?

M. TURCARET: Send that man away from here. You need only consent to it, Madame, and I have means to accomplish it.

THE BARONNE: Oh? What are they?

M. TURCARET: I will give him a directorship in the provinces.

THE BARONNE: A directorship!

M. TURCARET: That is my way of getting rid of those whose presence I find inconvenient . . . Oh, you have no idea how many cousins and uncles and husbands I have made directors in my time! I have representatives all the way to Canada.

THE BARONNE: But you have forgotten that my cousin the Knight is a gentleman of quality, and that employment of that kind would not be suited to him . . . Come, come, you need not trouble to send him away from Paris, for I swear to you that

131

in the whole world he is the man who should cause you the least disquiet.

M. TURCARET: Oh, I am choked with love and with joy! You said that with such simplicity that it convinced me . . . Farewell, my adored one, my all, my goddess . . . Tut, tut, I will repay you handsomely for my little misunderstanding, earlier. Your large mirror was flawed, to say the least, and I thought your china rather common.

THE BARONNE: So it was.

M. TURCARET: I will find others for you.

THE BARONNE: You see how costly your follies are.

M. TURCARET: A trifle! . . . Everything that I broke was not worth more than three hundred pistoles.

He starts to go, and THE BARONNE *detains him.*

THE BARONNE: Wait, Monsieur; I must entreat a favor of you before you go.

M. TURCARET: Entreat? A favor? Oh! your orders, your orders!

THE BARONNE: For the sake of the love you bear me, find some commission for that poor Belgian, your lackey. He's a boy whom I have conceived a liking for.

M. TURCARET: I would have pushed him out before this if I could have found him a position of any kind, but he's too trusting and honest by nature, and that's no use in business.

THE BARONNE: Find something simple for him to do.

M. TURCARET: I shall; this very day. It's as good as done.

THE BARONNE: That is not all. I should like you to replace him, in your service, with Frontin, who is my cousin the Knight's lackey, and a good child, too.

M. TURCARET: I will have him, Madame, and send the other on a commission at the first opportunity.

Scene VI

FRONTIN, M. TURCARET, THE BARONNE

FRONTIN, *to* THE BARONNE: Madame, the girl of whom I told you will be with you presently.

THE BARONNE, *to* M. TURCARET: Monsieur, this is the lad I recommended to your service.

M. TURCARET: He seems a trifle innocent.

THE BARONNE: What a shrewd judge of faces you are!

M. TURCARET: My glance is infallible . . .

To FRONTIN:

Approach, my friend. Now tell me: have you acquired any principles?

FRONTIN: What do you mean by "principles"?

M. TURCARET: Principles of business. For example, do you know how to prevent frauds, or to promote them?

FRONTIN: Not yet, Monsieur. But I feel sure that I will learn to, with no trouble.

M. TURCARET: Do you know arithmetic, at least? Can you do single-entry bookkeeping?

FRONTIN: Oh yes, Monsieur. I can even make double entries. And I know how to write both kinds of writing, the one just as well as the other.

M. TURCARET: You mean you can write a round hand?

FRONTIN: Yes; round, and oblique too.

M. TURCARET: What do you mean, oblique?

FRONTIN: That kind of writing . . . you know . . . that kind . . . that special way of writing which is not legitimate.

M. TURCARET, *to* THE BARONNE: He means bastard writing.

FRONTIN: Exactly. That is the word I was trying to remember.

M. TURCARET, *to* THE BARONNE: What ingenuousness! . . . Madame, he is a fledgling, this lad.

THE BARONNE: He will feather himself in your office.

M. TURCARET: Oh, of course, Madame, of course! Besides, his tasks will not require a particularly sparkling turn of mind. Except for myself and two or three others, there are none but fairly ordinary intelligences among us. A little practice, a certain acquaintance with our routine, which no one could fail to pick up—these are all he will need. We see so many people! We study how to obtain the best that the world has to offer; that is all there is to our science.

THE BARONNE: It is not the least useful of the sciences.

M. TURCARET, *to* FRONTIN: Well, there we are, my friend. You are in my service, and your wages start from this moment.

FRONTIN: In that case, Monsieur, I regard you as my new master . . . But as the former lackey of Monsieur the Knight, I must discharge a commission which he gave me. He invites you, and Madame his cousin, to dine with him this evening.

M. TURCARET: With pleasure.

FRONTIN: I must go to Fite's and order every sort of ragout, and twenty-four bottles of champagne. And to add to the gaiety of the occasion, you will be entertained with music and instruments.

THE BARONNE: Music, Frontin?

FRONTIN: Yes, Madame. The proof of it is that I am also to order a hundred bottles of Suresnes for the musicians to drink.

THE BARONNE: A hundred bottles!

FRONTIN: It's none too much, Madame. There will be eight ensemble players, four Italians from Paris, three sopranos, and two fat tenors.

M. TURCARET: Upon my word he's right. It will be none too much. It should be a delightful dinner.

FRONTIN: Oh, mark my words, when Monsieur the Knight gives that kind of a dinner he spares nothing, Monsieur.

M. TURCARET: I am convinced of it.

FRONTIN: One would think he had the purse of some benefactor at his disposition.

THE BARONNE, *to* M. TURCARET: He means that his arrangements are so lavish.

M. TURCARET: How open and unspoiled he is!

To FRONTIN:

Well, we shall taste of that presently.

To THE BARONNE:

And to supplement the festivities, I shall bring with me Monsieur Gloutonneau, the poet. Oh yes, I can't eat a mouthful if I don't have a wit at my table.

THE BARONNE: That would delight me. This author is noted, is he, for the brilliance of his conversation?

M. TURCARET: He doesn't utter four words during a whole meal, but he eats and thinks a prodigious amount. Damn me, he's a man of charm . . . Well, now, I shall go to Dautier the jeweller and buy you . . .

THE BARONNE: I beg you to be prudent. Do not rush headlong into expenses . . .

M. TURCARET, *interrupting her in his turn*: Oh! Tut, tut, Madame; you worry at trifles. I will not say good-bye, my queen.

THE BARONNE: I await your return with impatience.

M. TURCARET *goes*.

Scene VII

THE BARONNE, FRONTIN

THE BARONNE: There: at last you are on the way to making your fortune.

FRONTIN: Yes, Madame, and in a position not to injure yours.

THE BARONNE: Now is the moment, Frontin, to give wing to that superior genius . . .

FRONTIN: I shall prove, if I can, that it is not mediocre.

THE BARONNE: When will you fetch me this girl?

FRONTIN: I am waiting for her. She is to join me here.

THE BARONNE: Tell me when she arrives.

She goes into her bedchamber.

Scene VIII

FRONTIN

FRONTIN, *alone*: Courage, Frontin! Courage, my friend! Fortune summons you. Here you are, arrived at a man of affairs by way of a coquette. What joy! What a charming perspective! I feel as though everything that I touch will turn into gold.
Seeing LISETTE.
But here is my ward.

Scene IX

LISETTE, FRONTIN

FRONTIN: Welcome to this house, Lisette! . . . You are awaited here with impatience.

LISETTE: And I am happy to be here. I feel that is a promising start.

FRONTIN: I have informed you about everything that is going on here, and about everything that is likely to happen. You have only to act upon what I've told you. The one thing you must remember is to accommodate yourself to everything, without exception or hesitation.

LISETTE: You need not remind me of that.

FRONTIN: Lose no opportunity to encourage the Baronne's infatuation with the Knight. That, after all, is the point.

LISETTE: You weary me with unnecessary instruction.

Scene X

THE KNIGHT, FRONTIN, LISETTE

FRONTIN, *seeing* THE KNIGHT *arriving*: Here he is now.

LISETTE, *examining* THE KNIGHT: I never saw him before . . . Ah! He is not bad-looking, Frontin!

FRONTIN: One must not be bad-looking if one is to be the lover of a coquette.

THE KNIGHT, *to* FRONTIN, *without at first noticing* LISETTE: Frontin, I am happy to see you and have a chance to tell you . . .
Noticing LISETTE:
But what do I see? Who is this dazzling beauty?

FRONTIN: She is a girl whom I am giving to Madame to replace Marine.

THE KNIGHT: One of your friends, I don't doubt.

FRONTIN: Yes, Monsieur. We have known each other for some little time. I am her guardian.

THE KNIGHT: Excellent protection! You have spoken her eulogy in one word. She is, bless me, charming . . . Monsieur Guardian, I am grieved at you.

FRONTIN: How so?

THE KNIGHT: I say, I am grieved at you. All my affairs are known to you, but your own you hide from me. You are not a sincere friend.

FRONTIN: Monsieur, I did not wish . . .

THE KNIGHT, *interrupting him*: Whereas confidences should be reciprocated. Why have you kept me ignorant of so beautiful a discovery?

FRONTIN: Upon my word, Monsieur, I was afraid . . .

THE KNIGHT, *interrupting him*: What?

FRONTIN: Oh, confound it, Monsieur. You understand me quite well.

THE KNIGHT: The scoundrel! Where did he unearth this little charmer?
To FRONTIN:
Frontin, Monsieur Frontin, your discernment is exquisitely delicate when you are choosing for yourself. But your taste is less good where your friends are concerned . . . Oh, the pretty image! The adorable wench!

LISETTE, *aside*: How honest these young gentlemen are!

THE KNIGHT: No, I have never seen anything so beautiful as this creature.

LISETTE, *aside*: How pleasing their expressions! . . . I am not surprised that women pursue them.

THE KNIGHT, *to* FRONTIN: Let us strike a bargain, Frontin. Yield
me this girl here, and I will give up my old countess to you.

FRONTIN: No, Monsieur. My tastes are not so exalted. I will abide
by Lisette, for I have given her my word.

THE KNIGHT: Away with you. And you can boast of being the
luckiest good-for-nothing.

To LISETTE:

Yes, fair Lisette, you deserve . . .

LISETTE, *interrupting him*: A truce to your flatteries, Monsieur. I
must present myself to my mistress, who has not yet seen
me. You may come, if you like, and continue the conversation
before her.

She goes into THE BARONNE's *bedchamber.*

Scene XI

THE KNIGHT, FRONTIN

THE KNIGHT: Let us discuss more serious matters, Frontin. I have
not brought the Baronne the money for her note.

FRONTIN: How sad.

THE KNIGHT: I have been trying to find a certain usurer who has
lent me money before, but he is no longer in Paris. An
unexpected turn of affairs forced him to leave rather suddenly. And so, I must ask you to exchange the note.

FRONTIN: Why?

THE KNIGHT: Did you not tell me that you knew an exchange
broker who would give you the money immediately?

FRONTIN: That is true. But what will you say to Madame the
Baronne? If you tell her that you still have the note, she will
realize at once that we did not pawn her diamond. For she
is aware that a moneylender does not give up his collateral
for nothing.

THE KNIGHT: You are right. And therefore I have decided to tell
her that I have drawn her money, and left it at my lodgings,
whence you will fetch it to her tomorrow. In the meantime,
run to your exchange broker, and take home the money
which you receive. I shall await you there, as soon as I have
spoken with the Baronne.

He goes into THE BARONNE's *bedchamber.*

Scene XII

FRONTIN

FRONTIN, *alone*: Thank God I do not lack for occupation! I must go to the caterer, from him to the exchange broker; from the exchange broker to Monsieur the Knight's lodging; after that I must return here to join Monsieur Turcaret. That, I fancy, is what might be termed an active life . . . But patience! A little effort and fatigue now will bring me into my ease at last. Then what contentment! What peace of mind! . . . Then nothing will trouble me—except my conscience.

Act Three

Scene I

THE BARONNE, FRONTIN, LISETTE

THE BARONNE: Well, Frontin! Have you ordered the supper? May we expect a feast?

FRONTIN, *to* THE BARONNE: I will answer for it, Madame. Ask Lisette what sort of provision I make when I entertain on my own account, and judge from that as to how I might provide when I entertain at the expense of another.

LISETTE, *to* THE BARONNE: It is true, Madame. You may rely on him.

FRONTIN, *to* THE BARONNE: Monsieur the Knight awaits me. I must go and give him an account of the arrangements for this evening, and then I shall return here to take possession of Monsieur Turcaret, my new master.
He goes.

Scene II

THE BARONNE, LISETTE

LISETTE: There is a young man of sterling qualities, Madame.

THE BARONNE: It seems to me that you are not lacking in merit yourself, Lisette.

LISETTE: He is extremely capable.

THE BARONNE: I cannot think that you are less clever.

LISETTE: I should be most happy, Madame, if my small talents might prove to be of some use to you.

THE BARONNE: I am delighted with you. But there is one thing I must tell you: I do not like to be flattered.

LISETTE: I detest flattery.

THE BARONNE: When I consult you upon matters which concern me, do, above all else, be sincere.

LISETTE: Without fail, Madame.

THE BARONNE: And yet, it seems to me that you are too willing to agree with me.

LISETTE: I, Madame?

THE BARONNE: Yes. You do not disapprove sufficiently of my fondness for the Knight.

LISETTE: But why should I disapprove? It is so reasonable!

THE BARONNE: I confess that I believe the Knight deserves all my affection.

LISETTE: That is my opinion, too.

THE BARONNE: His passion for me is genuine and constant.

LISETTE: A knight who is faithful and sincere! You never find them like that nowadays.

THE BARONNE: He sacrificed a countess for my sake, this very day.

LISETTE: A countess!

THE BARONNE: She is not, it must be admitted, in the first flush of her youth.

LISETTE: That enhances the sacrifice. I know these young milords. It costs them more to sacrifice an old lady than another.

THE BARONNE: He has just delivered me an account of a note of credit which I entrusted to him. I think him a man of such good faith!

LISETTE: That is admirable.

THE BARONNE: He carries probity to the point of being positively scrupulous.

LISETTE: Well indeed, there is a knight who is unique among his species!

THE BARONNE: Hush. I see Monsieur Turcaret.

Scene III

M. TURCARET, THE BARONNE, LISETTE

M. TURCARET, *to* THE BARONNE: I have returned, Madame . . .
Noticing LISETTE.
Ah! Ah! Have you a new chambermaid?

THE BARONNE: Yes, Monsieur. What do you think of her?

M. TURCARET, *examining* LISETTE: What do I think of her? I like her looks well enough. We must get to know each other.

LISETTE: That should not take long, Monsieur.

THE BARONNE: Did you know that we are dining here? Order

them to lay the table, and see that the apartment is well
lighted.

LISETTE *goes*.

Scene IV

M. TURCARET, THE BARONNE

M. TURCARET: I think she is a most sensible girl.

THE BARONNE: In any case she has your interests at heart.

M. TURCARET: I find her delightful . . . Madame, I have just bought
you ten thousand francs worth of mirror, china, and furniture. They are all in exquisite taste: I chose them myself.

THE BARONNE: You are universal, Monsieur. You have a knowledge of everything.

M. TURCARET: Yes, thank heaven. Especially building. Wait till
you see, wait till you see the house that I intend to build.

THE BARONNE: What? You mean to build a house?

M. TURCARET: I have already bought the site, which covers four
acres, six rods, nine ells, three feet, and eleven square inches.
Would you not call that a fair extent?

THE BARONNE: Extremely fair.

M. TURCARET: The residence will be magnificent. I do not want
a single jot left out. I would rather they built it over two or
three times.

THE BARONNE: I have no doubt.

M. TURCARET: Confound it, I have no mind to construct something
common. I will build something that will make my colleagues
whistle.

THE BARONNE: I am sure of it.

M. TURCARET, *noticing the entrance of* THE MARQUIS: Who is this
gentleman?

THE BARONNE, *in an undertone*: It is the young marquis, whose
cause Marine espoused, as I told you. I wish he would spare
me his visits. I take no pleasure in them.

Scene V

THE MARQUIS, M. TURCARET, THE BARONNE

THE MARQUIS, *aside*: It looks as though I shall not find the Knight
here.

M. TURCARET: Oh! The devil take it! It's the Marquis de Tribau-
dière . . . What an embarrassing meeting.

THE MARQUIS, *aside*: I have been looking for him for the best part
of two days.

Catching sight of M. TURCARET.

Ah! What do I see? . . . Yes . . . No . . . Excuse me . . . It
is none other . . . It is Monsieur Turcaret himself.

To THE BARONNE:

What have you to do with this man, Madame? Do you know
him? Are you pawning your possessions? God's blood! He
will ruin you!

THE BARONNE: Monsieur le Marquis . . .

THE MARQUIS, *interrupting her*: He will plunder you, he will flay
you. I warn you. He has not his match among moneylenders:
he's the worst Jew of them all. He sells his silver for its
weight in gold.

M. TURCARET, *aside*: I should have gone.

THE BARONNE, *to* THE MARQUIS: You are mistaken, Monsieur le
Marquis. Monsieur Turcaret is known in the world as a man
of worth and of honor.

THE MARQUIS: So he is, Madame, so he is. He loves women's
honor and men for what they are worth. And he has a reputation for it.

M. TURCARET: You are a great one for jesting, Monsieur le Marquis . . .

To THE BARONNE:

He is a wag, Madame; he is a wag. You did not know that
side of him, perhaps?

THE BARONNE: Oh, I am aware that he is jesting, or else is misinformed.

THE MARQUIS: Misinformed! God's death, Madame, no one could
warn you on better authority. He is wearing an article of
mine at this moment.

M. TURCARET: An article of yours, Monsieur? I will swear to the
contrary.

THE MARQUIS: Oh yes, confound it, so you may! The diamond
belongs to you now, according to your ethic. My claim to it
has run out.

THE BARONNE: Explain me this riddle, both of you.

M. TURCARET: There is no riddle to it, Madame. I do not know
what it is about.

THE MARQUIS, *to* THE BARONNE: He is right. There is no riddle,
and that's certain. Some fifteen months ago I had need of

money. I had a jewel worth five hundred louis. I was directed to Monsieur Turcaret. Monsieur Turcaret, in turn, sent me to one of his clerks, a certain Monsieur Ra . . . Ra . . . Rafle. It is he who looks after his pawnshop. This honest Monsieur Rafle lent me 344 crowns, 6 florins and eight-pence on my stone. He prescribed me a term within which I might reclaim it. I am not a great one for exactitude. The time ran out; and my diamond was lost.

M. TURCARET: Monsieur le Marquis, Monsieur le Marquis, I beg you not to confuse me with Monsieur Rafle. He is a scoundrel whom I have thrown out of my establishment. If he has dealt unfairly with you, there is always the law. I know nothing of your stone; it has never passed through my hands, nor have I ever seen it.

THE MARQUIS: It came to me from my aunt. It was the most beautiful of stones. It was of a clearness, a cut, a size, rather like . . .

Looking at THE BARONNE'S *diamond.*

Ah! Is that not it, Madame? You are on terms with Monsieur Turcaret, it seems.

THE BARONNE: Mistaken again, Marquis. I bought it, and rather dearly, too, from a woman who deals in secondhand clothing.

THE MARQUIS: It came from him, Madame. He has women of that trade at his disposition; and, from what I hear, in his own family, too.

M. TURCARET: Monsieur, Monsieur!

THE BARONNE, *to* THE MARQUIS: Monsieur le Marquis, you are insulting.

THE MARQUIS: No, Madame. I did not intend to be insulting. I am too much indebted to Monsieur Turcaret, however hard he may use me. There was a time when we were on the best of terms. He was my grandfather's lackey; he carried me in his arms. We used to play whole days together, and were scarcely ever apart. The little ingrate has forgotten it entirely.

M. TURCARET: I remember . . . I remember . . . What's past is past. I am concerned only with the present.

THE BARONNE, *to* THE MARQUIS: Pray let us change the subject, Monsieur le Marquis. You are looking for the Knight?

THE MARQUIS: I have been looking for him everywhere, Madame: at the theatres, at the tavern, at the ball, at the gaming-table. I cannot find him anywhere. The rascal is turning into a rake. He is becoming a libertine.

THE BARONNE: I shall scold him.

THE MARQUIS: I beg you to . . . For my part, I never change. I
lead a regular life; I am always at the table, and they give
me credit at Fite's and La Morlière's because they know that
I should fall heir to the fortune of an old aunt before long,
and they see that I am fairly inclined to eat up all that she
leaves me.

THE BARONNE: You are a good customer for the caterers.

THE MARQUIS: Yes, Madame, and for the usurers too, am I not,
Monsieur Turcaret? However, my aunt desires me to mend
my ways. And in order to convince her of the change in my
conduct, I mean to go and see her in my present condition.
She will be astonished to find me so reasonable, for she has
hardly ever seen me sober.

THE BARONNE: It is indeed a novelty, Monsieur le Marquis, to
see you thus. You have attained an excess of sobriety today.

THE MARQUIS: I dined last night with three of the prettiest women
in Paris. We drank until dawn, and then I went to my lodgings for a little nap, so that I might present myself at my
aunt's on an empty stomach.

THE BARONNE: That was prudent.

THE MARQUIS: Farewell, my absolute charmer! Tell the Knight
not to hide from his friends. Lend him to us from time to
time, or else I shall come here more and more often until I
find him. Farewell, Monsieur Turcaret. For my part, I bear
no grudges.
Extending his hand.
Your hand; let us revive our old friendship. But pray tell
that helot of yours, that Monsieur Rafle, to treat me somewhat more humanely the next time I have need of his services.
He goes.

Scene VI

M. TURCARET, THE BARONNE

M. TURCARET: I know that one, Madame. He is the biggest fool
and the greatest liar in my acquaintance.

THE BARONNE: That is saying a great deal.

M. TURCARET: How I suffered in the course of that conversation!

THE BARONNE: I could see that.

M. TURCARET: I do not like dishonest people.

THE BARONNE: That is wise.

M. TURCARET: I was so surprised to hear the things he said, that I did not have the strength to answer. Did you notice that?

THE BARONNE: You behaved with great prudence. I admired your moderation.

M. TURCARET: I, a usurer! What a calumny!

THE BARONNE: The term befits Monsieur Rafle, rather than you.

M. TURCARET: Behaving as though it were a crime to lend people money on their possessions! . . . It is better to lend it on their possessions than to lend it on nothing.

THE BARONNE: Assuredly.

M. TURCARET: Comes and tells me to my face that I was his grandfather's lackey! Nothing could be further from the truth. I was never anything but his solicitor.

THE BARONNE: Even if it were true, what a thing to taunt you with now! It was so long ago! . . . It is obliterated.

M. TURCARET: Yes, I trust.

THE BARONNE: Those malicious tales make no impression on my mind. You are too deeply rooted in my heart.

M. TURCARET: You are too kind to me.

THE BARONNE: You are a man of worth.

M. TURCARET: You are jesting.

THE BARONNE: Truly a man of honor.

M. TURCARET: Oh! Not at all.

THE BARONNE: And you have too much the air and manners of a person of quality for anyone to suspect that you are not.

Scene VII

FLAMAND, M. TURCARET, THE BARONNE

FLAMAND, *to* M. TURCARET: Monsieur!

M. TURCARET: What do you want?

FLAMAND: There is someone below who is asking for you.

M. TURCARET: Who is it, blockhead?

FLAMAND: That Monsieur you know . . . that . . . that Monsieur . . . Monsieur . . . thing . . .

M. TURCARET: Monsieur thing!

FLAMAND: Yes, in a way. That clerk whom you are so fond of. The one who comes to chat with you, and as soon as he arrives, you send everyone else out of the room, and do not want anyone to overhear you.

M. TURCARET: Could it be Monsieur Rafle?

FLAMAND: Yes, precisely, Monsieur; that's the man.

M. TURCARET: I will join him. Tell him to wait.

THE BARONNE: Did you not say that you had dismissed him?

M. TURCARET: Yes, and that is why he has come here. He wishes to reinstate himself. At heart he is a decent fellow, and reliable. I will go and see what he wants.

THE BARONNE: By no means!

To FLAMAND:

Tell him to come up, Flamand.

FLAMAND *goes.*

Scene VIII

M. TURCARET, THE BARONNE

THE BARONNE: You may speak with him in this room, Monsieur. Are you not as much at home here as in your own house?

M. TURCARET: You are most obliging, Madame.

THE BARONNE: I will not disturb your conversation. I will leave you . . . Do not forget the favor I asked, regarding Flamand.

M. TURCARET: As to that, I have already given my orders. You will be satisfied.

THE BARONNE *goes into her bedchamber.*

Scene IX

M. RAFLE, M. TURCARET

M. TURCARET: What is it, Monsieur Rafle? Why have you come looking for me here? Do you not know that when one is visiting ladies it is not for the sake of attending to business matters?

M. RAFLE: The importance of the matters which I have to tell you should serve as my excuse.

M. TURCARET: Well, what are these affairs of such importance?

M. RAFLE: Can one speak freely here?

M. TURCARET: You can indeed. I am the master here. Speak.

M. RAFLE, *taking some papers from his pocket, and looking in a dossier:* First of all, that son of a good family, to whom we lent three thousand pounds last year. Following your orders, I again presented him with a demand for payment. He, em-

barrassed by the request, and unable to meet it, told his
uncle, the president, of the matter. And he, together with
the rest of the family, is at the moment plotting to ruin you.

M. TURCARET: Plotting in vain! A waste of effort . . . Let them
come; I do not panic easily.

M. RAFLE, *having consulted his dossier*: That cashier whom you stood
bail for, and who has just gone bankrupt owing two hundred
thousand crowns . . .

M. TURCARET, *interruting him*: It was by my order that he . . . I
know where he is.

M. RAFLE: But the case is being brought against you. The matter
is serious and urgent.

M. TURCARET: It can be settled. I have taken steps. It will all be
arranged tomorrow.

M. RAFLE: I am afraid that may be too late.

M. TURCARET: You are too timorous . . . Have you been to see
that young man on the Rue Quincampoix, whom I set up
in business?

M. RAFLE: Yes, Monsieur. He will be happy to lend you twenty
thousand francs out of his first takings, on the understanding
that he may be allowed to audit his share of the company to
his own profit, and that you will stand by him if his manip-
ulation is discovered.

M. TURCARET: That's all right and proper. Nothing could be more
fair. There's a sensible lad. Tell him, Monsieur Rafle, that
I will back him in all his dealings. Is there anything else?

M. RAFLE, *having consulted his dossier again*: That thin tall man who
gave you two thousand francs, two months ago, for an address in Valognes which you procured for him.

M. TURCARET, *interrupting him*: Well?

M. RAFLE: He has had a misfortune.

M. TURCARET: What?

M. RAFLE: His good faith has been abused. He has been robbed
of fifteen thousand francs . . . At heart, he is too good.

M. TURCARET: Too good! Too good! Then why the devil did he
go into business? Too good! Too good!

M. RAFLE: He wrote me an extremely touching letter, in which
he begs you to take pity on him.

M. TURCARET: Waste of paper. Vain entreaty.

M. RAFLE: And to save him from being dismissed.

M. TURCARET: Rather I shall see to it that he is. His post will
revert to me. I shall bestow it on another, at the same price.

M. RAFLE: That is what I thought.

147

M. TURCARET: I would be acting against my own interests. I would deserve to be cashiered in the presence of the entire company.

M. RAFLE: I am no more susceptible than you are to the whining of fools . . . I have already written him an answer, and told him in so many words that he is not to count on you.

M. TURCARET: I should think not!

M. RAFLE, *consulting his dossier again*: Are you interested in taking five thousand francs which an honest locksmith of my acquaintance has managed to save from his earnings? At seven per cent.

M. TURCARET: Yes, yes. Very well. I will do him that little kindness. Go fetch him to me. I will be at my house in a quarter of an hour. See that he brings the money. Now, be off with you.

M. RAFLE, *taking several steps, and then returning*: I forgot the most important thing of all. I had not put it down on my agenda.

M. TURCARET: Well, what is this most important thing?

M. RAFLE: A piece of news which will greatly surprise you. Madame Turcaret is in Paris.

M. TURCARET, *dropping his voice*: Not so loud, Monsieur Rafle, not so loud.

M. RAFLE, *under his breath*: I saw her yesterday, in a carriage with a sort of young milord whose face is not entirely unknown to me, and whom I noticed again, in this street, just now as I was coming here.

M. TURCARET, *under his breath*: You did not speak with her?

M. RAFLE, *under his breath*: No, but this morning she requested me to say nothing to you, except to remind you that you owe her fifteen months' arrears of the pension of four thousand francs which you give her to keep her in the country. She will not return until it has been paid.

M. TURCARET, *under his breath*: Oh, in the name of God, pay her, Monsieur Rafle! Let us rid ourselves of that creature at once. Take her the locksmith's five hundred pistoles today, if only she will go tomorrow.

M. RAFLE, *under his breath*: She will ask no better. I will go and fetch the goodman to your house.

M. TURCARET, *under his breath*: I will be there.

    M. RAFLE *goes.*

Scene X

M. TURCARET

M. TURCARET, *alone*: A plague on it! Only let it occur to Madame Turcaret to come to this house, and what a shambles there will be! She will ruin my Baronne's good opinion of me, for I have given the lady to believe that I am a widower.

Scene XI

LISETTE, M. TURCARET

LISETTE: Madame sent me to discover whether you were still engaged in business, Monsieur.
M. TURCARET: It was nothing worth the name, my child. A few trifles, things which puzzle the heads of clerks because the poor devils were not made for great things.

Scene XII

FRONTIN, M. TURCARET, LISETTE

FRONTIN, *to* M. TURCARET: I am overjoyed, Monsieur, to find you in conversation with this charming young person. Whatever my own interest in her, I should never permit myself to disturb so sweet a session.
M. TURCARET: You are not unwelcome. Come, Frontin; I am sure you are my man in everything, and I would enlist your aid in winning the girl's friendship.
LISETTE: That will not be difficult.
FRONTIN, *to* M. TURCARET: Oh, not at all! I do not know under which lucky star you were born, Monsieur! But everyone, quite naturally, has a great weakness for you.
M. TURCARET: That is no gift of the stars. That is a result of one's manners.
LISETTE: Yours are so exquisite, so attractive.
M. TURCARET: How do you know?
LISETTE: I have heard of nothing else, from Madame the Baronne, ever since I have been here.

M. TURCARET: All good?

FRONTIN: There, now, is a lady who cannot conceal her fondness. She loves you with such tenderness! Ask Lisette; ask her.

LISETTE: Oh, it is you whom he should believe, Monsieur Frontin.

FRONTIN: No, I do not myself understand everything that I know on that subject. And what further astonishes me, is the ardor, nay the excess, to which this passion of hers has grown, without Monsieur Turcaret, meanwhile, having even troubled much to deserve it.

M. TURCARET: What? What do you mean?

FRONTIN: Twenty times, Monsieur, I have remarked your negligence in certain respects . . .

M. TURCARET, *interrupting him*: Oh, God's my witness, I have nothing of that kind to reproach myself with.

LISETTE: Oh no! I am certain that Monsieur is not a man to neglect the slightest opportunity of giving pleasure to those he loves. It is those little attentions, and nothing else, that make one deserve to be loved.

FRONTIN, *to* M. TURCARET: Nevertheless, Monsieur does not deserve it as thoroughly as I might wish.

M. TURCARET: Explain yourself.

FRONTIN: Well . . . But would you not take it amiss if a sincere and faithful servant were to take the liberty of speaking to you from his heart?

M. TURCARET: Speak.

FRONTIN: You do not respond sufficiently to Madame the Baronne's love for you.

M. TURCARET: I do not respond!

FRONTIN: No, Monsieur . . . I call you to witness, Lisette:

To LISETTE:

Monsieur, with all his intelligence, is not always as attentive as he might be.

M. TURCARET: What do you mean, not as attentive as I might be?

FRONTIN: A certain thoughtlessness, a certain negligence . . .

M. TURCARET: Well?

FRONTIN: For example, is it not shameful that you have never thought to make her a present of a carriage?

LISETTE, *to* M. TURCARET: Oh, there he is right, Monsieur. Your clerks all give them to their mistresses.

M. TURCARET: What does she need a carriage for? Does she not have mine at her disposition, whenever she chooses?

FRONTIN: Oh, Monsieur; between having a coach of one's own,

on the one hand, and being obliged to borrow those of one's friends, on the other, there is all the difference.

LISETTE, *to* M. TURCARET: You are too much a man of the world not to be aware of such things. Most women are more susceptible to the vanity of having a carriage than to the actual pleasure of using it.

M. TURCARET: Yes, I understand that.

FRONTIN: Ah, this one's a girl of great good sense, Monsieur. There's point to what she says, it must be admitted.

M. TURCARET: I think you're not such a fool, either, as I at first took you for, Frontin.

FRONTIN: Ever since I had the honor of entering your service, I have felt myself growing more and more clever, every moment. Oh, I foresee that I shall profit greatly in your employ.

M. TURCARET: That depends upon no one but yourself.

FRONTIN: Oh, I promise you, Monsieur, I am not lacking in good will. I would, then, give Madame the Baronne a fine large carriage, well upholstered.

M. TURCARET: She shall have one. Your arguments are well considered: they have convinced me.

FRONTIN: I was positive that it was an oversight, and nothing more.

M. TURCARET: Quite, quite. And to prove it, I will go this moment and give order for a coach.

FRONTIN: For shame, Monsieur! You must not appear to have any connection with it. It would not be proper for everyone to know that you had given Madame the Baronne a carriage. You must make use of a third person, someone disinterested but loyal. I know two or three saddlers who are not yet aware that I am in your service. If you like, I will take the responsibility for it . . .

M. TURCARET, *interrupting him*: A pleasure. You seem to be fairly well acquainted with these things; I will leave the matter in your hands.

Giving him a purse.

Here: there are sixty pistoles left in my purse: put that on account.

FRONTIN, *taking the purse*: Without fail, Monsieur. As for the horses, I have a nephew in Brittany who is a senior horse-trader. He will supply you with superb beasts.

M. TURCARET: I daresay. At a price.

FRONTIN: No, Monsieur. He will make this sale a matter of conscience.

M. TURCARET: A horse-trader's conscience!

FRONTIN: Oh, I will answer for him as for myself.

M. TURCARET: In that case, I will give him my custom.

FRONTIN: Now, another little neglect of yours . . .

M. TURCARET: Oh, be off with you and your little neglects . . . This rascal will end by ruining me . . . Tell Madame the Baronne, from me, that I have been summoned home on a matter of business, but that I will not be kept long.

He goes.

Scene XIII

FRONTIN, LISETTE

FRONTIN: That's not bad for a beginning.

LISETTE: No. Excellent for Madame the Baronne. But for us?

FRONTIN: Well, we have made sixty pistoles, at the very least. I shall certainly make that much on the carriage. Lock them up. They are the foundation of our joint account.

LISETTE: Yes, but we must build on these foundations without delay. For I warn you, my mind has taken a moral turn.

FRONTIN: Of what sort, may I know?

LISETTE: I am weary of being a serving-maid.

FRONTIN: How's that? The devil! Ambitious already?

LISETTE: Yes, my boy. I fancy that the air of a house which is frequented by a financier is a foe to modesty. For in the short while that I have been here, I have formed ideas of grandeur such as I never conceived before. You must hurry to amass your wealth. Otherwise, whatever engagement there is between us, the first rich fop who offers to marry me . . .

FRONTIN, *interrupting her*: But give me time to get rich.

LISETTE: I will give you three years. That is enough for a man of wit.

FRONTIN: I ask no more . . . That is enough, my princess. I will stop at nothing in order to make myself worthy of you. And if I do not succeed, it will not be for any lack of trying.

He goes.

Scene XIV

LISETTE

LISETTE, *alone*: I cannot help but love this fellow Frontin. He is

152

my own true knight. And, if he continues as he has begun, I have a secret presentiment that with that lad I shall one day become a woman of quality.

Act Four

Scene I

THE KNIGHT, FRONTIN

THE KNIGHT: What are you doing here? Did you not say that you were going to call again on your exchange broker? Is he still not at home?

FRONTIN: Forgive me, Monsieur; but he was short of funds and did not have the full amount on the premises. He told me to come back this evening. I will return you the note, if you wish.

THE KNIGHT: Oh, keep it! What do you think I could do with it? . . . Is the Baronne within? What is she doing?

FRONTIN: She and Lisette are discussing a carriage, which I am to order a coach-builder to make for her, and a particular country house which has caught her fancy, and which she would like to rent, until such time as I can arrange for her to buy it.

THE KNIGHT: A carriage, and a country house? What folly!

FRONTIN: Yes; but all at the expense of Monsieur Turcaret. What good sense!

THE KNIGHT: That is a different matter.

FRONTIN: There is only one thing which has been troubling her.

THE KNIGHT: What is that?

FRONTIN: A mere trifle.

THE KNIGHT: Tell me what it is.

FRONTIN: This country house must be furnished. She did not know how to engage Monsieur Turcaret to do that. But the superior genius, whom she had placed in his service, has undertaken to supply that concern, too.

THE KNIGHT: How will you do that?

FRONTIN: I will go and look up an old rascal of my acquaintance, who will help us to realize the ten thousand francs which we need for our furnishings.

THE KNIGHT: Have you given your plan careful attention?

FRONTIN: Oh, indeed I have, Monsieur. Attention is my strong point. It is all exact in my head, never fear. A tiny fictitious document . . . a false writ . . .

THE KNIGHT, *interrupting him*: Take care, Frontin. Monsieur Turcaret is a shrewd man at business.

FRONTIN: My friend the old fox is shrewder still. He is the cleverest, the most intelligent penman . . .

THE KNIGHT: That is another story.

FRONTIN: He has lodged in kings' palaces for most of his life, because of his writing.

THE KNIGHT: I say no more.

FRONTIN: I know where I am certain to find him, and our instruments will be drawn up with all possible dispatch. Farewell. There is Monsieur the Marquis, who has been looking for you.
He goes.

Scene II

THE MARQUIS, THE KNIGHT

THE MARQUIS: Oh! God's my witness, sir, you have become an exceedingly rare bird. You are not to be found anywhere. I have been looking for you for the last twenty-four hours, to consult with you on an affair of the heart.

THE KNIGHT: Indeed! And since when have you allowed yourself to be drawn into affairs of that kind?

THE MARQUIS: Since three or four days ago.

THE KNIGHT: And have not taken me into your confidence on the subject until today? You have become wonderfully discreet.

THE MARQUIS: The devil take me if it didn't slip my mind entirely. An affair of the heart, as you know, occupies my heart only very vaguely. This one is a conquest which I made quite by chance, retain for the sake of amusement, and will cast off for a caprice, or perhaps even for a reason.

THE KNIGHT: What an idyllic attachment!

THE MARQUIS: We should not allow ourselves to take the pleasures of life too seriously. As for me, I never let anything trouble me . . . She gave me her portrait; I have lost it. Another man would have hanged himself.
Making a gesture of contemptuous dismissal.
I care no more than that.

THE KNIGHT: With sentiments like those, how can they fail to adore you? . . . But tell me: who is this woman?

THE MARQUIS: A woman of quality; a countess from the provinces, so she tells me.

THE KNIGHT: Ah! And when did you find time to make this conquest? You sleep all day and drink all night, usually.

THE MARQUIS: Oh, not at all, not at all, if you please. During the season I spend a few hours nightly at the ball. It is there that the best opportunities present themselves.

THE KNIGHT: Which is to say that you met her at the ball?

THE MARQUIS: Precisely. I went, the other evening, somewhat warmed with wine; in fact, rather flown. I ogled the pretty masks; I remarked a waist, the suggestion of a bosom, a curve of hips . . . I bore down upon her, I pled, I insisted; I prevailed upon her to remove her mask; I beheld a woman . . .

THE KNIGHT, *interrupting him*: Young, no doubt.

THE MARQUIS: No, rather old.

THE KNIGHT: But still beautiful, and thoroughly charming.

THE MARQUIS: Not very beautiful.

THE KNIGHT: Love, I see, has not blinded you.

THE MARQUIS: I am doing justice to my beloved.

THE KNIGHT: She is witty, then?

THE MARQUIS: Oh, when it comes to wit, she's a prodigy! What a flux of thoughts! What imagination! She told me a hunded droll and ridiculous things, which charmed me.

THE KNIGHT: What was the result of the conversation?

THE MARQUIS: The result? I took her back to her house, with her company; I offered her my services, and the old fool accepted them.

THE KNIGHT: Have you seen her since?

THE MARQUIS: The next evening, when I had got up, I presented myself at her house.

THE KNIGHT: Lodging-house, presumably.

THE MARQUIS: Yes, lodging-house.

THE KNIGHT: Well?

THE MARQUIS: Well. Another vivacious conversation, fresh follies, tender protestations on my part, lively rejoinders on hers. She gave me that accursed portrait which I lost the day before yesterday. I have not seen her since. She has written to me. I have answered her. She expects me today, but I do not know what I should do. Shall I go, or shall I not? What would you advise? That is why I was looking for you.

THE KNIGHT: It would be uncivil of you not to go.

THE MARQUIS: Yes; but equally, if I do go, it will appear that I am eager. It is a most delicate situation. To show so much eagerness is like running after a woman, which is dreadfully bourgeois, do you not agree?

THE KNIGHT: I cannot advise you until I have met the woman.

THE MARQUIS: I must arrange for you to meet her. I should like to invite you to dine at her house this evening, with your Baronne.

THE KNIGHT: That will not be possible this evening, for I have invited guests to dine here.

THE MARQUIS: To dine here? I shall bring my conquest.

THE KNIGHT: But the Baronne . . .

THE MARQUIS, *interrupting him*: Oh, the Baronne will not object to her; in fact it is a good thing that they should make each other's acquaintance; we can have little four-handed parties sometimes.

THE KNIGHT: But will not your countess make difficulties about coming with you, privately, into a house?

THE MARQUIS: Difficulties! Oh, my countess is not a one for difficulties. She is a woman who knows how to live, a woman undeterred by the prejudices of education.

THE KNIGHT: Well, then, bring her; we shall be delighted.

THE MARQUIS: You will be charmed, yourself. What pretty manners! You will see a woman who is lively, petulant, distracted, giddy, dissipated, and at all times stained with tobacco. You would never take her for a woman from the provinces.

THE KNIGHT: You paint a pretty picture! We shall see if your portrait is not too flattering.

THE MARQUIS: I shall go and fetch her. For the moment, then, Sir Knight.

THE KNIGHT: Your servant, Marquis.

THE MARQUIS *goes*.

Scene III

THE KNIGHT

THE KNIGHT, *alone*: This charming conquest of the Marquis' sounds like the same sort of countess as the one I sacrificed to the Baronne.

157

Scene IV

THE BARONNE, THE KNIGHT

THE BARONNE: What are you doing here alone, Sir Knight? I thought the Marquis was with you.

THE KNIGHT, *laughing*: He left not a moment ago, Madame . . . Ha, ha, ha!

THE BARONNE: Why are you laughing?

THE KNIGHT: This fool of a marquis is in love with a woman from the provinces, a countess who lives in a lodging-house. He has gone to fetch her and bring her here. What sport we shall have!

THE BARONNE: But tell me, Knight, have you invited them to dine here?

THE KNIGHT: Yes, Madame; the more guests, the greater the merriment. Monsieur Turcaret must be amused, be dissipated.

THE BARONNE: The Marquis' presence will not amuse him. You were not aware that they know each other. They are not fond of each other. In fact, there has been a scene between them, here . . .

THE KNIGHT, *interrupting her*: The pleasure of the table will heal everything. I trust they are not so hostile to each other that they may not be reconciled. I will see to it myself; leave it to me. Monsieur Turcaret is a good old fool . . .

THE BARONNE, *seeing* M. TURCARET *enter*: Hush: I think that is he . . . I fear he may have heard you.

Scene V

M. TURCARET, THE BARONNE, THE KNIGHT

THE KNIGHT, *to* M. TURCARET, *embracing him*: Monsieur Turcaret, I hope, will permit one to embrace him, and to proclaim how lively a pleasure it will give one, to see him, presently, with a glass in his hand.

M. TURCARET, *embarrassed*: The pleasure of that liveliness . . . Monsieur, will be . . . entirely reciprocal. The honor which you do me, on the one hand . . . together with . . . the satisfaction which . . . I take on the other . . .
Indicating THE BARONNE.

. . . in Madame, makes it true that . . . I assure you . . .
that . . . I am very happy to be dining here this evening.

THE BARONNE: Monsieur, you will involve yourself in compliments which will embarrass Monsieur the Knight also, and
which neither of you will be able to bring to a conclusion.

THE KNIGHT, *to* M. TURCARET: My cousin is right. Let us dispense
with ceremony, and consider nothing but our own amusement. Do you like music?

M. TURCARET: Oh, strike me dead, indeed I do! I have a sub-
scription to the Opéra.

THE KNIGHT: It is the ruling passion of everyone of breeding, wit,
and elegance.

M. TURCARET: It is mine.

THE KNIGHT: Music rouses the passions.

M. TURCARET: Terribly! A beautiful voice, accompanied by a
trumpet, will throw me into a sweet daydream.

THE BARONNE: What a refined taste!

THE KNIGHT: Is it not?

To M. TURCARET:

What a monstrous fool I am not to have thought of that
instrument!

He starts to go.

In God's name, since your taste is for trumpets, I must go
myself, and order . . .

M. TURCARET, *restraining him*: I will not hear of it, Monsieur. I
do not pretend that, for the sake of a trumpet . . .

THE BARONNE, *in an undertone, to* M. TURCARET: Let him go, Monsieur.

THE KNIGHT *goes.*

Scene VI

M. TURCARET, THE BARONNE

THE BARONNE: When we have the opportunity to be alone for a
few moments together, let us, for as long as possible, dispense
with the company of those whose presence, in any case, only
intrudes upon us.

M. TURCARET: You love me more than I deserve, Madame.

THE BARONNE: Who could fail to love you? My cousin the Knight,
for instance, has always been extremely fond of you . . .

M. TURCARET, *interrupting her*: I am deeply indebted to him.

THE BARONNE: And attentive to everything which might give you pleasure . . .

M. TURCARET, *interrupting her*: He seems a very decent fellow.

Scene VII

LISETTE, THE BARONNE, M. TURCARET

THE BARONNE: What is it, Lisette?

LISETTE: A man dressed in dark gray, with dirty linen and an old wig . . .
In an undertone:
It's the furniture for your country house.

THE BARONNE: Fetch him in.

Scene VIII

M. FURET, FRONTIN, M. TURCARET, THE BARONNE, LISETTE

M. FURET, *to* THE BARONNE *and* LISETTE: Which of you two Mesdames, is the mistress of this house?

THE BARONNE: I am the mistress. What do you want?

M. FURET: I will not answer until I have previously greeted you, Madame, and all the honorable company, with all due and requisite respect.

M. TURCARET, *aside*: Here's a merry odd one!

LISETTE: Without so much ceremony, Monsieur, tell us previously who you are.

M. FURET, *to* LISETTE: I am a bailiff, at your service, and my name is Monsieur Furet.

THE BARONNE: A bailiff! In my house!

FRONTIN: The impertinence!

M. TURCARET: Madame, would you like me to throw this clown out of the window? He would not be the first rascal whom I . . .

M. FURET: Gently, Monsieur; gently! Honest bailiffs like me are not exposed to such risks. I exercise my little office in so obliging a fashion that people of quality always deem it a pleasure to receive a writ at my hands.
Taking a paper from his pocket.

Here is one which, if you please, I will take the privilege—with your permission, Monsieur—which I will have the honor to present to Madame . . . with your kind permission, Monsieur.

THE BARONNE: A writ? For me?

To LISETTE.

See what it is, Lisette.

LISETTE: I, Madame? I know nothing of such things. I do not know how to read, except love letters.

To FRONTIN.

You see to it, Frontin.

FRONTIN: I am a mere child, at business matters.

M. FURET, *to* THE BARONNE: It concerns a debt of Monsieur le Baron de Porcandorf, deceased, your husband . . .

THE BARONNE, *interrupting him*: My late husband, Monsieur? It has nothing to do with me; I have dissolved all financial connection.

M. TURCARET: In that case, they cannot hold you responsible.

M. FURET: Forgive me, Monsieur, but since the document was signed by Madame . . .

M. TURCARET, *interrupting him*: It is still effective?

M. FURET: Yes, Monsieur; extremely effective. It even states what the money was to be used for . . . I will read you the terms; they are all set forth in the writ.

M. TURCARET: Let us see whether it is in order.

M. FURET, *having donned his spectacles*: "As witnessed by etc . . . the following, who were present in their own persons: the exalted and puissant Lord George-William de Porcandorf, and Lady Agnes-Ildegonde de la Dolinvillière, his wife, duly authorized by him for the purposes of this transaction, hereby declare that they owe to Eloi-Jerome Poussif, horse-merchant, the sum of five hundred pistoles . . .

THE BARONNE, *interrupting him*: Five hundred pistoles!

LISETTE: The vile obligation!

M. FURET, *continuing to read his document*: "For a train furnished by the abovementioned Poussif, consisting of twelve mules, fifteen chestnut Normandy horses, and three Auvergne nags, all complete with manes, tails and ears, and outfitted with harness, saddles, bridles and halters . . ."

LISETTE, *interrupting him*: Bridles and halters! Is it a woman's place to pay for that sort of trappings?

M. TURCARET: Let us not interrupt him.

To M. FURET:

Continue, my friend.

M. FURET, *continuing with his document*: "Against payment of which five hundred pistoles, the abovementioned debtors have impounded, attached, and generally mortgaged all their goods present and to come, renouncing all rights to division or discussion; and for the purpose of the present transaction, have appointed as their domicile the house of Innocent-Blaise the Just, formerly solicitor of Châtelet, currently residing in World's-End Lane. Given and approved, etc."

FRONTIN, *to* M. TURCARET: Is the document in order, Monsieur?

M. TURCARET: I would correct nothing, except the sum.

M. FURET: The sum, Monsieur! Oh, the sum is past correction. It is perfectly clear.

M. TURCARET, *to* THE BARONNE: This is most disturbing.

THE BARONNE: Disturbing? What do you mean? I cannot seriously be expected to pay five hundred pistoles, simply for signing my name.

LISETTE: There you see what it is to be too obedient to one's husband. Will women never be broken of that fault?

THE BARONNE: How unjust!

To M. TURCARET:

Is there no way to annul this document, Monsieur Turcaret?

M. TURCARET: None, that I can see. If you had not expressly renounced, in the writ, all rights to division and discussion, we might have been able to outmaneuver this Poussif.

THE BARONNE: One must resign one's self to paying, then, since it is you who condemn me, Monsieur. I do not appeal your decisions.

FRONTIN, *in an undertone, to* M. TURCARET: How pliant she is to your every wish!

THE BARONNE: It will inconvenience me, somewhat; it will alter the plans I had in mind for a certain creditory note which you know of.

LISETTE: No matter; let us pay it, Madame. Let us not contest a process against the advice of Monsieur Turcaret.

THE BARONNE: Heaven forfend! I would rather sell my jewels, my furniture.

FRONTIN, *in an undertone, to* M. TURCARET: Sell her furniture, her jewels; and all for the sake of her husband's carriage horses! The poor woman!

M. TURCARET, *to* THE BARONNE: No, Madame. You will sell nothing. I will take this debt upon myself. I will settle it.

THE BARONNE: You are jesting. I shall use that note of credit, as I said.

M. TURCARET: You must keep that for another use.

THE BARONNE: No, Monsieur; no. The nobility of your behavior embarrasses me more than the debt itself.

M. TURCARET: Not another word, Madame. I shall go this moment and arrange for it to be paid.

FRONTIN: The generous soul!

To M. FURET:

Follow us, tipstaff; you will be paid.

THE BARONNE, *to* M. TURCARET: At least do not let it keep you away for long. Remember that there are those who await your return.

M. TURCARET: The matter of a moment. And when I have settled it, I shall return from business to pleasure.

He goes, with M. FURET *and* FRONTIN.

Scene IX

THE BARONNE, LISETTE

LISETTE, *aside*: And we will send you back from pleasure to business again, upon my word! What clever rascals they are, Messieurs Furet and Frontin; and what a thorough dupe is Monsieur Turcaret!

THE BARONNE: Too thorough, it seems to me, Lisette.

LISETTE: It is true, we can take small credit for it, when he walks into the snare almost before it is well laid.

THE BARONNE: Do you know, I am beginning to feel sorry for him?

LISETTE: Oh, my dying breath! Let us have no indiscreet compassion! We must waste no pity on a man who never wastes any on others.

THE BARONNE: I am beginning to have scruples, in spite of myself.

LISETTE: You must stifle the things!

THE BARONNE: I can scarcely restrain them.

LISETTE: It is not yet time for having scruples. And it will be more comfortable, one day, to feel remorse at having ruined a financier, than to feel regret at having missed one's opportunity.

Scene X

JASMIN, THE BARONNE, LISETTE

JASMIN, *to* THE BARONNE: Someone who has come from Madame
    Dorimène.
THE BARONNE: Send her in.
    JASMIN *goes*.

Scene XI

THE BARONNE, LISETTE

THE BARONNE: No doubt she has sent to propose a gay evening;
    but . . .

Scene XII

MME. JACOB, THE BARONNE, LISETTE

MME. JACOB, *to* THE BARONNE: Madame, I beg you to forgive me
    for taking this liberty. I am a secondhand clothes merchant,
    and my name is Madame Jacob. I have the honor, from time
    to time, to sell lace, and all manner of pomades, to Madame
    Dorimène. I went, just now, to inform her of a great bargain
    which I shall be able to offer, presently; but she is without
    funds at the moment, and she told me that perhaps you might
    be able to avail yourself of the opportunity.
THE BARONNE: What is this bargain?
MME. JACOB: A circlet for the hair, worth three hundred crowns.
    It is the property of a squire's wife in Régrats, who wishes
    to sell it. She has not worn it more than twice. And now
    she dislikes it, and thinks it common, and wants to dispose
    of it.
THE BARONNE: I should not mind seeing this circlet.
MME. JACOB: I shall fetch it to you as soon as I have it, Madame;
    and I will make you a good price.
LISETTE: You will not lose by it. Madame is generous.
MME. JACOB: That is not my governing interest. And thank God,
    I have other talents besides selling at second hand.

THE BARONNE: I am convinced of that.

LISETTE, *to* MME. JACOB: One can see it at a glance.

MME. JACOB: Oh, indeed, if I had no other resources, how could I bring up my children as decently as I do? I have a husband, to tell the truth, but he does nothing but enlarge my family, without providing me with anything for its support.

LISETTE: There are many husbands who do just the opposite.*

THE BARONNE: What do you do, Madame Jacob, to supply all the expenses of your family yourself?

MME. JACOB: I arrange marriages, my dear. It is true, they are legitimate marriages; they do not bring in as much as the other kind. But, you understand, I do not want to have anything to reproach myself for.

LISETTE: Worthy principle!

MME. JACOB: Four months ago, I married a young musketeer to the widow of a government treasurer. There is a lovely match! They keep open house every day, and are consuming the treasurer's inheritance in the most agreeable way imaginable.

LISETTE: I can see that they would be well suited to each other.

MME. JACOB: Oh, all my marriages are happy!

To THE BARONNE.

And if Madame should take a fancy to marry, I have an excellent subject in hand.

THE BARONNE: For me, Madame Jacob?

MME. JACOB: A squire from the Limousin. Ah, he's superb husband material! He will let himself be led by a woman as tamely as any Parisian.

LISETTE, *to* THE BARONNE: There's another bargain for you, Madame.

THE BARONNE: I am not disposed to profit by it. I do not wish to marry so soon; I am not yet weary of the world.

LISETTE, *to* MME. JACOB: Oh; well, I am, Madame Jacob; I am. Put me down on your list.

MME. JACOB: I have your man. He is a big salesman, who has already some wealth, but little protection; he is looking for a pretty wife to protect him.

LISETTE: What a delightful prospect for a marriage! He will do nicely for me.

THE BARONNE, *to* MME. JACOB: You must be rich, Madame Jacob.

MME. JACOB: Alas! Alas! I should cut a considerable figure in Paris . . . I should be able to keep a carriage, having a brother in business, as I do.

* I.e., provide for families they have not begotten.—W.S.M.

THE BARONNE: You have a brother in business?

MME. JACOB: Yes, and not in petty trade: a financier! I am the sister of Monsieur Turcaret, since you would have me tell you . . . You may perhaps have heard someone speak of him.

THE BARONNE, *astonished*: You are Monsieur Turcaret's sister?

MME. JACOB: Yes. Madame; I am his sister, by the same father and the same mother.

LISETTE, *also with astonishment*: Monsieur Turcaret is your brother, Madame Jacob?

MME. JACOB: Yes, my brother; my own brother. And I am no nearer to being a great lady, for all that . . . I see that you are both amazed. I imagine that that is because you are astonished that he should let his own sister work for a living as I do.

LISETTE: Yes indeed! That is exactly what astonished us.

MME. JACOB: He does far worse things than that, the unnatural creature! He has forbidden me his house, and he is not even kind enough to employ my husband!

THE BARONNE: That cries out for vengeance.

LISETTE, *to* MME. JACOB: Oh, what a wicked brother!

MME. JACOB: As wicked a brother as he is a husband. Did he not turn his wife out of his house?

THE BARONNE: They did not enjoy each other's company?

MME. JACOB: They still do not, Madame; there is no longer anything between them, and my sister-in-law is in the country.

THE BARONNE: What? Is Monsieur Turcaret not a widower?

MME. JACOB: Widower indeed! He and his wife have been separated for ten years, and he pays her a pension in Valognes to keep her away from Paris.

THE BARONNE, *in an undertone, to* LISETTE: Lisette?

LISETTE, *in an undertone*: Upon my word, Madame; what an evil man!

MME. JACOB: Oh, heaven will punish him, sooner or later; he cannot escape it. I have already heard it said, in one house, that his financial affairs are suffering.

THE BARONNE: Suffering? His financial affairs!

MME. JACOB: Oh! How could they fail to? He is an old fool who has always loved every woman except his wife. When he is in love he throws everything out of the window; he is like a basket with a hole in the bottom.

LISETTE, *in an undertone*: To whom is she telling this? Who knows it better than we do?

MME. JACOB, *to* THE BARONNE: I do not know to whom he is

attached at the moment, but there are always a number of young ladies engaged in plucking and outwitting him, while he imagines that it is he who is outwitting them, because he promises to marry them. Now, I ask you, is he not a monstrous fool? What do you think, Madame?

THE BARONNE, *disconcerted*: Yes, that is not entirely . . .

MME. JACOB, *interrupting her*: Oh! I am delighted to see it! He entirely deserves it, the wretch; he deserves every bit of it! If I knew his mistress I would go to her and tell her to plunder him, to devour him, to gnaw him up, to ruin him.

To LISETTE:

Would you not do the same, Mademoiselle?

LISETTE: Without fail, Madame Jacob.

MME. JACOB, *to* THE BARONNE: I beg you to excuse me for assailing you with my troubles in this way. But when I come to consider them, I am so smitten that I cannot hold my tongue . . . Farewell, Madame; I shall not fail to bring you the circlet, as soon as it is in my hands.

THE BARONNE: There is no hurry, Madame; there is no hurry.

Scene XIII

THE BARONNE, LISETTE

THE BARONNE: Well, Lisette?

LISETTE: Well, Madame?

THE BARONNE: Would you have supposed that Monsieur Turcaret had a sister who was a merchant of secondhand apparel?

LISETTE: Would you, in your turn, have supposed that he had a real wife in the provinces?

THE BARONNE: The faithless thing! He assured me that he was a widower, and I took him at his word.

LISETTE: Oh, the old cheat!

Seeing THE BARONNE *looking pensive.*

But what is this? . . . What is troubling you? . . . You look quite sad. Heaven preserve me! You are taking the matter as seriously as though you were in love with Monsieur Turcaret.

THE BARONNE: Even though I do not love him, how can I lose the hope of marrying him, without a pang? The scoundrel! He has a wife! I must break with him.

LISETTE: Yes; but in the interest of your fortune you must ruin him first. Come, Madame; while we have him in our grasp, let us force his strongbox and seize his notes. Let us put Monsieur Turcaret to fire and sword. Let us render him at last so miserable that he may take pity, one day, even on his wife, and be a brother to Madame Jacob again.

Act Five

Scene I

LISETTE

LISETTE, *alone*: What a fine house this is for Frontin and me! We have sixty pistoles already, and the bailiff's writ may bring in quite as much. Courage! If we gain these little sums often, we shall have a reasonable total at last.

Scene II

THE BARONNE, LISETTE

THE BARONNE: It seems to me that Monsieur Turcaret should have returned by now, Lisette.
LISETTE: He must have been detained by some other affair . . .
Seeing FLAMAND *enter, but not recognizing him at first, since he is no longer in livery.*
But what can this Monsieur want?

Scene III

FLAMAND, THE BARONNE, LISETTE

THE BARONNE, *to* LISETTE: Why have they let him in unannounced?
FLAMAND: There is no harm done, Madame; it is I.
LISETTE, *to* THE BARONNE, *recognizing* FLAMAND: Oh, it's Flamand, Madame! Flamand without his livery! Flamand wearing a sword! What a metamorphosis!
FLAMAND: Gently, Mademoiselle, gently! You must not, if you please, call me plain Flamand. I am no longer Monsieur Turcaret's lackey, nothing of the sort. He has given me a much better position, indeed he has. I am in business now,

169

aha! And therefore I must be addressed as Monsieur Flamand, do you see?

LISETTE: You are right, Monsieur Flamand. Since you have become a clerk, you should no longer be treated as a lackey.

FLAMAND, *indicating* THE BARONNE: I am obliged to Madame for my promotion, and I have come here expressly to thank her. She is a good lady, and has been so good to me as to have had me entrusted with a good commission which will earn me a good hundred good crowns every year, and which is, besides, in a good locality, for it is at Falaise, which is such a good town, where there are, I am told, such good people.

LISETTE: There is a great deal of good in your news, Monsieur Flamand.

FLAMAND: I am the chief porter at the Guibrai gate. I will have the keys, and I will be able to allow anyone I please to come in or go out. I have been told that that is a good right to have.

LISETTE: Bless me!

FLAMAND: Oh! And what is still better, is that this post brings happiness upon those who fill it, for they all grow rich. They say that that was where Monsieur Turcaret began.

THE BARONNE: How glorious for you, Monsieur Flamand, to tread, thus, in the footsteps of your master.

LISETTE, *to* FLAMAND: And we beg you, for your own good, to be as honest as he is.

FLAMAND, *to* THE BARONNE: Madame, I will send you little presents from time to time.

THE BARONNE: No, my poor Flamand; I do not ask anything of you.

FLAMAND: Oh, indeed I shall! I know how clerks are expected to behave towards the ladies who have got them their positions. My only fear is that I may be recalled, because in positions of this kind one is greatly subject to that, do you see.

LISETTE: How disagreeable!

FLAMAND, *to* THE BARONNE: For example, the clerk who has been recalled today, so that I may have his place, obtained the position through the graces of a certain lady whom Monsieur Turcaret loved at one time, and whom now he does not love any more. Take care, Madame, lest I should be recalled too.

THE BARONNE: I will give it all my attention, Monsieur Flamand.

FLAMAND: I beg you to please Monsieur Turcaret permanently, Madame.

THE BARONNE: I will do my best, since it concerns you.

FLAMAND, *drawing closer to* THE BARONNE: Always wear that pretty rouge to take his eye.

LISETTE: Away with you Monsieur Chief Porter, be off to your Guibrai gate! We know our business . . . Indeed; we have no need for your advice . . . No; you will never be anything but a dunce. You can take my word for it; a dunce; do you understand?

FLAMAND *goes*.

Scene IV

THE BARONNE, LISETTE

THE BARONNE: That is the most ingenuous lad . . .

LISETTE, *interrupting her*: Nevertheless, he has been a lackey for some time; he should have learned a little something by now.

Scene V

JASMIN, THE BARONNE, LISETTE

JASMIN, *to* THE BARONNE: It is Monsieur the Marquis, with a very large and great lady.

He goes.

Scene VI

THE BARONNE, LISETTE

THE BARONNE: It is his lovely conquest. I am curious to see her.

LISETTE: I am no less anxious to see her than you are. I have formed a delightful picture of her in my mind.

Scene VII

THE MARQUIS, MME. TURCARET, THE BARONNE, LISETTE

THE MARQUIS, *to* THE BARONNE: I have come, my charming Baronne, to present to you this delightful lady, the wittiest, the most elegant, the most amusing person . . . So many good qualities which you share, should link you in mutual esteem and friendship.

THE BARONNE: I look forward to our union.

Aside to LISETTE:

She is the original of the portrait which the Knight sacrificed to me.

MME. TURCARET: I fear, Madame, that you will abandon those kind sentiments before long. Someone such as you, whose life is spent in the most fashionable and brilliant circles, cannot find much pleasure in the company of a woman from the provinces.

THE BARONNE: You do not seem like a provincial, Madame. And our most stylish ladies have no more agreeable manners than yours.

THE MARQUIS, *indicating* MME. TURCARET: Oh, strike me down, indeed they don't! I know what I'm about, Madame. And you will agree with me, upon seeing this figure and this face, that I have the best taste of any peer in France.

MME. TURCARET: You are too polite, Monsieur the Marquis. Such flattery might suit me in the country, where I shine well enough, as I may say without vanity. I keep a close eye on the fashions; I am sent the latest things as soon as they are invented, and I can boast of having been the first woman in the town of Valognes to wear spangles.

LISETTE, *aside*: What a ninny!

THE BARONNE: How splendid, to serve as a model for a town like that!

MME. TURCARET: I have given them something to live up to! I have attracted to myself the young, the decorative, and have assembled, as it were, a little Paris.

THE MARQUIS, *with irony*: What, a little Paris! Do you not know that it takes three months of Valognes to finish a courtier?

MME. TURCARET: Oh, I do not live like a country woman, at any rate. I do not keep myself walled up in a castle; I was born for society. I live in town, and I may describe my house as an academy of courtly ways and gallantry, for the young.

LISETTE: A kind of high school for all of lower Normandy.

MME. TURCARET, *to* THE BARONNE: We gamble there; we meet to destroy reputations; we read all the works of wit that are written in Cherbourg, Saint-Lô, and Coutances: they are worth all the writings of Vire and of Caen. Occasionally I hold courts of love, I give supper-collations. We have cooks who cannot make any single ragout in the canon; but they time their roasts so perfectly that one turn of the spit more or less and they would be ruined.

THE MARQUIS: That is the essential, in dining well . . . My word, long live the roasts of Valognes!

MME. TURCARET: And as for balls, we give them often. Oh, how we do amuse ourselves! It is all in the very best taste! The ladies of Valognes have no peer in the art of masking themselves well, and each has her favorite disguise. Can you guess mine?

LISETTE: Does Madame disguise herself as Love, perhaps?

MME. TURCARET: Oh, not that, not I!

THE BARONNE: You appear as a goddess, I fancy; one of the Graces?

MME. TURCARET: As Venus, my dear; Venus.

THE MARQUIS, *ironically*: Venus! Ah! Madame, how beautifully you are disguised!

LISETTE, *aside*: Completely, in fact.

Scene VIII

THE KNIGHT, THE BARONNE, MME. TURCARET, THE MARQUIS, LISETTE

THE KNIGHT, *to* THE BARONNE: Madame, we shall presently be treated to the most ravishing concert.
Aside, seeing MME. TURCARET.
But whom do I see?

MME. TURCARET, *aside*: Oh, heavens!

THE BARONNE, *aside, to* LISETTE: I suspected as much.

THE KNIGHT, *to* THE MARQUIS: Is that the lady whom you mentioned to me, Marquis?

THE MARQUIS: Yes; that is my countess. Why this astonishment?

THE KNIGHT: Oh, in God's name! I was not expecting to see her.

MME. TURCARET, *aside*: How unfortunate!

THE MARQUIS, *to* THE KNIGHT: Explain yourself, Knight. Do you know my countess?

THE KNIGHT: I do indeed; I have been paying court to her for a week.

THE MARQUIS: What's that? Oh, the faithless creature! The ingrate!

THE KNIGHT: And this morning she was so kind as to send me her portrait.

173

THE MARQUIS: The devil she did! Does she have portraits to hand out to everybody then?

Scene IX

MME. JACOB, THE BARONNE, THE MARQUIS, THE KNIGHT, MME. TUR-
CARET, LISETTE

MME. JACOB, *to* THE BARONNE: Madame, I have brought you the circlet which I promised to show you.

THE BARONNE: How very ill-timed your visit is, Madame Jacob! You see that I have guests.

MME. JACOB: I beg you to forgive me, Madame; I will return another time.

Seeing MME. TURCARET.

But what is this? My sister-in-law here! Madame Turcaret!

THE KNIGHT: Madame Turcaret?

THE BARONNE, *to* MME. JACOB: Madame Turcaret?

LISETTE, *to* MME. JACOB: Madame Turcaret?

THE MARQUIS, *aside*: What a merry caper!

MME. JACOB, *to* MME. TURCARET: By what chance do we meet in this house, Madame?

MME. TURCARET, *aside*: I must put a bold face on it.

To MME. JACOB:

I do not know who you are, my good woman.

MME. JACOB: You do not know Madame Jacob? . . . By Our Lady! Is it because you have been ten years separated from my brother, who could not bear to live with you, that you pretend not to know me?

THE MARQUIS: Madame Jacob, you have no idea; do you realize that you are speaking to a countess?

MME. JACOB: A countess! Ah! And exactly where, if you please, is her county situated? Oh, indeed, I like those swelling airs!

MME. TURCARET: You are insolent, my dear.

MME. JACOB: Insolent? I! I am insolent! . . . God's Holy Day, do not start that game. When it comes to name-calling I can take care of myself quite as well as you can.

MME. TURCARET: Oh, I do not doubt that. The daughter of a groom from Domfront would never lack for foul language.

MME. JACOB: The daughter of a groom! Bless me now! You're a well-bred lady to cast aspersions on my birth! You seem to have forgotten that Monsieur Briochais, your father, was a pastry cook in the town of Falaise. Away with you, Madame la Comtesse, since that's what you call yourself; we know each other . . . My brother will split with laughing when he hears of the preposterous name that you have assumed, to come and preen in Paris. Oh, I wish, for the sheer pleasure of it, that he would walk in at this moment.

THE KNIGHT: Your wish will be granted, Madame; we are expecting Monsieur Turcaret to dinner.

MME. TURCARET, *aside*: Ohh!

THE MARQUIS, *to* MME. JACOB: And you will dine with us too, Madame Jacob; for I love family dinners.

MME. TURCARET: How I regret that I ever set foot in this house!

LISETTE, *aside*: I can believe that.

MME. TURCARET, *starting to go*: I will leave at once.

THE MARQUIS, *preventing her*: You will not go, if you please, before you have seen Monsieur Turcaret.

MME. TURCARET: Do not hold me, Monsieur le Marquis; do not hold me.

THE MARQUIS: Oh, in the name of heaven, Mademoiselle Briochais, you will not leave here; depend upon it.

THE KNIGHT: Oh, Marquis! Let her go.

THE MARQUIS: I shall do nothing of the sort. In order to punish her for having deceived us both, I intend to bring her face to face with her husband.

THE BARONNE: No, Marquis. Take pity on her. Let her go.

THE MARQUIS: Waste of breath. The utmost that I will do for you, Madame, is to permit you to disguise yourself as Venus, so that your husband will not recognize you.

LISETTE, *Seeing* M. TURCARET *entering*: Oh! bless me, here is Monsieur Turcaret.

MME JACOB, *aside*: I am overjoyed.

MME. TURCARET, *aside*: Oh, wretched day!

THE BARONNE, *aside*: Why must this scene take place in my house?

THE MARQUIS, *aside*: I am overcome with delight!

Scene X

M. TURCARET, MME. TURCARET, THE BARONNE, MME. JACOB, THE MARQUIS, THE KNIGHT, LISETTE

M. TURCARET, *to* THE BARONNE: I have sent the bailiff on his way, Madame, and settled . . .

Aside, as he notices his sister.

Oh! Can I believe my eyes? My sister, here?

Seeing his wife.

And, even worse, my wife!

THE MARQUIS: Here you are in familiar country, Monsieur Turcaret . . .

Indicating MME. TURCARET.

You behold here a beautiful countess, whose chains I bear. Would you not like me to present her to you, not forgetting Madame Jacob?

MME. JACOB, *to* M. TURCARET: Ah, brother!

M. TURCARET: Ah, sister! . . . Who in the devil's name fetched them here?

THE MARQUIS: I did, Monsieur Turcaret; you are indebted to me for that. Embrace these two cherished creatures . . . Oh, he seems quite overcome! I am touched at the power of kinship and of conjugal love.

M. TURCARET, *aside*: I do not dare to look at her. I am afraid I will see my evil genius.

MME. TURCARET, *aside*: I cannot face him without horror.

THE MARQUIS, *to* M. *and* MME. TURCARET: Use no restraint, tender pair. Give rein to all the joy which you must feel, at seeing each other again after ten years of separation.

THE BARONNE, *to* M. TURCARET: You did not expect, did you, Monsieur, to meet Madame Turcaret here; and I can imagine your embarrassment. But why did you tell me that you were a widower?

THE MARQUIS: Did he tell you that he was a widower? Oh, I'll be blessed, his wife told me that she was a widow. They have a passion for being bereft, both of them.

THE BARONNE, *to* M. TURCARET: Tell me, why did you deceive me?

M. TURCARET, *confused*: I thought, Madame . . . that if I led you to think that . . . I thought that if I were a widower . . . you would think that . . . that I did not have a wife . . .

Aside.

My brain is confused; I do not know what I am saying.

THE BARONNE: I can guess your intention, Monsieur, and I forgive you for a deceit which you considered necessary in order to gain my ear. I will go even further: instead of reproaching you, I should like to see you and Madame Turcaret reconciled.

M. TURCARET: Who, I! Madame! Oh, not I, not that! You do not know her: she is a demon. I would rather live with the wife of the Great Mogul.

MME. TURCARET: Ah, Monsieur, you need not resist with such fury. I am certainly no more anxious to return to you than you are to have me; and I would not come to Paris to disrupt your pleasures, if you were more prompt at paying the pension which you give me to keep me in the country.

THE MARQUIS, *to* M. TURCARET: To keep her in the country! . . . Ah, Monsieur Turcaret, you do her wrong; Madame deserves to be paid quarterly in advance.

MME. TURCARET: He is five quarters behind in his payments. If he does not give me what he owes me, I will not go; I will stay in Paris and drive him mad. I will go to all his mistresses and raise bedlam . . . and I will begin with this house, I warn you.

M. TURCARET, *aside*: Oh, the insolent creature!

LISETTE, *aside*: This conversation can come to no good.

THE BARONNE, *to* MME. TURCARET: You have insulted me, Madame.

MME. TURCARET: I have eyes, thank God! I have eyes! I can see everything that is going on in this house. My husband is the greatest dupe . . .

M. TURCARET, *interrupting her*: What impudence! Oh, damnation! Jade! If it were not for the respect I have for the present company . . .

THE MARQUIS, *interrupting him*: Do not let that deter you, Monsieur Turcaret. You are among friends; follow your inclinations.

THE KNIGHT, *to* M. TURCARET, *stepping between him and his wife*: Monsieur . . .

THE BARONNE, *to* MME. TURCARET: Remember that you are in my house.

Scene XI

JASMIN, M. TURCARET, MME. TURCARET, THE BARONNE, MME. JACOB, THE MARQUIS, THE KNIGHT, LISETTE

JASMIN, *to* M. TURCARET: A carriage has just drawn up at the door. There are two gentlemen in it who say they are colleagues of yours. They wish to speak to you about a matter of great importance.
He goes.

Scene XII

M. TURCARET, MME. TURCARET, THE BARONNE, MME. JACOB, THE MARQUIS, THE KNIGHT, LISETTE

M. TURCARET, *to* MME. TURCARET: Oh, I shall return . . . And I will teach you, you impudent creature, to respect a house . . .

MME. TURCARET, *interrupting him*: I am not afraid of your threats.

M. TURCARET *goes*.

Scene XIII

MME. TURCARET, THE BARONNE, MME. JACOB, THE MARQUIS, THE KNIGHT, LISETTE

THE KNIGHT, *to* MME. TURCARET: Calm your anxieties, Madame; let Monsieur Turcaret find you in a sweeter temper when he returns.

MME. TURCARET: Oh, all his outbursts do not frighten me.

THE BARONNE: We shall pacify him, in your favor.

MME. TURCARET: I understand you, Madame. You wish to reconcile me to my husband, so that, out of gratitude, I shall allow him to continue to favor you with his attentions.

THE BARONNE: Your anger has blinded you. I have no other end in view than the reunion of your hearts. As for Monsieur Turcaret, I give him up to you. I do not wish ever to see him again.

MME. TURCARET: That is too generous.

THE MARQUIS, *to* THE KNIGHT, *indicating* THE BARONNE: Since Madame has renounced the husband, I for my part, renounce the wife. Come, Knight, you renounce her too. It is a fine thing to master one's passions.

Scene XIV

FRONTIN, MME. TURCARET, THE BARONNE, MME. JACOB, THE MARQUIS, THE KNIGHT, LISETTE

FRONTIN, *aside*: Oh, unforeseen catastrophe! Oh cruel disgrace!

THE KNIGHT: What is it, Frontin?

FRONTIN: Monsieur Turcaret's associates have put the bailiff's men into his house, because of two hundred thousand crowns, which a cashier whom he stood bail for, has made off with . . . I came here posthaste to warn him, so that he could escape; but I arrive too late: his creditors have already laid hands on him.

MME. JACOB: My brother, in the hands of his creditors? . . . Unnatural though he is, I am grieved at his misfortune. I will go and use all my credit to help him. I cannot forget that I am his sister.

She goes.

Scene XV

MME. TURCARET, THE BARONNE, THE MARQUIS, THE KNIGHT, LISETTE, FRONTIN

MME. TURCARET: As for me, I will go and find him and cover him with abuse. I cannot forget that I am his wife.

She goes.

Scene XVI

THE BARONNE, THE MARQUIS, THE KNIGHT, LISETTE, FRONTIN

FRONTIN, *to* THE KNIGHT: We envisaged the pleasure of ruining him, but justice was jealous of that pleasure, and has been before us.

THE MARQUIS: Well, well! He has enough money to get out of this scrape.

FRONTIN: I do not think so. It is said that he has foolishly dissipated his enormous wealth . . . But it is not that which troubles me at the moment; what most distresses me is that I was in his house when his colleagues came with the bailiff's men.

THE KNIGHT: Well?

FRONTIN: Well, Monsieur, they seized me too, and searched me, to see whether I might perchance have been entrusted with some paper which could be turned to the creditors' profit . . .

Indicating THE BARONNE.

I could not prevent them from confiscating Madame's note of credit, which you had placed in my keeping.

THE KNIGHT: What is this? Just heaven!

FRONTIN: They took from me also another note for ten thousand francs, which Monsieur Turcaret had given me to settle the process for debt, and which Monsieur Furet had returned to me.

THE KNIGHT: And why, villain, did you not tell them that you were my man?

FRONTIN: Oh, Monsieur, I did tell them, indeed I did. I told them that I was a knight's man, but when they saw the notes of credit, they refused to believe me.

THE KNIGHT: I cannot contain myself! I am in despair!

THE BARONNE: And as for me, my eyes have been opened. You told me that my note had been exchanged, and that you had the money at your house. I realize now that my diamond was never put in pawn; and I know what I may think of that moving oration, which Frontin made me, on the subject of your sufferings last night. Ah! Knight, I would not have thought you capable of such behavior . . .

Turning to LISETTE.

I dismissed Marine because she was opposed to your interests, and I am dismissing Lisette because she has embraced them . . . Farewell. I want never to hear from you again as long as I live.

She retires into the interior of her apartment.

Scene XVII

THE MARQUIS, THE KNIGHT, FRONTIN, LISETTE

THE MARQUIS, *laughing, to* THE KNIGHT, *who is quite disconcerted*: Ha ha! Upon my word, Knight, I cannot help but laugh at you. Your consternation has so amused me . . . Let us go and dine at the caterer's, and spend the night drinking.

FRONTIN, *to* THE KNIGHT: Shall I come with you, Monsieur?

THE KNIGHT: No, I discharge you. Let me never see you again.

He goes, with THE MARQUIS.

Scene XVIII

FRONTIN, LISETTE

LISETTE: And as for us, Frontin, what shall we do?

FRONTIN: I have a proposition to make. Long live wit, my child! I have just played a bold hand: I was never searched at all.

LISETTE: You still have the notes?

FRONTIN: I have already changed them, and have the money. It is safe under lock and key. I have forty thousand francs. If your ambition can be contained within the limits of that humble fortune, we can set about begetting a line of honest folk.

LISETTE: Here is my hand.

FRONTIN: And so the reign of Monsieur Turcaret is ended; and mine is just about to begin.

The False Confessions

Pierre de Marivaux

Characters

ARAMINTE, *Mme. Argante's daughter*

DORANTE, *M. Remy's nephew*

M. REMY, *solicitor*

MME. ARGANTE

HARLEQUIN, *Araminte's valet*

DUBOIS, *Dorante's former valet*

MARTON, *an attendant of Araminte's*

THE COMTE

A SERVANT

A YOUNG JEWELLER

THE BOY

Act One

Scene I

DORANTE, HARLEQUIN

HARLEQUIN, *leading* DORANTE *in*: Have the goodness, Monsieur, to make yourself comfortable in this room for a moment. Mademoiselle Marton is with Madame, and will be down presently.

DORANTE: I'm much obliged to you.

HARLEQUIN: I will keep you company, if you like, to insure you against boredom. We can pass the time in talk.

DORANTE: I'm grateful to you, I'm sure, but it's quite unnecessary. Please don't trouble yourself on my account.

HARLEQUIN: Not at all, Monsieur; pray do not stand on ceremony. Madame insists that we be polite, and you are witness to my civility.

DORANTE: No, believe me, I should be most happy to find myself alone for a moment.

HARLEQUIN: Then, Monsieur, pray excuse me; I leave you to your fancies.

Scene II

DORANTE, DUBOIS (*entering with an air of mystery*)

DORANTE: Ah, there you are!

DUBOIS: Yes, I was waiting for you.

DORANTE: I was afraid I should not be able to rid myself of a certain domestic who was set most absolutely on waiting with me as my charm against tedium. Tell me, has Monsieur Remy arrived yet?

DUBOIS: No, but it's very nearly the hour when he said you might expect him.

He looks cautiously about.

Are you sure there is no one about to observe us together?

It is imperative that the servants here should not realize that I know you.

DORANTE: I cannot see anyone.

DUBOIS: You have said nothing of our project to your uncle, Monsieur Remy?

DORANTE: Not a syllable. In the most innocent good faith in the world he has commended me, in the quality of a steward, to this lady, whose solicitor he happens to be. He does not suspect that it was you who urged me to apply to him. He spoke to her about it yesterday, and bade me present myself here this morning, saying that most probably he would be here before me to introduce me to her, but that if he had not yet come I was to address myself to a certain Mademoiselle Marton. And that is all. I took care not to divulge our scheme to him, nor to anyone else: it seemed preposterous even to me, who am committed to the attempt. I am none the less sensible of your good will, Dubois. You were my servant and I was unable to retain you; I could not even reward your zeal. And in spite of that you concern yourself with making my fortune. Indeed, you have made me everlastingly your debtor.

DUBOIS: Oh, Monsieur, say no more of that, for you always used me with kindness, and in a word I was happy in your service. Your excellent nature surely deserves my affections, and if I stood master of a great fortune, I should place it all at your disposal.

DORANTE: When shall I be able to reward such sentiments? Whatever I might win should rightfully be yours. But I expect nothing better from our enterprise than the shame of being dismissed tomorrow.

DUBOIS: Well, and if you are! You will come back and try again.

DORANTE: This lady enjoys a position in the world; she is connected with every kind of quality and eminence; she is the widow of a noted financier. And you suggest that she will accord me the least attention; nay, that she will marry me? Me? Who have neither distinction nor capital?

DUBOIS: No capital indeed! Your good looks are a very Peru. Turn round a bit and let me look at you. Upon my word, Monsieur, you do yourself an injustice: you have not your peer among the greatest lords in Paris. Here, I say, is a figure and presence worthy of every possible distinction. And our design is infallible, absolutely infallible. I fancy I can already see you in your morning undress in Madame's apartment.

DORANTE: What an illusion!

DUBOIS: Is it not? And to pursue it: at this very moment you are standing in your own salon, and your carriages are in the coach-house.

DORANTE: She has an income of fifty thousand and upwards, Dubois.

DUBOIS: Well, you command sixty at least.

DORANTE: And you say she is utterly virtuous?

DUBOIS: So much the better for you, and the worse for her. If you capture her fancy she will be so consumed with shame, she will resist so desperately, she will languish into such an exhaustion that marriage will become her only hope of survival, mark what I say. You have seen her, and you love her.

DORANTE: I love her passionately. It is just that that makes me tremble.

DUBOIS: Oh, you madden me with your trepidations! Damn me, show a bit of confidence. You will triumph, I tell you. I desire it; I have made myself responsible for its success; I have arranged it; all our actions have been agreed upon; all our stratagems are in motion. I am acquainted with the humour of my mistress, I am sensible of your merit, I know my own talents. I will conduct you to Madame; Madame will love you, for all her virtue; Madame will marry you, for all her pride; Madame will make you rich, for all your poverty, do you see? Pride, virtue, riches, all must yield. When love speaks, he is the master and will have his way. Farewell; I leave you. I hear someone: Monsieur Remy, perhaps. We are launched now; let us hold to our course.

He takes a few steps and returns.

While we are on the subject, try to induce Mademoiselle Marton to conceive a tender inclination for you. Love and I will take care of the rest.

Scene III

M. REMY, DORANTE

M. REMY: Good morning, nephew; I'm delighted you're punctual. Mademoiselle Marton will be with us presently; I have sent to inform her that I am here. Have you met her?

DORANTE: No, Monsieur. Why do you ask?

187

M. REMY: Simply a notion which occurred to me on the way here. She is pretty, to say the least.

DORANTE: I believe so.

M. REMY: And of an extremely good family. I, in fact, have been a father to her since she lost her own, who was a cherished friend of your own father's, albeit a somewhat erratic gentleman, leaving his daughter totally unprovided for. Madame here sent for her, loves her, retains her far less as an attendant than as a friend, has been most generous towards her, will be more so, and has even offered to settle a dowry on her. Mademoiselle Marton has besides an old asthmatic aunt, comfortably off, whose heir she will be. You will both be in the same house: it is my opinion that you should marry her. What do you say?

DORANTE, *looking away, smiling*: Oh . . . But I had not considered her.

M. REMY: Very well, take my advice and consider her now; try to catch her fancy. After all, nephew, you have nothing; nothing, I say, but certain remote expectations, for you are, in fact, my heir, but my health is excellent, and I shall spin it out as long as I can, not to mention the possibility that I might marry. I have no inclinations that way, but then that particular inclination is notorious for striking without warning; the world is alive with pretty young things; and in the eyes of any one of them it may be lurking in ambush. With a wife one gets children, that's the custom; and then farewell mortgaged hopes and pawned collateral. Therefore, nephew, you must look to your little precautions, and put yourself in a position where you need not depend on my fortune, which today I intend for you, but may deprive you of tomorrow.

DORANTE: You are quite right, Monsieur. I shall apply myself to precisely that.

M. REMY: Do. Here is Mademoiselle Marton. Stand over there for a moment to give me a chance to ask her impression of you.

DORANTE *moves to one side.*

Scene IV

M. REMY, MARTON, DORANTE

MARTON: I am distressed at having kept you waiting, Monsieur, but Madame required me.

M. REMY: No great harm done, Mademoiselle; I have just arrived myself.

Indicating DORANTE.

What is your opinion of that great boy there?

MARTON, *laughing*: Ah, and why do you want to know, Monsieur Remy?

M. REMY: Simply because he is my nephew.

MARTON: Indeed! Your nephew bears showing. He's a credit to the family looks.

M. REMY: He is the one I bespoke to Madame as a steward and I'm charmed to find that he suits your taste. He has already seen you—oh, more than once—at my house when you called there, do you remember?

MARTON: No. No, not at all.

M. REMY: Well, one can't notice everything. Do you know what he said to me the first time he saw you? "Who is that pretty girl?"

MARTON *smiles*.

Approach, nephew. Mademoiselle, your father and his cherished the profoundest affection for one another; should not their children, in turn, love each other? My nephew here, for one, desires nothing better—oh, with a most fervent heart.

DORANTE, *embarrassed*: Yes. Indeed. How could I fail to?

M. REMY: See how he gazes at you. You could strike a worse bargain, I assure you.

MARTON: Yes, I'm convinced; Monsieur is most tempting in his favour. It will bear looking into.

M. REMY: Looking into! Good, good; yes, of course it will. I shan't move a step till it's been looked into.

MARTON, *laughing*: Such haste! I tremble.

DORANTE: You urge Mademoiselle too importunately, Monsieur.

MARTON, *laughing*: Still, I trust I do not seem utterly inflexible.

M. REMY: Ah, there, you're agreed; now I'm content. Oh! my little ones . . .

Joining their hands.

I hereby betroth you to each other, at any rate until we can arrange something better. Now I must go. I shall return very shortly.

To MLLE. MARTON.

I leave you to present your prospects to Madame. Farewell, niece.

MARTON, *laughing*: Farewell, uncle.

189

Scene V

MARTON, DORANTE

MARTON: And yet, and yet, all this seems like a dream. Monsieur Remy is so precipitate. I can't help feeling that your love is rather sudden, and wondering whether it can be as enduring.

DORANTE: As enduring as it was sudden, Mademoiselle.

MARTON: I fear it may exhaust itself in too great haste at the start. There: Madame is coming, and since, thanks to Monsieur Remy's arrangements, your interests are virtually my own, have the goodness to step out onto the terrace for a moment, till I have spoken with her.

DORANTE: As you wish, Mademoiselle.

MARTON, *watching him go*: I am delighted with this turn of fancy which allows one of us suddenly to take the place of the other.

Scene VI

ARAMINTE, MARTON

ARAMINTE: Marton, who is that man who greeted me so charmingly just now, and has gone off there along the terrace? Was it you he came to see?

MARTON: No, Madame, it was to see you.

ARAMINTE, *a bit too eager*: Very well, then, send him in; what is he going away for?

MARTON: He begged me to speak with you before he did. He is that nephew of Monsieur Remy's; the one whom Monsieur Remy proposed to you as a steward.

ARAMINTE: Ah, he's the one! His appearance is certainly satisfactory.

MARTON: He has an excellent reputation. I can vouch for it.

ARAMINTE: Oh, I can believe it; you can see he deserves it. But Marton, he is so handsome that I am piqued with a scruple as to whether I dare take him into my service. Would not people talk?

MARTON: What could they say? Is one to be obliged to have nothing but lumps and monsters in one's service?

ARAMINTE: You are right. Tell him to come in. There was no need to prepare me to receive him; since Monsieur Remy recommends him, I am quite satisfied. I will employ him.

MARTON, *starting to go*: You could do no better.
Then coming back.
Have you fixed on what salary to give him? Monsieur Remy asked me to speak to you about it.
ARAMINTE: There's no need to. There will be no disagreement about that. If he is honest and capable he will have reason to be content. Call him.
MARTON, *hesitating to go*: You will give him the little apartment that opens out onto the garden, will you not?
ARAMINTE: Yes, whichever he likes. Send him in.
MARTON *goes out into the corridor.*

Scene VII

DORANTE, ARAMINTE, MARTON

MARTON: Monsieur Dorante, Madame will receive you now.
ARAMINTE: Come in, Monsieur; I am obliged to Monsieur Remy for having thought of me, but when he sends me his nephew I am overcome by his generosity. One of my friends spoke to me the day before yesterday about sending me a possible steward today; but I have made up my mind: I will have you.
DORANTE: I hope, Madame, that my zeal will justify the preference with which you honour me, and I beg you to retain me. Nothing could cause me greater affliction, at the moment, than to lose this position.
MARTON: Madame has given her word.
ARAMINTE: No, Monsieur, the affair is closed; I will dismiss all the others. You are acquainted with this sort of work, I presume; have you undertaken such business before?
DORANTE: Yes, Madame; my father was a lawyer, and I should have been one myself.
ARAMINTE: Which is to say that you are a young man of extremely good family, in fact rather above the salary which you must now seek?
DORANTE: Madame, I am in no way ashamed to accept this position. The honour of serving a lady such as you is inferior to none. I will envy no man's station.
ARAMINTE: The manner of my employment will give you no cause to qualify those sentiments. You will have all the consideration that you deserve, and if in time there should arise some

opportunity for me to render you a service, I should not fail to do so.

MARTON: Indeed, Madame, I can vouch for that.

ARAMINTE: Oh, if the truth were known, I am always distressed to see someone of merit and worth lacking a fortune, when there is such a multitude of persons with no virtue nor quality to recommend them, who without a thought can indulge in dazzling opulence. It pains me. Above all in people of your own age. For I should suppose you are not yet thirty, at most?

DORANTE: Not quite thirty, Madame.

ARAMINTE: You can console yourself with the thought that you may yet achieve happiness.

DORANTE: Happiness, Madame, begins for me today.

ARAMINTE: You will be shown the apartment which I have chosen for you. If it does not suit you, there are others; you may choose for yourself. You must also have someone to wait upon you; I must see to that. Who would be best for him, Marton?

MARTON: It will have to be Harlequin, Madame. There he is at the door of the salon; I'll call him. Harlequin, Madame wishes to speak to you.

Scene VIII

ARAMINTE, DORANTE, MARTON, HARLEQUIN, A SERVANT

HARLEQUIN: Madame?

ARAMINTE: Harlequin, in the future you will answer to Monsieur as his servant. I have given you to him.

HARLEQUIN: Given me to him? Madame! Will I not belong to me any more? Will I not be able to call myself my own ever again?

MARTON: The dunce!

ARAMINTE: I mean, you will wait upon Monsieur instead of me.

HARLEQUIN, *near tears*: I don't know why Madame should want to dismiss me. I have not deserved this treatment. I have always tried to serve your pleasure.

ARAMINTE: I am not dismissing you; I will pay you to wait upon Monsieur.

HARLEQUIN: I make exposition to Madame that that would not be just. I could not disburse my labours on the one hand while the money was coming to me on the other. You must have my service, as long as I enjoy your wages, otherwise I should be cheating Madame.

ARAMINTE: No. I cannot. I cannot make him understand.

MARTON: Blockhead! When I send you somewhere, or say to you, "Do this, do that," do you not obey me?

HARLEQUIN: Always.

MARTON: Very well. It will be Monsieur who will say it to you, just as I do; and he will do so in Madame's name and by her order.

HARLEQUIN: Ah, that is another matter. It is Madame who will order Monsieur to endure my service, which I will lend him at Madame's command.

MARTON: Exactly.

HARLEQUIN: You can see how it might have confused me.

A SERVANT, *entering*: Madame, the merchant has come with those materials.

ARAMINTE: I must go and see them; I shall return presently. Monsieur, there are certain affairs I wish to discuss with you. Do not go away.

Scene IX

DORANTE, MARTON, HARLEQUIN

HARLEQUIN: Well, Monsieur, here we are, indissoluble to each other, and you're one ahead of me. I shall be the valet who serves, and you the valet who is ordered to be served.

MARTON: The gnat, with his comparisons! Go away!

HARLEQUIN: One moment, with your permission. Monsieur, will you not pay anything at all? Have you been commanded to be served gratis?

DORANTE *laughs*.

MARTON: Oh, do go. Let us alone. Madame will pay you; can't you be content with that?

HARLEQUIN: But oh dear, Monsieur, will I cost you nothing at all? I will be the cheapest valet that ever was.

DORANTE: Harlequin is right. Here: that's an earnest of what I'll give you.

HARLEQUIN: There, that's the gesture of a master. You can give me the rest at your own convenience.

DORANTE: Go drink to my health.

HARLEQUIN: Oh, if your health requires nothing but my drinking to it to insure its soundness, I can promise you it will flourish as long as I live.
Aside:
Well, what a liberal colleague luck has found for me there!

Scene X

DORANTE, MARTON, MME. ARGANTE (*who arrives a moment later*)

MARTON: You have every reason to congratulate yourself upon Madame's welcome. She seems to have taken a fancy to you. So much the better; we will not lose by that. But here comes Madame Argante. Be warned: she is Madame's mother, and I think I know what has brought her here.

MME. ARGANTE, *a brusque, vain woman*: Indeed, Marton: my daughter tells me that she has suited herself with a new steward. Some person provided by her solicitor. How vexing, to be sure! And how disobliging towards Monsieur le Comte, who had set one aside for her. She should have waited, at least, till she had seen them both. What was so preferable about this one? What sort of man is it?

MARTON: It . . . is Monsieur, Madame.

MME. ARGANTE: Ah! It's Monsieur. I might have suspected as much: he's terribly young.

MARTON: At thirty, one is quite old enough to manage the business of an estate, Madame.

MME. ARGANTE: That depends. Is your engagement quite definite, Monsieur?

DORANTE: Yes, Madame.

MME. ARGANTE: And from whose house do you come?

DORANTE: From my own, Madame. I have not been in anyone's employment until now.

MME. ARGANTE: From your own! You mean to use this house for your apprenticeship?

MARTON: Not at all. Monsieur is thoroughly acquainted with business matters. His father was an extremely clever man.

MME. ARGANTE, *aside to* MARTON: I've no great opinion of this one. Is that, do you fancy, what a steward should look like? He has not the air . . .

MARTON, *aside*: We can manage without that: I will answer for his other qualities. He is exactly what was required.

MME. ARGANTE: Provided Monsieur does not in any way obstruct certain plans of ours, it is immaterial to me whether it be he or another.

MARTON: Might one be admitted to those plans, Madame?

MME. ARGANTE: Do you know Monsieur le Comte Dorimont? An illustrious name. My daughter and he were on the point of going to law against each other over a certain considerable piece of land. They could come to no agreement as to its rightful ownership, and it was suggested that they should marry to avoid having to take it to court. My daughter is the widow of a man of considerable reputation in the world, who left her extremely rich. But Madame la Comtesse Dorimont would enjoy so exalted a rank, would converse on equal footing with persons of such immense distinction, that I will have no rest until I have seen the marriage performed. And I must confess it would delight me to be the mother of Madame la Comtesse Dorimont, and, perhaps of someone still more exalted one day, for to Monsieur le Comte Dorimont all things are possible.

DORANTE: Have they pronounced their betrothal?

MME. ARGANTE: Not entirely, yet, but very nearly. My daughter is not reluctant. She merely says that she wishes, first, to determine the rights of the dispute exactly, and whether she has not a better claim than Monsieur le Comte, so that if she were to marry him he would be under an obligation to her. But there are moments when I fear that that may be only an excuse. My daughter has only one fault, and that is that sometimes I find her wanting in a proper taste for the sublime: the illustrious name of Dorimont, and the rank of countess do not sway her as they should. She is not sensible of the chagrin of being nothing but a bourgeoisie. She has sunk into a complacency with her present station, in spite of the immensity of her fortune.

DORANTE, *sweetly*: Perhaps she would be no happier if her lot were improved.

MME. ARGANTE, *sharply*: Your opinion is neither interesting nor welcome. Keep your plebeian little reflections to yourself and look to our convenience, if you hope for our condescension.

MARTON: Just a minor moral consideration, which need not concern us.

MME. ARGANTE: A vulgar consideration, and not to my taste.

DORANTE: What was it you wanted me to do, Madame?

MME. ARGANTE: Tell my daughter, when you have perused the documents, that her claim to the property is less tenable than Monsieur le Comte's; that, if she were to take it to law, she would lose.

DORANTE: If her position is, in fact, weaker than his, I shall not fail to advise her so, Madame.

MME. ARGANTE, *aside to* MARTON: Humph! Feeble wit!

To DORANTE:

You have not entirely understood. That is not quite what you were told. You are to advise her as I said, whether her case is assured or hopeless.

DORANTE: But Madame, it would not be honest to deceive her.

MME. ARGANTE: Honest! You question my honesty, sirrah? Insufferable reasoning! I am her mother, and I order you to deceive her for her own good, do you understand? I do; I.

DORANTE: It would be I, even so, who would have acted in bad faith.

MME. ARGANTE, *aside, to* MARTON: He's an ignoramus, this one. She'll have to dismiss him. Farewell, monsieur man of affairs, who have never handled any.

She goes.

Scene XI

DORANTE, MARTON

DORANTE: There is a mother who does not take after her daughter.

MARTON: Yes, there is a certain difference, and I'm distressed that I had not time to warn you of that brusqueness in her disposition. She is set absolutely upon this marriage, as you see. But in any case, when the mother gives you her warrant, why should you scruple as to what you say to the daughter? Your conscience would have no cause, that I can see, to reproach you: it could not, under such circumstances, be called deceit.

DORANTE: Ah, you must excuse me: I hesitate to commit her to a decision which perhaps, without my inducements, she would not make. If my influence is felt to be so necessary, is Madame, then, averse to this marriage?

MARTON: Only through indolence.

DORANTE: Come now, let us have the truth.

MARTON: Oh well, there is one small point which you should take into consideration: Monsieur le Comte has promised me a thousand crowns the day the contract is signed. And, what with Monsieur Remy's plans, that money concerns you now, as well as me.

DORANTE: Mademoiselle Marton, hear me, you are the most delightful young lady in the world, but it is due merely to lack of consideration on your part that those thousand crowns tempt you.

MARTON: On the contrary, it is by consideration on my part that they tempt me; the more I think of them, the more desirable they seem.

DORANTE: But you are devoted to your mistress: and if she were to be anything less than happy with this man, would you not reproach yourself for having enticed her to the connection for a paltry sum?

MARTON: Save your sentiments, sir: I'm deaf to you. Besides, the count's a decent enough gentleman; I've no time for these over-niceties. Here is Madame. She had something to discuss with you. I'll go. Meditate on the money; turn a thousand crowns over in your own mind for a while. You'll relish it quite as much as I do.

DORANTE: I'm not so distressed, now, at the thought of deceiving her.

Scene XII

ARAMINTE, DORANTE

ARAMINTE: You have met my mother, I believe?

DORANTE: Yes, Madame; just a moment ago.

ARAMINTE: So she told me, and said how heartily she wished I had engaged almost anyone rather than you.

DORANTE: I sensed something of the kind.

ARAMINTE: Yes, but do not be disheartened by that. You suit me perfectly.

DORANTE: To do so, Madame, is my sole ambition.

ARAMINTE: Now for what I wished to discuss with you; but I beg you to keep the matter a secret entirely between ourselves.

DORANTE: I would rather betray myself.

ARAMINTE: Oh, I do not hesitate to trust you. The substance is this: there is a design afoot to marry me to Monsieur le Comte Dorimont, in order to avoid an interminable lawsuit, which threatens between us, over a piece of land which belongs to me.

DORANTE: I know, Madame; it was on that very subject that I had the misfortune, just now, to provoke Madame Argante's displeasure.

ARAMINTE: Indeed! How?

DORANTE: She requested me, if your case in the impending suit should appear the stronger, to tell you the contrary, so as to hasten you into agreeing to this marriage; and I begged her to excuse me from that service.

ARAMINTE: What a mischief my mother is! I am not surprised at your loyalty: I counted on it. Continue as you have begun, and do not allow yourself to be shaken by what my mother says. I disapprove of what she has done. Did she go so far as to be disagreeable to you?

DORANTE: It's of no matter, Madame. It served merely to inflame my zeal and redouble my devotion to you.

ARAMINTE: And for that reason also, I will not countenance your being subjected to impertinences and embarrassment. I will see to this. What does she mean by it? I shall be worse than annoyed if she persists. Indeed! So you are not to be left in peace! But to have misconduct and ill manners thrust upon you because your own are impeccable. That is a pleasant prospect!

DORANTE: Madame, in the name of all for which I am indebted to you, do not think of it. I am overwhelmed by your kindnesses, and I am too happy to be at odds with anyone.

ARAMINTE: I applaud your sentiments. Let us return to this matter of the lawsuit: if I do not marry Monsieur le Comte . . .

Scene XIII

DORANTE, ARAMINTE, DUBOIS

DUBOIS, *entering*: Madame la Marquise is feeling better, Madame . . .

He pretends surprise at the sight of DORANTE.

. . . and is very much obliged to you . . . very much obliged for your solicitude.

DORANTE *pretends to turn his face away to conceal his identity from* DUBOIS.

ARAMINTE: I am delighted to hear it.

DUBOIS: Madame, there was also an urgent message which I was to repeat to you.

ARAMINTE: Pray do.

DUBOIS: I was requested to divulge it to you only, in private.

ARAMINTE, *to* DORANTE: I have not yet finished what I wished to say to you. Be so good as to withdraw for a moment, and then return.

Scene XIV

ARAMINTE, DUBOIS

ARAMINTE: What was the meaning of that air of astonishment which you manifested, I thought, at the sight of Dorante? Why that incredulous stare you fixed upon him?

DUBOIS: Nothing, nothing; but I am compelled to resign the honour of serving you, Madame, and beg you to discharge me at once from your employment.

ARAMINTE, *surprised*: What? Merely because you have seen Dorante here?

DUBOIS: Are you aware who it is you are dealing with?

ARAMINTE: With Monsieur Remy's—my solicitor's—nephew.

DUBOIS: Indeed. And by what means, Madame, did he enter your acquaintance? How does he contrive to be here?

ARAMINTE: Monsieur Remy sent him to me as a steward.

DUBOIS: He, your steward! And Monsieur Remy sent him? Alas, the good gentleman, all unknowing what he was urging upon you—this fellow's a very devil.

ARAMINTE: What do you mean, with your exclamations? Explain yourself. Do you know him?

DUBOIS: Do I know him, Madame! Do I know him! Ah, only too well, and ah too well he knows me. Did you not notice how he turned his face from me, lest I should recognize him?

ARAMINTE: It is true, he did. Now it is my turn to be surprised. Could there be some villainy you know him to be capable of? Is he not an honest man?

DUBOIS: He? For his virtues there's not a man could compare with him in the whole country. He has, I should hazard, more

199

honour in him than you could make up out of fifty others. Oh, a marvellous probity, a very marvel. I might say unequalled.

ARAMINTE: Then what grounds is there for apprehension? Why did you seek to alarm me? Really, I am quite unsettled.

DUBOIS: His weakness . . . is here.
Touching his forehead.
It's in his head that it takes him.

ARAMINTE: In his head?

DUBOIS: Yes, he is cracked. Cracked: like a bell, like a carillon.

ARAMINTE: Dorante? I thought him in excellent sense. What proof of his madness have you?

DUBOIS: Proof? He has been mad these six months; for six months he has gone raving of love, his wits flown as birds, like a man beside himself. I should know; I was his man; I waited on him. It was that which obliged me to quit his service, and it's that which now forces me to leave yours also. Aside from that, he's an admirable—I might say incomparable—gentleman.

ARAMINTE, *rather sulkily*: You don't say! Well, he can be what he pleases, I shall not retain him. A great help he'd be to me, with his wits all worn backwards. And driven to this extremity, I should wager, for the sake of some object unworthy of his attentions; for I know how men are, with their fancies . . .

DUBOIS: Oh, you must forgive me, but as for the object of his passion, not a word could be said against it. No, God's truth, his madness is in the best of taste.

ARAMINTE: No matter, I shall dismiss him. Do you know her, by any chance—this person?

DUBOIS: I have the honour of seeing her daily; the person is you, Madame.

ARAMINTE: Me, did you say?

DUBOIS: He worships you. For six months he has been like a ghost, and he would have given what life he had merely to gaze upon you for one instant. You must have noticed what ecstasy his manner betrays when he speaks to you.

ARAMINTE: There is, to be sure, some little thing in his demeanour which I have remarked as extraordinary. Oh, merciful heaven! The poor boy; what can be done for him?

DUBOIS: You would not believe the ends to which this folly of his drives him; it's destroying him; it's cutting his throat. His looks are presentable; a middling to decent figure, well brought up, of a good family; but he is not rich, and as you can imagine, there was nothing for him but to marry some lady who was; and very nice ones there were, too, who offered to make his fortune, and who would have deserved to have had theirs made for them. There is one who will not be put off by any means and still pursues him relentlessly. I know, I have met her.

ARAMINTE, *with feigned negligence*: Recently?

DUBOIS: Yes, Madame, recently. She never lets a whole day go by. A tall brunette, pretty in a very pointed sort of way, whom he flees the sight of. Nothing will make him see reason: Monsieur refuses them all. "I should be deceiving them," he told me; "I could not love them; my heart is elsewhere." Several times when he said it there were tears in his eyes, for he knows quite well how hopeless it is.

ARAMINTE: I am distressed to hear it. But where did he ever see me before he came here today, Dubois?

DUBOIS: Alas, Madame, it was one day as you were coming out of the Opéra that he lost his reason. It was a Friday, as I remember. Yes, a Friday. He had seen you come down the stairs, he told me, and he had followed you as far as the door of your carriage. When I found him he was in a kind of ecstasy; he had learned your name. He never recovered after that.

ARAMINTE: How surprising!

DUBOIS: It was no use my shouting, "Monsieur!" He was beyond it: nobody home. However, finally he came to himself again, though all bewildered; I flung him into a carriage and we returned home. I hoped it would pass off, because I was fond of him. He was the best of masters! Not at all, he was past cure: that excellent good sense, that genial wit, that delightful humor, you had sent them all packing; and, starting the next morning, we did nothing further, we two, but minister to his folly: he, dreaming of you, vaporing of his love, and I spying after you from morning to night, wherever you went.

ARAMINTE: I cannot express my astonishment!

DUBOIS: I even went so far as to make friends with a certain retainer of yours who is no longer with you: a fellow of most precise information, whom I rewarded out of a bottle. "She's going to the theatre," he'd say, and I'd run to make my report, whereupon my man would be ready from four in the afternoon onwards, and waiting at the door. "She's gone to call on madame this, or madame that" and on receipt of that news we would go and spend the whole evening camped in the street to see—I mean no offense—Madame go in and come out, he in a carriage and I behind it, both of us blue and shivering, for of course it was mid-winter. But he not so much as noticing the time or the weather, and I swearing at this and cursing that to soothe myself.

ARAMINTE: Is it possible?

DUBOIS: Yes, Madame. But in the end I grew bored with that manner of living; my health began to go, and his also. I gave him to understand that you were in the country; he believed me, and things were almost peaceful for a bit; and then didn't he happen upon you, two days later, in the Tuileries, where he had gone to be gloomy about your absence? When he got back he was furious; he would have beaten me, for all his goodness. But that I would not stay for, and I left him. My good fortune then led me to secure a place with Madame, only to find that by some desperate contrivance he has succeeded to the stewardship of your household, a post which he would not trade for an emperor's throne.

ARAMINTE: Is it surprising that I should have engaged him? I am so weary of retainers who do nothing but deceive me, that I rejoiced at finding him, for I could perceive his integrity. Do not suppose I am angry, for I am above that.

DUBOIS: It would be kindest to dismiss him. The more he sees of you, the less hope there is for him.

ARAMINTE: Oh, most certainly I would dismiss him, but I fear that would not cure him. Besides, I should never be able to explain it to Monsieur Remy, who recommended him to me; it would be most embarrassing. I am quite at a loss to see how I can extricate myself gracefully.

DUBOIS: Yes. But you will render him incurable, Madame.

ARAMINTE: Oh! So much the worse for him. As things are, I cannot do without a steward; and furthermore, the risk is less grave than you suppose: on the contrary, if there were one thing which might restore the gentleman to his senses, it would be an habitual familiarity with the sight of me, which till now has been impossible to him. I would be doing him a service.

DUBOIS: Ah, Madame, that is the remedy of an innocent. In the first place, never a word of it will he let fall to you; you will never hear him speak of his love.

ARAMINTE: Are you quite sure?

DUBOIS: Oh, you need have no fear: he would rather die. Such respect, such adoration as he cherishes for you, with such humility, you cannot imagine. Do you suppose he so much as dreams of his love being returned? Never for a moment. He says that in the entire universe there is not one person worthy of your love. He desires nothing more than to see you, contemplate you, behold your eyes, the grace of your bearing, the shape of your beauty, and that's all. He's told me so a thousand times.

ARAMINTE: Poor gentleman: it is obvious that he merits every compassion. Well, then, I shall be patient for a few days, until I find someone to replace him. As for you, you may rest assured: I am pleased with you. I shall reward your zeal, and I should be unhappy to lose you, do you understand, Dubois?

DUBOIS: Madame, I am devoted to you for life.

ARAMINTE: I shall see that you have no cause to regret it. But above all, he must never suspect that I know. You must keep it an absolute secret: no one, not even Marton, must know what you have told me. Things of this sort must not be blazoned abroad, but require the utmost discretion.

DUBOIS: I have never mentioned it, save to Madame.

ARAMINTE: There: he is coming back. Go.

Scene XV

DORANTE, ARAMINTE

ARAMINTE, *alone for a moment*: This is one confidence, if the truth were known, that I had far rather I had not been honoured with.

DORANTE, *entering*: Madame, I await your pleasure.

ARAMINTE: Yes, Monsieur. What was I talking about? I have forgotten.

DORANTE: A lawsuit, with Monsieur le Comte Dorimont.

ARAMINTE: So I was. I mentioned that there had been a proposal that he and I should marry.

DORANTE: Yes, Madame, and you were on the point of saying, I believe, that you were not disposed to this marriage.

ARAMINTE: True. I had hoped to set you to study the case, so that I should know whether I would be risking anything if

I took it to law, but I feel I must relieve you of that task: I am not sure that I shall be able to keep you.

DORANTE: Oh, Madame, you had the kindness to give me every assurance that you would retain me.

ARAMINTE: Yes, but I did not take into account my promise to Monsieur le Comte to engage a steward whom he would send me. You can see, surely, that it would not be honest of me to fail to keep my word. At the very least I must speak to the person he has provided.

DORANTE: Wretch that I am, I succeed at nothing, and now I must suffer the affliction of being dismissed.

ARAMINTE, *out of weakness*: I do not say that; nothing has yet been decided.

DORANTE: Do not leave me in this uncertainty, Madame.

ARAMINTE: Oh, of course I shall do all that I can to retain you; I shall try.

DORANTE: Do you wish me to study the case for you, then, as you suggested?

ARAMINTE: But think: if I were to marry the comte you would have gone to much trouble for nothing.

DORANTE: I thought I understood you to say, Madame, that he held no attraction for you.

ARAMINTE: Not yet.

DORANTE: And besides, your situation is so tranquil and pleasant just as it is!

ARAMINTE, *aside*: I have not the courage to torment him! . . . Very well, then, do so: study away, study to your heart's content. I have some of the documents in my desk. Come to fetch them, and I will give them to you.
As she goes.
I hardly dare look at him!

Scene XVI

DORANTE, DUBOIS

DUBOIS, *entering with an air at once mysterious and casual, as though he were merely passing through*: Marton is looking for you to show you the apartment they have chosen for you. Harlequin has gone drinking: I said I would come and tell you. How did she behave towards you?

DORANTE: How kind she is! I am enchanted! How did she receive what you told her?

DUBOIS, *as though in a hurry to be off*: She is sweetly disposed to keep you here, out of pity. She hopes that the familiarity with the sight of her may cure you.

DORANTE, *charmed*: Does she really?

DUBOIS: She'll not escape now: she's too far gone. I will come back at once.

DORANTE: No, stay; I think that is Marton coming. Tell her that Madame is waiting for me, to give me certain papers, and that I shall rejoin her as soon as I have them.

DUBOIS: Go, go; I too have something to say to Marton. Into each mind drop those suspicions that will prove most useful to us: that's the way.

Scene XVII

DUBOIS, MARTON

MARTON: Where is Dorante? I thought I saw him with you.

DUBOIS, *brusquely*: He says Madame is waiting for him with certain papers, and that he will return at once. In any case, what need is there for him to see this apartment? If he didn't fancy it, he would be delicate indeed. 'Sdeath, I'd advise him . . .

MARTON: It's no concern of yours. I am simply following out Madame's orders.

DORANTE: Madame is good, and wise; but have a care. Have you not noticed this trifling libertine making pretty eyes at her?

MARTON: His eyes are pretty.

DUBOIS: I'm heartily deceived if I did not see this puppy's glance linger, I will not say where, on Madame's countenance.

MARTON: Indeed! And must you fly into a rage because someone finds her beautiful?

DUBOIS: No. But sometimes I suspect him of having come here only so that he might be able to look at her from nearer-to.

ARAMINTE, *laughing*: Ha! Ha! What a notion! Away with you, you understand nothing at all: quite, quite astray.

DUBOIS, *laughing*: Ha! Ha! Well, what a fool I am, then.

MARTON, *laughing as she goes*: Ha! Ha! The wit, with his observations!

205

DUBOIS, *alone*: As you will, as you will, just as you will. And yet your opinion of those observations will improve, if pains of mine can give it grounds. Now is the moment to shout "fire" to our whole artillery.

Act Two

Scene I

ARAMINTE, DORANTE

DORANTE: No, Madame, you have nothing to lose. It is quite safe: you can take the matter to law. I have even gone so far as to consult several opinions; your case is excellent, and if the expedient you mentioned is all that urges you to marry Monsieur le Comte, now there is no reason why you need contract such a marriage.

ARAMINTE: It would distress him terribly. It is so difficult to decide.

DORANTE: It would not be right for you to sacrifice yourself to your fear of causing him distress.

ARAMINTE: But have you truly and carefully examined the case? You said to me not long since that my present situation is tranquil and pleasant: are you certain you have not been swayed by a wish to keep me in it? Are you not perhaps rather too prejudiced against this marriage, and so against Monsieur le Comte?

DORANTE: Madame, I love your interests better than I do his, or anyone else's in the world.

ARAMINTE: I cannot object to that, of course. However, if I marry him and he should wish to install another here in your place, you will lose nothing by it: I promise you I will find you a still better position.

DORANTE, *sadly*: No, Madame, if I am so unhappy as to lose my position with you, I will devote myself to no one else. And I see that I shall lose it; I expect no less.

ARAMINTE: Nevertheless, I think I shall bring this suit against him; we shall see.

DORANTE: There was one other small thing I wished to say to you, Madame. I have just heard that the custodian of one of your estates has died. I thought you might send one of your servants to take his place, and it occurred to me that Dubois might go. I would replace him here with a certain domestic whom I can vouch for.

207

MARTON: No, send this person of yours to the château and leave Dubois here with me. He is a young man whom I trust, who serves me well, and I wish to keep him here. By the way, he tells me, unless I have mistaken him, that he was at one time in your employment; is that so?

DORANTE, *feigning a certain embarrassment*: It is true, Madame. He is loyal, but hardly accurate. Furthermore, that sort seldom have any good to say of their former masters. Will he not damage what esteem you may have for me?

ARAMINTE, *with negligence*: He has spoken very highly of you, and that is all . . . What has brought Monsieur Remy?

Scene II

ARAMINTE, DORANTE, M. REMY

M. REMY: Madame, I am your most humble servant. I have come to thank you for your goodness in taking my nephew into your service on my recommendation.

ARAMINTE: I did not hesitate, as you can see.

M. REMY: Accept my thanks a thousandfold. Did you not tell me, too, that you had been offered another?

ARAMINTE: Yes, Monsieur.

M. REMY: So much the better, for I've come to ask for this one back again on a matter of some importance.

DORANTE, *with an air of refusal*: Importance to whom, Monsieur?

M. REMY: Patience!

ARAMINTE: But Monsieur Remy, this is somewhat sudden. You have chosen your moment, I am afraid, badly; and I have refused the other person.

DORANTE: As for me, I shall never leave Madame unless she dismisses me.

M. REMY, *brusquely*: You do not realize what you are saying. In any case, you must come, as you will see. Consider, Madame, and judge for yourself when you hear what it concerns. A woman of thirty-five, whom they say is good-looking, and decent, and of some distinction; who will not divulge her name; who states that I have acted as her solicitor; who has at least fifteen thousand pounds rent and will prove it; who has seen Monsieur at my house, who has spoken to him, who knows that he has nothing, and who offers to marry him without delay; and the person whom she sent to me with this offer will return presently for the reply and take you back with her at the same time. Is that clear? Is that definite? Is there anything to discuss about that? You must be at her house within two hours. Am I not right, Madame?

ARAMINTE, *coldly*: It is for him to answer.

M. REMY: Well, then. What is he waiting for? Are you coming?

DORANTE: No, Monsieur, I am not so inclined.

M. REMY: Hum! What? Do you hear what I say? She has fifteen thousand pounds in rent, do you hear?

DORANTE: Yes, Monsieur, and had she twenty times as much again, I would not marry her. Neither she nor I would be happy. My heart is fixed elsewhere. I love another.

M. REMY, *in a tone of mockery, drawing out his words*: My heart! The bother of it! Fixed elsewhere! Ah! Ah! The heart is an admirable possession. I never could quite grasp the beauty of those scruples the heart proffers, which insist that one remain a steward in someone else's house when one might be a lord of one's own. Is that your final word, faithful shepherd?

DORANTE: My sentiments will never change, Monsieur.

M. REMY: You and your half-witted heart! Nephew, you are an imbecile, a lunatic, and in my opinion the person you love is a Barbary ape if she does not agree with me; am I not right, Madame? Do you not think he is out of his senses?

ARAMINTE, *sweetly*: Do not quarrel with him. It does seem that he is mistaken, I must confess.

M. REMY, *hotly*: What! Madame, it seems . . .

ARAMINTE: I cannot condemn him for thinking as he does. All the same, Dorante, do try to overcome this fancy of yours if you can; though I realize how difficult it must be.

DORANTE: Hopeless, Madame: my love is dearer to me than life itself.

M. REMY, *with an air of astonishment*: Well, the collectors of fine sentiments should be pleased: that one is as great a curio as they could find anywhere. Do you call that reasonable, Madame?

ARAMINTE: I will leave you to speak to him by yourself.
Aside:
He so melts me, I dare not stay.
She goes.

DORANTE: He cannot guess how aptly he serves me.

Scene III

DORANTE, M. REMY, MARTON

M. REMY: Dorante, I hope you have bethought yourself how poor a belfry you can afford for your bats.

MARTON *enters*.

Approach, Mademoiselle Marton.

MARTON: I learned only this minute that you had come.

M. REMY: Treat us to your opinion on a little matter: what would you say of someone who was penniless, and yet refused to marry a respectable and quite pretty woman with a clear fifteen thousand pounds' rent per annum?

MARTON: That one is easy to answer: your someone is in a dream.

M. REMY: This is the dreamer. And for excuse he pleads his heart, which he has consigned to you. But since apparently he has not collected yours, and since I trust you are still more or less in your right mind (if only because of how briefly you have been exposed to his acquaintance) I beg you to help me restore him to a measure of reason. You are very pretty, there's no denying it, but you would not set that in the scales against vested interests such as I have described. No eyes are pretty enough to be worth that price.

MARTON: What, Monsieur Remy? Was it Dorante that you meant? And is it for my sake that he refuses to be rich?

M. REMY: Just so, and you are too generous to allow it.

MARTON, *with a show of passion*: You are mistaken, Monsieur. I love him too well myself to discourage him, and I am enchanted with his decision. Ah, Dorante, you have won my admiration! I would never have believed that you loved me with such a passion.

M. REMY: Steady, steady! I do no more than display him to you and before I know it you have tried him on! God's truth, the heart of a woman is a matter for amazement: the promptitude with which it bursts into flame!

MARTON, *in mock sorrow*: Ah, Monsieur, must one have riches in order to be happy? I am assured of Madame's goodness to me; she will make up a part at least of all this that his generosity sacrifices for my sake. Oh, Dorante, how deeply I am indebted to you!

DORANTE: Not at all, Mademoiselle, by no means. You have no cause to thank me for what I have done: I have acted according to my own sentiments, and in doing so have considered no one but myself. You owe me nothing, and I do not expect your gratitude.

MARTON: Oh, you charm me! What delicacy! Nothing could be more tender than what you have just said to me.

M. REMY: My faith, then, I'm more at a loss than ever for it sounded flat enough to me.

To MARTON:

Farewell, pretty child; I would never have said you were worth the price you're fetching, upon my word I would not.

To DORANTE:

Menial, idiot. Well, keep your raptures, and I'll keep my patrimony.

He goes.

MARTON: He's angry, but we'll find ways to soothe him.

DORANTE: I hope so. Someone is coming.

MARTON: It is Monsieur le Comte, whom I told you of: the one who, most probably, will marry Madame.

DORANTE: I will leave you, in that case. He might speak to me of his lawsuit. You remember what I told you about that, and it would do no good for me to see him.

Scene IV

THE COMTE, MARTON

THE COMTE: Good day, Marton.

MARTON: You have returned, then, Monsieur?

THE COMTE: Yes. I was told that Araminte was walking in the garden, and her mother has just told me something which disturbs me: I had provided a steward for her, who should have entered her service today, but since I last saw her she has engaged another, a person who does not meet with her mother's approval, and from whom we may hope for nothing.

MARTON: Oh, there's no cause for alarm there, Monsieur. Put your mind at rest, he's a man after your own heart; and if her mother's not happy with the choice, she's partly to blame, for at her first encounter she assailed him in a manner so exaggeratedly brusque that it's not surprising that she did not win his immediate devotion. Imagine: she found fault with him for being good-looking.

THE COMTE: Was that he who went from you just now?

MARTON: It was.

THE COMTE: Handsome, as you say. Not quite the mien one might expect in a steward.

MARTON: Yet, I beg your pardon, Monsieur, he is an honest man.

THE COMTE: Is there no way of rectifying that? Araminte does not, I believe, entirely dislike me, yet she is slow in coming to a decision, and it would complete her resolution if she were told that the outcome of our dispute might not be in her favour. She would not then wish to endure the vexations of a lawsuit. As for this steward, if money alone may serve to recruit him to our interests, I shall not leave him unfurnished.

MARTON: Oh no! He is not a man to be influenced by such means. He's the most disinterested fellow in the whole of France . . .

THE COMTE: Worse luck! They're a good-for-nothing lot.

MARTON: Leave him to me.

Scene V

THE COMTE, HARLEQUIN, MARTON

HARLEQUIN: Mademoiselle, there is a man here looking for another man; have you any idea who it might be?

MARTON, *sharply*: And who is this "other"? Who is he looking for?

HARLEQUIN: Upon my word I've no idea; that's what I came to ask you.

MARTON: Send him in.

HARLEQUIN, *motioning* THE BOY *in from the wings*: Ho, boy! Come in here and tell them why you've come.

Scene VI

THE COMTE, THE BOY, MARTON, HARLEQUIN

MARTON: Whom did you want?

THE BOY: Mademoiselle, I am looking for a certain gentleman to whom I must deliver a portrait with its case which he ordered from us; he left instructions that it was to be delivered to none but himself, and that he would come to fetch it, but since my father must depart on a short journey tomorrow, he has sent me to deliver it to the gentleman, and I was told that here I should learn where I might find him. I know him at sight, but not his name.

MARTON: Is it not for you, Monsieur le Comte?

THE COMTE: No indeed; I know nothing of it.

THE BOY: My business is not with Monsieur, Mademoiselle; it is a different gentleman.

MARTON: And where was it that you got your instructions to look here?

THE BOY: At the house of a certain solicitor named Monsieur Remy.

THE COMTE: Ah, is that not Madame's solicitor? Show us the case.

THE BOY: Monsieur, I have been forbidden to do so; I am not at liberty to give it to anyone but its owner: the lady's portrait is inside.

THE COMTE: A lady's portrait! What is the meaning of this? Might it be a portrait of Araminte? I will hear an explanation of this matter, and presently.

Scene VII

MARTON, THE BOY

MARTON: It was a mistake to mention the portrait in front of him. I know who it is you are looking for: Monsieur Remy's nephew.

THE BOY: I think that must be the gentleman, Mademoiselle.

MARTON: A great gentleman whose name is Monsieur Dorante.

THE BOY: That sounds as though it might be his name.

MARTON: Yes, he has told me about it; I am in his confidence. Have you examined the portrait?

THE BOY: No, I did not even notice who it looked like.

MARTON: Ah, did you not? It is, in fact, a portrait of me. Monsieur Dorante is not here, and is not expected for some time. Your only course is to entrust the portrait, case and all, to me; you can do so in perfect safety; you will, in fact, be doing Monsieur Dorante a favour. As you can see, I am thoroughly acquainted with the affair.

THE BOY: It does seem so, I must say. Here you are Mademoiselle. Be so good as to deliver it to him when he returns.

MARTON: Oh, never fear!

THE BOY: There is a certain trifling sum which he still owes us for it, but if I can I shall call again soon, and perhaps if he is not here you will have the goodness to pay it.

213

MARTON: Without hesitation. Go.
  Aside:
  Here is Dorante.
  To THE BOY:
  Go now, quickly.

Scene VIII

MARTON, DORANTE

MARTON, *alone for a moment; elated*: A portrait of me! It must be. Oh, the delightful man! Monsieur Remy was right when he said that Dorante's attention had been fixed on me for some time.

DORANTE, *entering*: Mademoiselle, have you not seen a certain person who came here just now? Harlequin thinks he was looking for me.

MARTON, *gazing tenderly at him*: What a dear, delightful person you are, Dorante! I should be lacking in all reason if I did not love you. There, set your mind at rest: the artisan has come, I have spoken to him, I have the case and the portrait; I have it.

DORANTE: I've no idea . . .

MARTON: Now, now, no need for mystery. I have it, I say, and I'm not in the least annoyed. I will give it to you when I've seen it. Now go: here is Madame with her mother and the comte. Discussing this very matter, perhaps. Leave me to appease them; don't wait.

DORANTE, *laughing as he goes*: Success, oh complete, in that quarter! She's taken the change better than anything I could have hoped for.

Scene IX

ARAMINTE, THE COMTE, MME. ARGANTE, MARTON

ARAMINTE: Marton, what is this that Monsieur le Comte tells me about a portrait which was brought here for someone whose name was not divulged, and which, it has been suspected, is a likeness of me? Enlighten me.

MARTON, *dreamily*: It's nothing, Madame. I will tell you all about it. I unravelled the mystery after Monsieur le Comte had gone; there is nothing to alarm yourself about. It does not even concern you.

THE COMTE: How do you know, Mademoiselle? You have not seen the portrait.

MARTON: Never mind; it is just as though I had seen it. I know who the original is; there is no need for you to fret.

THE COMTE: It is a portrait of a woman, so much is certain; and it was to this house that it was brought for delivery to the person who commissioned it; and that person is certainly not I.

MARTON: Agreed. But must I repeat that it has nothing to do with Madame, nor with you either?

ARAMINTE: Very well, if you have discovered the secret, pray tell us whom it does concern, for I should like to know. There have been theories bruited which have been not at all to my liking. Speak.

MME. ARGANTE: Yes, there is an air of mystery about it all which is disagreeable. Still, you must not vex yourself overmuch, daughter: Monsieur le Comte loves you, and a little jealousy, however groundless, is not unbecoming in a suitor.

THE COMTE: I am not jealous of anyone but this unknown person who dares indulge in the pleasure of having a portrait of Madame.

ARAMINTE, *hotly*: As you please, Monsieur. But I have understood your insinuations, and I mistrust that species of wit. Well, Marton?

MARTON: Well, Madame; what a turmoil! It's a portrait of me.

THE COMTE: Of you?

MARTON: Yes, of me. And why not, pray? There's no call for your astonishment.

MME. ARGANTE: I am rather with Monsieur le Comte; it does strike me as singular.

MARTON: Upon my word, Madame, and without vanity: they paint people every day, just because they're swells, who could not compare with me.

ARAMINTE: And who was it who entailed so much expense on your account?

MARTON: A most charming gentleman who loves me, who is rich in delicacy and choice sentiments, and who pays me court; and since I must name him, it is Dorante.

ARAMINTE: My steward?

215

MARTON: None other.

MME. ARGANTE: The ass, with his sentiments!

ARAMINTE, *sharply*: Indeed! You are trying to deceive us. I ask you when he has had time to have you painted since he has been here.

MARTON: Today was not the first he saw me.

ARAMINTE, *hotly*: Give it to me.

MARTON: I have not yet opened the case, but it is my face you will see there.

ARAMINTE *opens it, and all look.*

THE COMTE: Ah! Just as I suspected: it is Madame.

MARTON: Madame! . . . It is true, and oh how sadly I have been mistaken.

Aside:

Dubois was right, after all.

ARAMINTE, *aside*: As for me, I see quite clearly.

To MARTON:

By what chance did you come to suppose it was a portrait of you?

MARTON: Upon my word, Madame, it might have deceived another as utterly as it did me. Monsieur Remy told me that his nephew loved me, and that he hoped to marry us; Dorante was present and did not say no. He rejected, before my very eyes, a marriage which would have made him indescribably rich; whereupon his uncle turned on me and said I was the cause of his refusal. Then a man came bringing this portrait, inquiring here for the person who had commissioned it; I questioned him; in every reply he made me I recognized Dorante. It was a small portrait of a woman; Dorante loved me sufficiently to refuse a fortune for me; I concluded that it would be I whose portrait he would have had painted. Was it absurd to think that? My conclusion was mistaken. I abjure it; so much honour was not meant for me. I think I see now the full extent of my error, and I shall say no more.

ARAMINTE: Ah, there is nothing so difficult to divine in this. You make pretense of outrage, of astonishment, Monsieur le Comte; there has been a certain misunderstanding over the very extremity of your feigned passion; but I am not to be duped so. It was to you that the portrait was to be delivered. A gentleman whose name is not known, who is to be sought here: it is you, Monsieur, it is you.

MARTON, *gravely*: I do not think so.

MME. ARGANTE: Yes, yes, it is Monsieur; what is the use of denying it? When you are on such terms as you are with my daughter, there is no great crime in it. Come, come: confess.

THE COMTE, *coldly*: No, Madame, it is not I, upon my honour. I am not acquainted with this Monsieur Remy: how could he or his know to direct inquiries after me to this house? It is not possible.

MME. ARGANTE, *assuming a thoughtful air*: I had not considered that circumstance.

ARAMINTE: Well, and what is a circumstance more or less? I do not scorn it, in any case. And, come what may, I shall keep it, no one else shall have it. But what is this noise I hear? Marton, go and see.

Scene X

ARAMINTE, THE COMTE, MME. ARGANTE, MARTON, DUBOIS, HAR-
LEQUIN

HARLEQUIN, *as he enters with* DUBOIS: You're a sweet baboon!

MARTON: What is the matter between you?

DUBOIS: If I uttered a single word of what I know, your master would be dismissed immediately.

HARLEQUIN: You? That's how much we care for you and your whole scummy clan.

DUBOIS: What a beating I should give you, but for my respect for Madame!

HARLEQUIN: Approach, approach; there she is, there is Madame.

ARAMINTE: What are you quarrelling over? What is it about?

MME. ARGANTE: Come, Dubois. Tell us what you were saying to Dorante's discredit. It would be interesting to know what it was.

HARLEQUIN: Tell her what you said.

ARAMINTE: Be still; let him speak.

DUBOIS: For the past hour he has been assailing me with every abuse, Madame.

HARLEQUIN: I look after my master's interests, that is what I receive wages for doing, and I will not suffer an Ostrogoth to threaten my master with a single word; I have come to you to seek justice, Madame.

MME. ARGANTE: But once again, may we know what it was that moved Dubois to speak? That is the first consideration.

HARLEQUIN: I defy him to repeat so much as a single letter.

DUBOIS: I was carried away with anger, Madame, when I uttered that threat. And the cause of our dispute is as follows: when I was putting Monsieur Dorante's apartment to rights, my glance fell, quite by chance, upon a painting in which Madame is depicted. I deemed it necessary to remove it, for it had no business where it was, and decency forbade me to leave it there. And so reasoning, I was just reaching up to unhook it, when this oaf rushed in, forced me to desist, and very narrowly indeed we escaped coming to blows.

HARLEQUIN: I should think so; and what should possess you to want to remove that picture? It is a lovely painting, a painting which my master, not a moment before, had been gazing at with the keenest appreciation. It is true: I saw him, drinking it in with all his heart; and then this clod takes a fancy to deprive the good man of a painting which gives him pleasure. There is malice for you! Relieve him of some other article if you think him overfurnished, but leave him that picture, pachyderm.

DUBOIS: And I tell you it shall not be left there; that I will take it down myself; that you will rue every word you have spoken, and that Madame would insist that I remove it.

ARAMINTE: Why, what does it matter? The absurdity: to take it upon yourselves to brew up such a tempest over an old picture that was hung there for want of another place, and has happened to remain there. Go; leave us. Is it worth the words to dismiss it?

MME. ARGANTE, *sourly*: You will excuse me, daughter, but the picture does not belong there, and without question should be removed. Your steward would do well to discontinue his artistic meditations.

ARAMINTE, *smiling, teasing*: You are right, of course! I doubt that he will miss them.

To HARLEQUIN *and* DUBOIS:

Go, both of you.

Scene XI

ARAMINTE, THE COMTE, MME. ARGANTE, MARTON

THE COMTE, *mocking*: It is evident, at least, that in this bookkeeper you have a man of taste.

ARAMINTE, *ironically*: Yes, your observation is correct. It is, as you infer, extraordinary that he should have noticed that painting.

MME. ARGANTE: Daughter, I have never for an instant approved of that man; you know it; my judgement is not commonly unreliable, and I do not like him. Now mark what I say; you heard the threat Dubois made when he spoke of him, and I repeat, he most assuredly had some grounds for what he said. Question him; let us find out what it is. I am convinced that our little Monsieur is not the man for you at all. It is quite apparent to all of us; only you persist in not seeing it.

MARTON, *negligently*: As for me, I am not satisfied.

ARAMINTE, *laughing ironically*: And just what, pray, is so apparent to you, that I do not see at all? I am without the necessary powers of penetration; I confess, it entirely escapes me; I can see no good cause to deprive myself of a man who came to me on excellent recommendation, a man of some not inconsiderable merit, who has served me well, perhaps only too well: that much, I may tell you, has not escaped my penetration.

MME. ARGANTE: Oh, how blind you are!

ARAMINTE: Not so blind, perhaps, as you suppose; to each his own lights. I consent, however, to listen to what Dubois may have to say; that advice is sound, and I approve. Marton, go and tell him that I wish to speak with him. If he can present me with sufficient reasons why I should dismiss this steward who was so abandoned as to glance at a painting, the man shall not long remain in my house. Otherwise, you will be so good as to subscribe to my retaining him in my service until such time as he should provoke my displeasure.

MME. ARGANTE, *hotly*: Ha! He will provoke it. I'll say no more, but wait for stronger proofs.

THE COMTE: As for me, Madame, I confess that I am afraid he might do me a disservice where you are concerned, that he might inspirit you with a determination to take your case to law, whereas the tender inclination I bear you had led me to hope that he might dissuade you from such a course. However, he will counsel you in vain, for I hereby declare that I renounce all disputes between us, that I desire, as arbiter of our disagreement, no one but you and your agents, and that I had rather lose everything than debate the smallest trifle.

MME. ARGANTE, *positively*: But what would there be to dispute?
The marriage would liquidate your differences, and so your
account is settled.

THE COMTE: As for Dorante, I shall say nothing. I shall return
later to determine what opinion you then entertain towards
him, and if you discharge him, as I trust you will, it rests
entirely with you to decide whether or not to engage the
person whom at first I offered to you, and whom I shall
retain still for a time.

MME. ARGANTE: I shall do as Monsieur has done: I will not further
discuss anything with you, either. You would only accuse
me of having hallucinations, and your obstinacy in the end
would carry you beyond our help. I am counting heavily
upon Dubois, whom I see coming, and with whom we will
leave you.

Scene XII

DUBOIS, ARAMINTE

DUBOIS: I was told that you wished to speak with me, Madame.

ARAMINTE: Come here. You are most imprudent, Dubois, most
indiscreet. To think how exceptionally I esteemed you, when
you did not so much as heed what I said to you. I commended
you to keep silence concerning this matter of Dorante. You
were aware of the ridiculous consequences; you gave me your
promise. Why, then, must you make an issue of this miserable painting, with a fool whom you might have known
would create an unimaginable uproar and would come here
hot to uphold a flock of suggestions exactly suited to fill the
company with notions I despair to think of them entertaining?

DUBOIS: Upon my word, Madame, I thought it was a trifling thing
that would proceed no further, and in any case my action
was motivated by nothing but respect and zeal.

ARAMINTE, *heatedly*: Oh, bother your zeal! It was not that that I
asked for, and it is not that that I need. It is your silence
that I require in order to extricate myself from my present
absurd predicament, into which I have been precipitated by
no one but you. For had it not been for you, I should never

have been aware of his love for me, since I should certainly not have taken it upon me to discover it for myself.

DUBOIS: I fully perceive my error.

ARAMINTE: So much for your quarrel. But then why cry out, "If I uttered a single word"? Is anything else the matter with you?

DUBOIS: That was a further case of my mistaken zeal.

ARAMINTE: Oh, enough! But from now on silence, do you hear, silence. I wish I could make you forget what you have told me.

DUBOIS: Oh, I stand utterly corrected.

ARAMINTE: You may thank your heedless blundering for it, for I have been forced to call you here, on pretext of asking you what you know of him. My mother and Monsieur le Comte expect you to ply me with startling revelations: what report can I give them, at present?

DUBOIS: Ah, nothing is easier to accommodate. You can report that certain persons acquainted with him have told me that he is a man incapable of performing the duties you require of him in your household, although he is extremely clever, to say the least: it is not that in which he is lacking.

ARAMINTE: Well and good; but there is one disadvantage, if he is in fact competent: they will tell me to dismiss him, and it is not yet time for that. I have given the matter further thought: prudence forbids me to do anything so rash. I must adopt strategems, and proceed with the utmost circumspection, to deal with a passion as violent as you have described in him. Otherwise, who knows, perhaps in his grief he might lose all restraint and resort to anything. How could I be sure of my own safety, if he were driven to desperation? It is no longer my need for his services, but a consideration for my own well-being that constrains me.

Softening her tone.

Unless what Marton says should be true, and in that case I should have nothing to fear. She pretends that Dorante had already seen her, some time since, at Monsieur Remy's, and that the solicitor has gone so far as to tell her, in Dorante's presence, that the young man had loved her all that time, and that they must marry. I should like to think that that were true.

DUBOIS: Nonsense! Dorante never saw Marton, either at close hand or at a distance. It was Monsieur Remy himself who sold Marton that fable, as a device to get them married, and

"I did not dare contradict him," Dorante told me, "for fear of gaining the girl's ill will, for her mistress thinks highly of her, and heeds what she says; and so afterwards she thought it was for her sake that I refused the fifteen thousand pounds' rent that were offered me."

ARAMINTE, *casually*: He has told you the whole story, then?

DUBOIS: Yes; only a moment ago in the garden, where he flung himself at my feet, pleading with me to reveal nothing of his passion, and to forget what a tempest of rage he hurled upon me when I left him. I told him that I would say nothing, but that I would under no circumstances remain in the same house with him, and that he must go; which wrung from him sighs and torrents of tears, so that I left him in the saddest state imaginable.

ARAMINTE: Oh, the poor man! You must not torment him. You see, I have reason to insist that we must proceed cautiously with a temper such as his; you can see that quite well. Ah, and I cherished hopes for this marriage with Marton; I thought he would forget me; and not at all, there is nothing in it.

DUBOIS, *as though going*: Pure fable. Did Madame have anything further to say to me?

ARAMINTE: Wait. What can I do? If only he had given me, in his conversation with me, some cause to complain of him! But not the smallest hint has escaped his lips; I know nothing of his love except what you have told me, which is not sufficient grounds to justify his dismissal. It is true that I should be offended if he were to speak; on the other hand, such offense would be convenient.

DUBOIS: True, true; Monsieur Dorante is unworthy of Madame. If he were heir to a larger fortune, since his birth is above reproach, it would be a different matter; but he is not rich except in merit, which is not enough.

ARAMINTE, *sadly*: No, it's true; such are the decrees of decorum. I do not know what I shall do with him. I do not know at all. I will see.

DUBOIS: Oh, Madame, it's quite simple. You have a superb pretext: that portrait which Marton thought was hers, or so she's told me.

ARAMINTE: Oh no, I could not use that against him. It was the comte who commissioned it.

DUBOIS: Not at all. It was Dorante; I've heard him speak of it, and it was still unfinished two months ago when I left his service.

ARAMINTE: You are excused now. I cannot spend the whole day chattering with you. If anyone should ask me what you have told me about him, I shall repeat what we agreed upon a moment ago. Here he is: I will try to lay a trap for him.

DUBOIS: Yes, Madame; perhaps he will declare himself, and then, without another word I will say to him, "Go."

ARAMINTE: Leave us.

Scene XIII

DORANTE, ARAMINTE, DUBOIS

DUBOIS, *as he goes, pretending to hurry past* DORANTE: I cannot possibly give him instructions, but whether he tells her now, or not, things cannot go other than well.

DORANTE: Madame, I have come to beg your protection. I am wretched, and tormented by uncertainty. I have refused everything for the honour of being with you, and I am more ardently devoted to you than I can express; no one could serve you more faithfully or with more entire disinterest; and nevertheless I cannot be certain of retaining my position. Everyone here is hostile to me, everyone persecutes me, and conspires to accomplish my dismissal. I am in despair; I dread to think that you might yield to the enmity they all bear me, and then I should know the utter depths of affliction.

ARAMINTE, *softly, sweetly*: Set your mind at ease. You are not dependent upon those who dislike you. They have not succeeded in damaging my opinion of you, and all their little intrigues will come to nothing: I am the mistress.

DORANTE, *feigning worry*: I have no support but yours, Madame.

ARAMINTE: It will not fail you. But let me give you one word of advice. Do not let them see your disquiet, for that would bring them to doubt your capabilities, and in such case it would appear to them that you were extraordinarily indebted to me for retaining you in my service.

DORANTE: They would not be mistaken, Madame: I am overwhelmed with gratitude for your goodness.

ARAMINTE: Well, well; but you need not impress it upon them. I am pleased with your devotion and obliged to you for your loyalty, but dissimulate a little: it is perhaps precisely those qualities which have turned them against you. In that matter of the lawsuit, for example, you refused to impose upon my

223

trust for the sake of their interests; do, now, make yourself agreeable to their demands in that; recover their favour in that way; I authorize you to. The outcome will convince them that you have served them well, for, all things considered, I have determined to marry Monsieur le Comte.

DORANTE, *distraught*: Determined, Madame?

ARAMINTE: Yes, my mind is made up. The comte will believe that your influence contributed to my decision; I shall tell him so myself, and I promise you that you will retain your position here; I give you my word.
Aside:
He has turned quite pale.

DORANTE: What a difference, to me, Madame!

ARAMINTE, *with decision*: None whatever; do not let it trouble you. And now write the letter which I shall dictate to you; you will find all that is necessary there on the table.

DORANTE: Ah . . . to whom, Madame?

ARAMINTE: To the comte, who left here gravely troubled and anxious. I intend to give him a most pleasant surprise in the little note which you are about to write to him, in my name.
DORANTE *continues to stare off into space; in his distraction he neglects to go to the table.*

ARAMINTE: Well, will you not go to the table? What are you dreaming about?

DORANTE, *still distracted, as though in his sleep*: Yes, Madame.

ARAMINTE, *aside, as he seats himself*: He does not know what he is doing. We shall see how long that can go on.

DORANTE, *looking for paper*: Oh, Dubois has deceived me!

ARAMINTE, *businesslike*: Are you ready to begin?

DORANTE: Madame, I cannot find any paper.

ARAMINTE, *going to the table*: Find no paper! It is there in front of you.

DORANTE: So it is.

ARAMINTE: Write: "Come at once, Monsieur; your offer of marriage has been accepted." Have you written that?

DORANTE: What, Madame?

ARAMINTE: Have you not been listening to me? "Your offer of marriage has been accepted; I am writing to you at Madame's bidding, who awaits your arrival to tell you herself."
Aside:
He is in torment, yet he does not say a word; will he never speak? "Do not ascribe this decision to any fear of Madame's as to the outcome of a dubious lawsuit."

DORANTE: I have assured you that you would win the case, Madame. Your claim is by no means dubious.

ARAMINTE: No matter. To conclude: "No, Monsieur; I have been instructed by her to assure you that nothing but a true recognition of your merits has led her to this decision."

DORANTE: Heavens! I am lost. But Madame, he does not hold the least attraction for you.

ARAMINTE: Conclude, I say. "Recognition of your merits has led her to this decision." Your hand: it seems to be trembling. You are quite altered. What is the cause of this? Do you feel ill?

DORANTE: I do not feel well, Madame.

ARAMINTE: What? Overtaken so suddenly! Extraordinary. Fold the letter and address it: "To Monsieur le Comte Dorimont." Tell Dubois to take it to him.

Aside:

My heart is pounding!

To DORANTE:

You have written it all crooked. The address is hardly legible.

Aside:

He will never be persuaded this way.

DORANTE, *aside*: May this not be merely to try me? Dubois gave me no hint of anything.

Scene XIV

ARAMINTE, DORANTE, MARTON

MARTON: Madame, I am delighted to find Monsieur in your company: he will give immediate confirmation to what I am about to tell you. On several occasions you have offered to lend your most generous auspices to my marriage, and until now my inclinations have never led me to profit by your goodness. Today Monsieur asked for my hand; he has just refused an offer entailing infinitely greater riches, all for my sake, or at least so he has led me to believe, and I should welcome his further explanation; but as I desire to be dependent upon no one but you, Madame, it is from you that he must ask for my hand in marriage. Therefore, Monsieur, your only course is to address yourself to Madame. If she will confer me upon you, you will need to ply no further suasions to obtain my consent.

Scene XV

DORANTE, ARAMINTE

ARAMINTE, *aside, in great agitation*: The fool!
To DORANTE:
I am delighted to learn what she has told me. You have made a wise choice; she is a charming girl, and her character is excellent.

DORANTE, *prostrate*: Alas! Madame, I have never given her a thought.

ARAMINTE: Never given her a thought! She says that you love her, and that you had seen her sometime before you came here.

DORANTE, *sadly*: That is an error which Monsieur Remy threw in without consulting me at all, and I did not dare to contradict him for fear of making an enemy of someone so close to you. The same is true of the wealthy match she thinks I refused for her sake; I had nothing to do with that. I am not in a position to bestow my heart upon anyone; I have lost it forever, and the most brilliant fortune imaginable would not tempt me for a moment.

ARAMINTE: You were wrong. You should have informed Marton that she had been deluded.

DORANTE: She might have influenced you not to receive me. Besides, my indifference should have told her the truth.

ARAMINTE: But if the disposition of your heart is such as you have described, what could prompt you to seek service in my house, and to prefer it to another?

DORANTE: I find deeper contentment with you, Madame.

ARAMINTE: There is something incomprehensible about all this! Do you often see the person whom you love?

DORANTE, *downcast as ever*: Not as often as I should like, Madame. And if I saw her every moment of the day, I should still not think it enough.

ARAMINTE, *aside*: How tender are some of the things he says!
Aloud:
Is she unmarried? Has she ever been married?

DORANTE: She is a widow, Madame.

ARAMINTE: And will you not marry her? She loves you, I suppose?

DORANTE: Alas, Madame, she is not even aware that I adore her. Forgive me for using so ardent a term; but I can scarcely mention her without being overcome with passion!

ARAMINTE: It is nothing but my astonishment that makes me question you. You say she does not know that you love her? And yet you have sacrificed your future for her sake? That is quite incredible. How is it, if your love is so fierce, that you have been able to remain silent? One must make some attempt to awaken a love in return, surely; and to do so is natural and pardonable.

DORANTE: Heaven preserve me from daring to conceive the slightest hope! I, be loved! No, Madame. Her station is far above my own. My respect condemns me to silence; and at least I shall die without having suffered the torment of causing her displeasure.

ARAMINTE: I cannot imagine any woman who is worthy of inspiring so extraordinary a passion; I cannot believe that such a woman exists. She is beyond all comparison, then?

DORANTE: Spare me the hazard of praising her, Madame: I should grow distraught in the description of her. There is nothing so beautiful, so delightful, so sweet as she is; and she cannot speak to me nor look at me without redoubling my love.

ARAMINTE, *lowering her eyes*: But your conduct violates good sense. What can you hope from this love for someone who will never know that you love her? That is bizarre indeed. What can you hope for?

DORANTE: The pleasure of seeing her sometimes, and of being with her, is the end of my aspirations.

ARAMINTE: With her? Can you forget that you are here?

DORANTE: I mean with her portrait, when I do not see her.

ARAMINTE: Her portrait? Have you had one painted?

DORANTE: No, Madame, but for my own amusement I have learned to paint, and I painted her myself. I should have been without a portrait of her if I had to rely upon the talents of another.

ARAMINTE, *aside*: I must force this to an issue.

Aloud:

Show me this portrait.

DORANTE: I beg you to excuse me from that, Madame. Though my love may be hopeless, I owe it none the less to the object of my passion to preserve her identity an inviolable secret.

ARAMINTE: There is a portrait that has fallen, quite by chance, into my hands. It was found here.
Showing him the case.
See if this is not the portrait in question.

DORANTE: It cannot be.

ARAMINTE, *opening the case*: It would, in fact, be something of a surprise: but examine it for yourself.

DORANTE: Oh, Madame, believe me, I would have lost my life a thousand times over, rather than have confessed to what has been disclosed to you by accident. How can I expiate . . .
He throws himself at her feet.

ARAMINTE: Dorante, I am not angry with you. Your distress moves me to take pity on you. Come, I pardon you.

MARTON, *who appears, and then flees*: Ah!
DORANTE *rises hastily.*

ARAMINTE: Oh, heavens, it was Marton! She saw you.

DORANTE, *pretending to be disconcerted*: No, Madame, no; I do not think so; she did not come in.

ARAMINTE: She saw you, I say. Leave me; go at once. I cannot bear the sight of you. Give me my letter.
When he has gone.
This is what comes of keeping him in my service!

Scene XVI

ARAMINTE, DORANTE

DUBOIS: Has Dorante declared himself, Madame? Will it be necessary for me to speak to him?

ARAMINTE: No, he said nothing of it to me. I remarked nothing remotely resembling what you described to me, and to avoid any more such complications, do not meddle further in the matter.
She goes.

DUBOIS: Well, so it has come to the crisis!

Scene XVII

DUBOIS, DORANTE

DORANTE: Ah, Dubois.

DUBOIS: Go away.

DORANTE: I do not know what I should expect to result from the conversation I have just had with her.

DUBOIS: What are you dreaming of? She is not two steps from here: do you want to lose everything?

DORANTE: You must relieve me . . .

DUBOIS: Go into the garden.

DORANTE: Of a doubt . . .

DUBOIS: Into the garden, I tell you; I will come to you presently.

DORANTE: But . . .

DUBOIS: I am not listening.

DORANTE: I am more apprehensive than ever.

Act Three

Scene I

DORANTE, DUBOIS

DUBOIS: No, I say; we must lose no time. Is the letter ready?

DORANTE, *showing it to him*: Yes, here it is, and I've written on the outside "Rue du Figuier."

DUBOIS: Are you quite sure that Harlequin is not acquainted with that part of the city?

DORANTE: He told me he had no knowledge of it.

DUBOIS: Have you instructed him to ask for directions either from Marton or me?

DORANTE: Certainly, and I shall tell him again.

DUBOIS: Go, then, and give it to him: I will see to the rest as far as it concerns Marton. I shall go now and find her.

DORANTE: I must confess to you that I feel somewhat hesitant. Are we not being overhasty with Araminte? Do you wish to further embarrass her, in her present agitation, by presenting her with the sudden revelation of our whole venture?

DUBOIS: Yes, yes, we must give her no quarter. It must be struck home while she is still dazed with the last blow. She no longer knows what she is doing. Didn't you notice how she fibbed to me, pretending that you had told her nothing? Ah, I will teach her to try to solicit my offices as a confidant, for the purposes of her fraudulent love for you!

DORANTE: How I suffered during that last conversation with her! Why, since you knew that she wanted me to declare myself, did you not make some signal to tell me?

DUBOIS: That would have been pretty, my word! She wouldn't have noticed or anything, would she? And besides, as it was, your distress was the more convincing. Are you grieving over the effect you produced? Monsieur has suffered! God's truth, I'd say this venture was worth a bit of disquietude.

DORANTE: Do you know what will happen? She will make up her mind, and dismiss me on the instant.

DUBOIS: I defy her to. It is too late; the moment for courage is past; now she will have to marry us.

DORANTE: Have a care: you see how her mother is tiring her out.

DUBOIS: I should be most annoyed if she let her get her rest.

DORANTE: Marton's catching sight of me at her feet has thrown her into confusion.

DUBOIS: Confusion indeed! She is not confused. She has not yet begun to be confused! It was I, when I saw the trend that the conversation was taking, who sent Marton back again.

DORANTE: Be that as it may; Araminte told me that she could not bear the sight of me.

DUBOIS: And with good provocation. Would you expect her to retain her good humour with a man whom she must love in spite of herself? Do you suppose such a position agreeable? You plunder her of her most treasured possession, her heart, and do you expect the woman not to cry out? Come, come, show a little more sense; allow yourself to be led.

DORANTE: But you cannot imagine: I love her, and if our too great haste were to prove our undoing, you would plunge me into desperation.

DUBOIS: But I know very well that you love her: that is precisely why I refuse to listen to you. Are you in a fit condition to weigh and decide anything? Come, you make a mock of yourself. Leave it to a man of cool judgement. Go; the more particularly since I see Marton coming, which is most convenient and to the point: I must try to keep her amused while you give Harlequin the message.

Scene II

DUBOIS, MARTON

MARTON, *sadly*: I was looking for you.

DUBOIS: What service can I render you, Mademoiselle?

MARTON: It was true, just as you told me, Dubois.

DUBOIS: What did I tell you? I cannot remember.

MARTON: That this steward had dared to fix his eyes upon Madame.

DUBOIS: Oh yes! You speak of that look which I saw him turn upon her. Indeed, I have never forgotten it. The glance itself was nothing. But there was something in it which was not precisely what it should have been.

MARTON: There, then! Dubois, we must apply ourselves to getting that man dismissed from the house.

231

DUBOIS: Upon my soul, as hard as you like; I will not spare myself. I have already told Madame that I have been assured that he is utterly ignorant of business.

MARTON: But is that all that you know about him? I speak as well for Madame Argante and Monsieur le Comte: we are afraid that you may not have told Madame everything, or else that she may be keeping it from us. Use no pretenses with us; you will not be sorry.

DUBOIS: Upon my word, I know of nothing but his incompetence, and I have informed Madame of that.

MARTON: Do not dissemble.

DUBOIS: I a dissembler! I keep a secret! You have come to the wrong man! When it comes to discretion, I might as well have been a woman. I beg you to forgive me for the comparison, but I make it only to set your mind at rest.

MARTON: He loves Madame; that is quite certain.

DUBOIS: No one could doubt it; I have gone so far as to treat her to my own thoughts on that subject.

MARTON: And what was her answer?

DUBOIS: That I was a fool. She is so prejudiced . . .

MARTON: Prejudiced to a point I dare not say, Dubois.

DUBOIS: Oh, the devil stands to lose nothing, and I don't either: I get your meaning.

MARTON: Your face tells me that you know more than I do about that.

DUBOIS: Not at all, I swear to you. But more immediately, he called Harlequin to him only a moment ago to give him a letter to deliver: if we could seize that, perhaps we might learn something more.

MARTON: A letter! I should say so. We must neglect nothing. I will go this minute and speak to Harlequin, if he has not already left.

DUBOIS: You need not go far: I think that is he coming.

Scene III

DUBOIS, MARTON, HARLEQUIN

HARLEQUIN, *catching sight of* DUBOIS: Ah, there you are, botched face!

DUBOIS: Oh, come, do you think that your own countenance is so lovely that you can afford to mock at mine?

MARTON: What do you want, Harlequin?

HARLEQUIN: To ask you: do you perhaps know where the Rue du Figuier lives, Mademoiselle?

MARTON: Yes.

HARLEQUIN: Because my colleague, whom I serve, told me to take this letter to someone who is in that street, and since I do not know where it is, he told me to ask you or that animal there for directions, but that animal there is not worthy that I should speak to him, except to insult him. I would rather the devil had run off with all the streets than learn to make out one of them through the offices of a lout like him.

DUBOIS, *aside to* MARTON: Take the letter.

Aloud:

No, no, Mademoiselle, do not tell him anything. Let him find it for himself.

HARLEQUIN: Will you be still?

MARTON, *casually*: Do not interrupt him, Dubois. Would you like to give me the letter? I shall have occasion presently to send into that part of the city, and the bearer will see that it reaches its address.

HARLEQUIN: Ah, now that is pleasant! You are a considerate and accommodating young lady, Mademoiselle.

DUBOIS, *as he goes*: You are little less than a saint to waste your efforts on that good-for-nothing.

HARLEQUIN: Oh, the pickthief! Go, go find the picture and see how it mocks you.

MARTON, *alone with* HARLEQUIN: Do not answer him; give me your letter.

HARLEQUIN: Here you are, Mademoiselle. You render me a service which contributes not a little to my comfort. When you require someone to run an errand for your most obliging self, see that you employ no other postillion than me.

MARTON: It will be delivered with the greatest care.

HARLEQUIN: Yes, I beg you, commend them to be precise, because of Monsieur Dorante, who deserves every kind of fidelity.

MARTON, *aside*: The wretch!

HARLEQUIN, *as he goes*: I am your eternal servant.

MARTON: Adieu.

HARLEQUIN, *returning*: If you see him, do not tell him that someone else is looking for the address instead of me.

Scene IV

MME. ARGANTE, THE COMTE, MARTON

MARTON, *alone for a moment*: Not a word to disclose that I have seen the contents of this.

MME. ARGANTE, *entering*: Well, Marton, what have you learned from Dubois?

MARTON: Nothing which you did not already know, Madame, and that is not enough.

MME. ARGANTE: Dubois is a rascal, and is deceiving us.

MARTON: It is true that there was a certain portent about him which seemed to signify something further.

MME. ARGANTE: Whatever it may be, I shall await Monsieur Remy, whom I have sent for; and if he does not relieve us of this person, my daughter shall know that he dares to love her; I have made up my mind. We have the strongest presumptions, and were it only in the interests of propriety, she must rid herself of him. At the same time I have summoned the steward whom Monsieur le Comte proposed. He is here; I will present him there and then.

MARTON: I doubt whether you will succeed, if we learn nothing new. But perhaps I, perhaps I myself may have his dismissal in my grasp . . . Here is Monsieur Remy; I have no time to tell you more; I shall go and see.
She starts out.

Scene V

M. REMY, MME. ARGANTE, THE COMTE, MARTON

M. REMY, *to* MARTON, *as she goes*: Good day, niece, since after all you will be my niece soon enough. Do you know why I was called here?

MARTON, *brusquely*: Go on, Monsieur, and look somewhere else for your niece; I have no taste for dreary wags.
She goes.

M. REMY: There's an uncivil little girl!
To MME. ARGANTE:
I was told you had sent for me to come here, Madame; what is the nature of the business?

MME. ARGANTE, *sourly*: Ah, it is you, Monsieur solicitor?

M. REMY: Yes, Madame, I warrant you it is none other than myself.

MME. ARGANTE: And whatever prompted you, may I ask, to encumber us with a steward of your stamp?

M. REMY: And by what chance has Madame found any cause to complain of him?

MME. ARGANTE: Let us say simply that we would most happily dispense with the present which you have made us.

M. REMY: My word, Madame, if he does not suit your taste, you are confoundedly hard to please.

MME. ARGANTE: He is your nephew, I believe.

M. REMY: Yes, Madame.

MME. ARGANTE: Well, his kinship to you notwithstanding, you would do us a great favour in taking him away.

M. REMY: It was not to you that I presented him.

MME. ARGANTE: No, but it is we whom he displeases, myself and Monsieur le Comte there, who is to marry my daughter.

M. REMY, *raising his voice*: That is news! But Madame, since he is no retainer of yours, it strikes me that it is not essential that he should meet with your approval. It was never stipulated that he must please you; that was not so much as considered; and as long as he suits Madame Argante everyone should be content, and if they aren't, so much the worse for them. What is the meaning of all this?

MME. ARGANTE: Your tone is insolent, Monsieur Remy.

M. REMY: Upon my word, your compliments are not well chosen to soften it, Madame Argante.

THE COMTE: Gently, Monsieur Solicitor, gently; it seems to me that you are in the wrong.

M. REMY: As you please, Monsieur le Comte, as you please; but it is no affair of yours. As you are well aware, I have not the honour of your acquaintance, and there is nothing to be considered between us, not the smallest thing.

THE COMTE: Whether you know me or not, your insistence that your nephew must please Madame is not so inconsiderable a thing. She is not a stranger in this house.

M. REMY: As far as this is concerned, a complete stranger, Monsieur; she could not be more of a stranger. Furthermore, Dorante is a man of honour, and known to be such, a man whom I have vouched for, as I shall continue to do, and Madame has spoken of him just now in a shocking manner.

MME. ARGANTE: Your Dorante is an impertinent fellow.

235

M. REMY: Piffle! The words are meaningless, coming from you.

MME. ARGANTE: Coming from me! Who is this petty practitioner speaking to, Monsieur le Comte? Will not you impose silence upon him?

M. REMY: How's that? Impose silence on me, me, a lawyer? Are you aware that I have been speaking for fifty years, Madame?

MME. ARGANTE: That makes fifty years, then, that you have not known what you were saying.

Scene VI

ARAMINTE, MME. ARGANTE, M. REMY, THE COMTE

ARAMINTE: What's this, what's this? One would have said you were quarrelling.

M. REMY: We are not suffering from a surfeit of peace, and you have come just at the right moment, Madame; we have been discussing Dorante; have you any cause to complain of him?

ARAMINTE: None, that I know of.

M. REMY: Have you noticed in him any lapses from honesty?

ARAMINTE: He? Certainly not. I am satisfied that he is worthy of the highest esteem.

M. REMY: In Madame's argument he figures, nevertheless, as a scoundrel, whom I must deliver you from; and one would be happy to dispense with the present I have made you, and he is an impertinent fellow who displeases Madame, who displeases Monsieur, speaking in his capacity of future husband; and I, for daring to defend him, have been given to understand that I speak gibberish.

ARAMINTE, *coldly*: Gross excesses have been indulged in, in this. I have had no part in it, Monsieur. I would not dream of according you such shameful treatment. As regards Dorante, the best justification he could have is the fact that I retain him. But I came here to inquire one thing, Monsieur le Comte. I am told that there is a man of affairs, a steward, waiting below, whom you have fetched here for me: obviously there has been some mistake.

THE COMTE: Madame, it is true that he came here with me; but it was Madame Argante . . .

MME. ARGANTE: Wait; I will answer her. Yes, daughter, it was I who requested Monsieur to be so kind as to bring this man, to replace the one whom you now have, and whom you will discharge presently; I know what I am about. Furthermore, I have allowed your solicitor to have his say; but he exaggerates.

M. REMY: God bless me!

MME. ARGANTE, *hotly*: Peace! You have said enough.

To ARAMINTE:

I did not say that his nephew was a scoundrel. It is not impossible that he may be one; it would not surprise me.

M. REMY: A misleading parenthesis, with your permission; a damaging supposition, and entirely out of order.

MME. ARGANTE: An honest man he may be; at least we have not the means to prove otherwise, and I should like to believe him so. I have said that he was an impertinent fellow, in fact highly impertinent, and I am right. You say that you will retain him; you will do nothing of the kind.

ARAMINTE, *coldly*: He will remain, I assure you.

MME. ARGANTE: Not at all; you do not know. Would you be disposed to retain a steward who loves you?

M. REMY: Ah, and to whom would you have him attach himself? To you, whom he has nothing to do with?

ARAMINTE: But is it, in fact, essential that my steward should detest me?

MME. ARGANTE: Let us have no equivocations. When I say that he loves you, I mean that he is in love with you, in good French; that he is what is called smitten with love for you; that he sighs for you, that you are the secret object of his affection.

M. REMY: Dorante?

ARAMINTE, *laughing*: The secret object of his affection! Oh, indeed, very secret, I am sure. Dear me, I had no idea that the mere sight of me was so dangerous. But if you have managed, in his case, to uncover secrets of that nature, who knows, perhaps you may be able to reveal that all my retinue is in the same condition. Perhaps they love me too, who can tell? Monsieur Remy, you come to see me rather frequently: I should be delighted to learn that you are in love with me too.

M. REMY: Upon my word, Madame, at my nephew's age I would have come off no better than he has.

MME. ARGANTE: This is no matter for levity, daughter. It has nothing to do with your Monsieur Remy; let us leave the good man at that, and discuss the affair somewhat more seriously. Your other servants do not commission portraits of you; your other servants do not give themelves up in the contemplation of portraits of you; your other servants do not give themselves gallant airs, nor gaze at you as though they were about to swoon.

M. REMY, *to* ARAMINTE: "The good man." I let it pass that time on your account, I may say; but "the good man" is sometimes not so gentle.

ARAMINTE: Indeed, Mother, you would be the first to call me ridiculous if what you are saying were to make the slightest impression upon me. It would be childish of me to dismiss him upon a mere suspicion of that sort. Is it impossible for anyone to see me without falling in love with me? I do not know what I am to do; I must simply get used to it and order my life accordingly. You say you have remarked a certain gallantry in his manner? I had not noticed it, and I shall not reprimand him. That would be bizarre, truly, to be angry with him because he was born handsome. When it comes to that I am like everyone else: I prefer people to present a pleasant appearance.

Scene VII

ARAMINTE, MME. ARGANTE, M. REMY, THE COMTE, DORANTE

DORANTE: I beg you to excuse me for interrupting you, Madame, I have been given reason to presume that my services are no longer agreeable to you, and in the present circumstances it is natural that I should want to learn my fate.

MME. ARGANTE, *ironically*: His fate! The fate of a steward: that is sublime!

M. REMY: And why should he not have a fate?

ARAMINTE, *sharply, to her mother*: His agitation concerns no one but me.

To DORANTE:

What are these circumstances, Monsieur, and what is the cause of your anxiety?

DORANTE: You know it, Madame. There is someone here whom you sent for to occupy my place.

ARAMINTE: That someone has been shamefully deluded. Put your mind at ease: it was not I who fetched him here.

DORANTE: Everything has conspired to deceive me, the more so since Mademoiselle Marton came and informed me most emphatically that within an hour I should no longer be here.

ARAMINTE: Marton has regaled you with nonsense.

MME. ARGANTE: The term she mentioned was too long: he should be leaving almost at once.

M. REMY, *as though aside*: We shall see about that.

ARAMINTE: Dorante, you may proceed with entire composure; if you were the man who in the whole world were least suited to my convenience, you should remain; on this occasion I owe myself no less. I am offended at the conduct which has been adopted with regard to me, and I shall send word to that steward to withdraw; let those who brought him here without consulting me, take him back again, and let there be no further discussion of the matter.

Scene VII

ARAMINTE, MME. ARGANTE, M. REMY, THE COMTE, DORANTE, MARTON

MARTON, *coldly*: Do not be too hasty about sending him away, Madame. I have here a letter of recommendation for him, and it was Monsieur Dorante who wrote it.

ARAMINTE: What!

MARTON, *giving the letter to* THE COMTE: One moment, Madame; it is worth hearing. The letter, I repeat, is from Monsieur.

THE COMTE, *reading aloud*: I beg you, my dear friend, to be at home tomorrow at nine in the evening. I have many things to tell you. I think I must leave the service of the lady whom you know. She cannot longer remain ignorant of the wretched passion for her which I have contracted, and of which I shall never be cured.

MME. ARGANTE: Passion, do you hear, daughter!

THE COMTE, *reading*: A miserable workman, whom I did not expect, came here to deliver to me the case containing that portrait of her which I had painted.

MME. ARGANTE: Am I to understand that this person knows how to paint?

THE COMTE, *reading*: I was absent when he arrived; he left it with a young woman of the house.

MME. ARGANTE, *to* MARTON: Young woman of the house: that concerns you.

THE COMTE, *reading*: It was suspected that the portrait might belong to me: therefore I think it best to reveal all, and in addition to the misery of being dismissed, and of forfeiting the delight of daily seeing her whom I adore . . .

MME. ARGANTE: Whom I adore; oh! Whom I adore!

THE COMTE, *reading*: I shall suffer the knowledge that she despises me.

MME. ARGANTE: He was not far wrong that time, I feel, daughter.

THE COMTE, *reading*: Not because of the meanness of my fortune, for I should not dare to suppose her capable of scorning me for such a reason . . .

MME. ARGANTE: Oh! And why not?

THE COMTE, *reading*: But only because of how slight is my worth in comparison with her, even when it is considered that I am honoured with the esteem of so many worthy persons.

MME. ARGANTE: And what is there about him, pray, that they esteem so highly?

THE COMTE, *reading*: My intention, therefore, is to remain no longer in Paris. You are on the eve of embarking: I am determined to follow you.

MME. ARGANTE: Bon voyage to our gallant.

M. REMY: What a reason for taking a trip!

MME. ARGANTE: Well, are you satisfied now, daughter?

THE COMTE: I should say the clarification was complete.

ARAMINTE, *to* DORANTE: What! Is this letter not a counterfeit? Do you not deny this handwriting?

DORANTE: Madame . . .

ARAMINTE: Leave us.

M. REMY: Well, what of it? He is in love. It was not this morning that handsome young people started the custom. And take him as he is, he did not fling his love at the feet of any of the ones, and there were not a few of them, who would have been delighted to love him in return. This love of his has cost him fifteen thousand pounds per annum rent, not counting the seas which he now intends to traverse; and that is the heart of the trouble. Because after all, if he were rich one person of note would be worthy of another; he would be free to disclose his adoration.

Mimicking MME. ARGANTE.

And it would not be so utterly ridiculous. Settle it as you will; for the rest, account me, Madame, your servant.

He goes.

MARTON: Shall I send for the steward whom Monsieur le Comte brought, Madame?

ARAMINTE: Am I to hear of nothing but stewards? Go: you are most unfortunate in the moments you choose for putting your questions to me.

MARTON *goes.*

MME. ARGANTE: But daughter, she is right. Since it is Monsieur le Comte who answers for this person, there is nothing for you to do but engage him.

ARAMINTE: And I tell you I prefer not to.

THE COMTE: Is it because I am his sponsor, Madame?

ARAMINTE: You may command what interpretation you please, Monsieur, but I prefer not to employ him.

THE COMTE: You explain yourself in this matter with an air of vivacity which astonishes me.

MME. ARGANTE: But indeed, I do not understand you. What have you to be vexed about?

ARAMINTE: Everything; the egregious awkwardness of this whole affair, so disagreeably contrived, and employing means so invidious that I find everything about it offensive.

MME. ARGANTE, *astonished*: I do not understand you at all.

THE COMTE: Although I have had no part in what has happened, I cannot but be too sensible, Madame, of the fact that I am not excluded from your annoyance, and I should be distressed to contribute further to it by my presence.

MME. ARGANTE: No, Monsieur, I will come with you. Daughter, I shall retain Monsieur le Comte with me; I trust you will come and find us before long. You cannot imagine, Araminte: one does not know what to think.

Scene IX

ARAMINTE, DUBOIS

DUBOIS: At last, Madame, judging by what I have seen, you are delivered of him: let him do what he likes with himself now, everyone has seen for themselves how mad he is, and you have nothing further to fear from his sorrows; he has not a word to say. In fact I met him, more dead than alive, just now as I came: he was walking through the gallery on his way to his apartment. How you would have laughed if you could have seen him sigh. I was even a little sorry for him:

he was so wan, so pale, and so sad, that I was afraid he might be ill.

ARAMINTE, *who until now has not looked at him, but remained gazing off into space; her voice raised*: But send someone to look to him! Did no one go after him? Will not you minister to him? Must he be killed, this man?

DUBOIS: I have seen to it, Madame; I called Harlequin, who will not leave him, and I think nothing else will befall him; it is finished, after all. I came merely to tell you one thing, which is that I think he may ask to speak with you, and I would not not advise Madame to see him again: it is not worth the trouble.

ARAMINTE, *dryly*: Do not fret yourself, it is my own affair.

DUBOIS: In a word, you are quit of him, and all by means of that letter which was read to you, and which Mademoiselle Marton, at my suggestion, took from Harlequin. It crossed my mind that the letter might prove useful to you; and what an excellent idea it was, was it not, Madame?

ARAMINTE, *coldly*: What are you saying? Is it to you that I am indebted for the scene which I have just endured?

DUBOIS, *openly*: Yes, Madame.

ARAMINTE: Spiteful lackey! Do not enter my presence ever again.

DUBOIS, *as though astonished*: Alas, Madame, I thought I was acting for the best.

ARAMINTE: Go, wretch! You disobeyed me: I told you not to meddle any further. You have precipitated me into all the vexations that I wished to avoid. It was you who spread all those rumours about him, and it was not devotion to me that urged you to tell me of his love for me, but merely the pleasure of doing harm. I need not have been told; I would never have learned of his love, and I account him most unfortunate to have had anything to do with you, ever; he, who was your master, who was fond of you, who treated you kindly, and who came, and that barely a moment ago, to beg you on his knees to keep his secret. You assassinate him, and you betray me; obviously you are capable of anything. Let me never see you again; I will not hear a word of reply.

DUBOIS, *laughing, as he goes*: There we are: perfect, perfect.

Scene X

ARAMINTE, MARTON

MARTON: Your manner when, a moment ago, you sent me from

the room, persuades me that my presence is no longer a pleasure to you, Madame, and I feel certain therefore that I am doing what would please you most in asking your permission to leave your service.

ARAMINTE, *coldly*: You have it.

MARTON: Do you intend that I should leave this very day, Madame?

ARAMINTE: As you will.

MARTON: Oh, what a sad occasion this is for me!

ARAMINTE: We will not go into details, if you please.

MARTON: I am in despair!

ARAMINTE, *impatiently*: Is it the thought of going that distresses you? Very well then, stay, Mademoiselle, stay: I consent to that too, only let us hear no more of it.

MARTON: After the benefits which you have showered upon me, how could I remain at your side now that I have become an object of your suspicions and lost all your confidence?

ARAMINTE: But what do you want me to confide in you? Am I to invent secrets to tell you?

MARTON: It is true nevertheless that you have given me my dismissal, Madame. What is the cause of my disgrace?

ARAMINTE: It is in your own imagination. You asked my leave to go, and I gave it to you.

MARTON: Ah, Madame, why have you exposed me to the misery of displeasing you? In my ignorance I have persecuted the most charming gentleman in the world, who loves you more than anyone was ever loved.

ARAMINTE, *aside*: Alas!

MARTON: And against whom I bear no ill will. We have just spoken together. I was his enemy, and I am so no longer. He has told me everything. He had never seen me before he came here: it was Monsieur Remy who deceived me, and I have forgiven Dorante.

ARAMINTE: I am glad to hear it.

MARTON: Why were you so cruel as to deliver me up to the risk of loving a man who is not meant for me, who is worthy of you, and upon whom I have inflicted this misery which in its turn pierces me?

ARAMINTE, *sweetly*: You loved him, then, Marton?

MARTON: Never mind my sentiments. Let me have your affection as I had it formerly, and I shall be content.

ARAMINTE: I give it you, unimpaired.

MARTON, *kissing her hand*: I am consoled, then.

ARAMINTE: No, Marton, you are not. You are weeping. You melt me.

MARTON: Do not heed it. Nothing is so dear to me as you.

ARAMINTE: There, I will see if I cannot make you forget your sorrows. Here is Harlequin.

Scene XI

ARAMINTE, MARTON, HARLEQUIN

ARAMINTE: What do you want?

HARLEQUIN, *sobbing and weeping*: It would be very difficult for me to tell you, for I am in such distress that it is absolutely impossible for me to speak, because of Mademoiselle Marton's treachery. Oh, the ungrateful perfidious . . .

MARTON: Pass on from the perfidy, and tell us what you want.

HARLEQUIN: Oh, that poor letter! What a swindle!

ARAMINTE: Your business.

HARLEQUIN: Monsieur Dorante begs you on his knees to let him come here to render you an account of all those old papers he has received into his keeping since he has been here. He is waiting for me at the door, where he is weeping.

MARTON: Tell him to come in.

HARLEQUIN: Do you wish him to come in, Madame? Because I do not trust her. When I have been abused by somebody once, I do not give them a second chance.

MARTON, *sadly, and with emotion*: Speak to him, Madame; I will leave you.

HARLEQUIN, *when* MARTON *has gone*: You have not answered me, Madame.

ARAMINTE: He may come in.

Scene XII

DORANTE, ARAMINTE

ARAMINTE: Come in, Dorante.

DORANTE: I hardly dare show myself before you.

ARAMINTE, *aside*: Ah, I have no more assurance, any longer, than he.

Aloud:

244

Why do you wish to render me an account of my papers? I have complete trust in you. It is not in that connection that I might have any cause to complain.

DORANTE: Madame . . . there is something else I wish to say . . . I am so at a loss, and tremble so, that I can scarcely speak.

ARAMINTE, *aside, with considerable agitation*: Oh, how I fear the outcome of all this!

DORANTE, *greatly agitated*: One of your farmers came just now, Madame.

ARAMINTE, *greatly agitated*: One of my farmers! . . . It is possible.

DORANTE: Yes, Madame . . . he came.

ARAMINTE, *agitated, as before*: I do not doubt it.

DORANTE, *agitated*: And I have some money to return to you.

ARAMINTE: Ah, some money! . . . We shall see.

DORANTE: Whenever you please, Madame; to receive it.

ARAMINTE: Yes . . . I will take it . . . you will give it to me.
Aside:
I do not know what to say to him.

DORANTE: Would it not be soon enough if I were to bring it to you this evening or tomorrow, Madame?

ARAMINTE: Tomorrow, you say! Do you suggest that I could keep you until then, after what has happened?

DORANTE, *plaintively*: Out of the whole lifetime which I must endure far away from where you are, might I not have this one day, which I would treasure?

ARAMINTE: It cannot be, Dorante: we must part. Your love for me is known, and it would appear as though I condoned it.

DORANTE: Alas, Madame, what a pitiable wretch I shall be!

ARAMINTE: Come, Dorante, everyone has his sorrows.

DORANTE: I have lost everything! I had a portrait, and even that is gone.

ARAMINTE: Why do you need it? You can paint another.

DORANTE: It would be long indeed ere I could compensate myself for the one I have lost. Besides, that one was especially dear to me: you had held it in your hands, Madame.

ARAMINTE: But you are not reasonable.

DORANTE: Ah, Madame, I shall be far away from you. You will be amply revenged upon me: do not add to my suffering.

ARAMINTE: Give you my portrait! Do you not realize that that would be as much to admit that I love you?

DORANTE: You, love me, Madame! What a notion! Who could imagine such a thing?

ARAMINTE, *her tone lively and naïve*: And nevertheless, that is what I have come to.

DORANTE, *throwing himself at her feet*: Oh, it is too much for me!

ARAMINTE: I no longer know where I am. Restrain your joy; rise, Dorante.

DORANTE, *rising; tenderly*: I do not deserve it. I am overwhelmed with the joy of it. I do not deserve it, Madame. You will deprive me of it again, but no matter: you must be told.

ARAMINTE, *astonished*: What? What do you mean?

DORANTE: In the whole course of what has happened here, nothing has been genuine except my passion, which is infinite, and the portrait of you which I painted. All the incidents which have occurred were sprung from the industry of a domestic who knew of my love, who was sorry for me, and who, by dangling before me as a charm the prospect of seeing you often, forced me, you might say, to consent to his stratagem: all his ingenuity was to make me shine in your eyes. There, Madame, you have what my respect, my character, and my love alike forbid me to conceal from you. I had rather regret the loss of your love, than owe the enjoyment of it to the success of an artifice; I had rather suffer your hate than the remorse for having deceived her whom I adore.

ARAMINTE, *after looking at him for some time without speaking*: If I had learned that from anyone but you, I would without doubt have hated you. But the confession which you yourself have made, in such a moment as this, alters everything. Your sincerity disarms me; it seems incredible to me; you are in the whole world the most honest of men. After all, since your love for me is genuine, what you have done in order to win me is not blameworthy; a lover is to be permitted to find whatever ways he can to please his beloved, and if he succeeds he should be forgiven.

DORANTE: What? Does the enchanting Araminte deign to find excuses for me?

ARAMINTE: Here is the comte, with my mother; do you say nothing, and let me speak to them.

Scene XIII

DORANTE, ARAMINTE, THE COMTE, MME. ARGANTE, DUBOIS, HARLEQUIN

246

MME. ARGANTE, *catching sight of* DORANTE: What! Is he still here?

ARAMINTE, *coldly*: Yes, Mother.

To THE COMTE:

Monsieur le Comte, there was some question of marriage between you and me; it is no longer to be considered. You are worthy of being loved; my heart is not at liberty to do you justice, and my position is not suited to yours.

MME. ARGANTE: What is this? What do you mean?

THE COMTE: I understand you, Madame, and without disclosing my intention to Madame . . .

Indicating MME. ARGANTE.

. . . I had made up my mind to withdraw. I had guessed the complexion of things: Dorante came here for no other reason than because he loved you. He has won you, and you mean to make his fortune: that is what you were about to tell me.

ARAMINTE: I have nothing to add to that.

MME. ARGANTE, *outraged*: That man's fortune!

THE COMTE, *sadly*: There is nothing more to be done except for us to settle our differences; I have said that I would not take the matter to law, and I shall keep my word.

ARAMINTE: You are most generous; send me someone who can draw up the terms, and that will do.

MME. ARGANTE: Oh, the thudding descent! Oh, this accursed steward! He can be your husband as much as he likes, but he will never be son-in-law of mine.

ARAMINTE: Let us leave her anger to cool, and make an end.

They go.

DUBOIS: Ooh! My glory swallows me up! I may call that woman my daughter-in-law; I have deserved it.

HARLEQUIN: God's truth, so much for your portrait now! We can have as many copies as we like, from the original.

W.S. Merwin

W.S. Merwin was born in New York City in 1927 and grew up in Union City, New Jersey, and in Scranton, Pennsylvania. From 1949 to 1951 he worked as a tutor in France, Portugal, and Majorca. After that, for several years he made the greater part of his living by translating from French, Spanish, Latin and Portuguese. Since 1954 several fellowships have been of great assistance. In addition to poetry, he has written articles, chiefly for *The Nation*, and radio scripts for the BBC. He has lived in Spain, England, France, Mexico and Hawaii, as well as New York City. His books of poetry are *A Mask for Janus* (1952), *The Dancing Bears* (1954), *Green with Beasts* (1956), *The Drunk in the Furnace* (1960), *The Moving Target* (1963), *The Lice* (1967), *The Carrier of Ladders* (1970), for which he was awarded the Pulitzer Prize, *Writings to an Unfinished Accompaniment* (1973), *The Compass Flower* (1977), and *Opening the Hand* (1983). His translations include *The Poem of the Cid* (1959), *Spanish Ballads* (1960), *The Satires of Persius* (1961), *Lazarillo de Tormes* (1962), *The Song of Roland* (1963), *Selected Translations 1948-1968* (1968), for which he won the P.E.N. Translation Prize for 1968, *Transparence of the World*, a translation of his selection of poems by Jean Follain (1969), *Osip Mandelstam, Selected Poems* (with Clarence Brown) (1974), *Selected Translations, 1968-1978* (1979), *From the Spanish Morning* (1985), and *Four French Plays* (1985). He has also published three books of prose, *The Miner's Pale Children* (1970), *Houses and Travellers* (1977) and *Unframed Originals* (1982). In 1974 he was awarded The Fellowship of the Academy of American Poets. In 1979 he was awarded the Bollingen Prize for Poetry.